Challenging Territoriality in Human Rights Law

Human rights have traditionally been framed in a vertical perspective with the duties of States confined to their own citizens or residents. Interpretations of international human rights treaties tend either to ignore or downplay obligations beyond this 'territorial space'. This edited volume challenges the territorial bias of mainstream human rights law. It argues that with increased globalisation and the impact of international corporations, organisations and non-State actors, human rights law will become less relevant if it fails to adapt to changing realities in which States are no longer the only leading actor.

Bringing together leading scholars in the field, the book explores potential applications of international human rights law in a multi-duty-bearer setting. The first part of the book examines the current state of the human rights obligations of foreign States, corporations and international financial institutions, looking in particular at the ways in which they address questions of attribution and distribution of obligations and responsibility. The second part is geared towards the identification of common principles that may underpin a human rights legal regime that incorporates obligations of foreign States as well as of non-State actors.

As a marker of important progress in understanding what lies ahead for integrating foreign States and non-State actors in the human rights duty-bearer regime, this book will be of great interest to scholars and practitioners of international human rights law, public international law and international relations.

Wouter Vandenhole holds the UNICEF Chair in Children's Rights – a joint venture of the University of Antwerp and UNICEF Belgium – at the Faculty of Law of the University of Antwerp (Belgium). He is the spokesperson of the Law and Development Research Group and chairs the European Research Networking Programme GLOTHRO. He has published widely on economic, social and cultural rights, children's rights and transnational human rights obligations and is a founding member of the Flemish Children's Rights Knowledge Centre and co-convener of the advanced summer course on human rights for development (HR4DEV).

Routledge Research in Human Rights Law

Available titles in this series include:

The Right to Development in International Law
The Case of Pakistan
Khurshid Iqbal

Global Health and Human Rights
Legal and Philosophical Perspectives
John Harrington and Maria Stuttaford

The Right to Religious Freedom in International Law
Between group rights and individual rights
Anat Scolnicov

Emerging Areas of Human Rights in the 21st Century
The role of the Universal Declaration of Human Rights
Marco Odello and Sofia Cavandoli

The Human Right to Water and its Application in the Occupied Palestinian Territories
Amanda Cahill

International Human Rights Law and Domestic Violence
The effectiveness of international human rights law
Ronagh McQuigg

Human Rights in the Asia-Pacific Region
Towards Institution Building
Hitoshi Nasu and Ben Saul

Human Rights Monitoring Mechanisms of the Council of Europe
Gauthier de Beco

The Positive Obligations of the State under the European Convention of Human Rights
Dimitris Xenos

Vindicating Socio-Economic Rights
International Standards and Comparative Experiences
Paul O'Connell

The EU as a 'Global Player' in Human Rights?
Jan Wetzel

Regulating Corporate Human Rights Violations
Humanizing Business
Surya Deva

The UN Committee on Economic, Social and Cultural Rights
The Law, Process and Practice
Marco Odello and Francesco Seatzu

State Security Regimes and the Right to Freedom of Religion and Belief
Changes in Europe Since 2001
Karen Murphy

The European Court of Human Rights in the Post-Cold War Era
Universality in Transition
James A. Sweeney

The United Nations Human Rights Council
A Critique and Early Assessment
Rosa Freedman

Children and International Human Rights Law
The Right of the Child to be Heard
Aisling Parkes

Litigating Transnational Human Rights Obligations
Alternative Judgements
Mark Gibney and Wouter Vandenhole

Reproductive Freedom, Torture and International Human Rights
Challenging the Masculinisation of Torture
Ronli Noa Sifris

Applying an International Human Rights Framework to State Budget Allocations
Rights and Resources
Rory O'Connell, Aoife Nolan, Colin Harvey, Mira Dutschke and Eoin Rooney

Human Rights Law in Europe
The Influence, Overlaps and Contradictions of the EU and the ECHR
Kanstantsin Dzehtsiarou, Tobias Lock, Theodore Konstadinides and Noreen O'Meara

Nomadic Peoples and Human Rights
Jérémie Gilbert

Children's Lives in an Era of Children's Rights
The Progress of the Convention on the Rights of the Child in Africa
Afua Twum-Danso Imoh & Nicola Ansell

China's Human Rights Lawyers
Advocacy and Resistance
Eva Pils

The Right to Equality in European Human Rights Law
The Quest for Substance in the Jurisprudence of the European Courts
Charilaos Nikolaidis

Business and Human Rights in South East Asia
Risk and Regulatory Turn
Mahdev Mohan & Cynthia Morel

Indigenous Peoples, Title to Territory, Rights and Resources
The Transformative Role of Free Prior and Informed Consent
Cathal M. Doyle

Challenging Territoriality in Human Rights Law
Building Blocks for a Plural and Diverse Duty-Bearer Regime
Wouter Vandenhole

Reconciling Cultural Diversity and International Human Rights Obligations
The Compatibility Approach in the Practice of International Human Rights Institutions
Michael K. Addo

Social and Economic Rights in Theory and Practice
A Critical Assessment
Helena Alviar Garcia, Karl Klare & Lucy A. Williams

The Human Rights Approach to Disability
Cases and Materials
Andreas Dimopoulos

Socio-Economic Rights in Emerging Free Markets
Comparative Insights from India and China
Surya Deva

Capturing Caste in Law
The Legal Regulation of Caste Discrimination
Annapurna Waughray

Care, Migration and Human Rights
Law and Practice
Siobhán Mullally

The Protection of Vulnerable Groups under International Human Rights Law
Ingrid Nifosi-Sutton

Forthcoming titles in this series include:

Jurisdiction, Immunity and Transnational Human Rights Litigation
Xiaodong Yang

Extraterritoriality and International Human Rights Law
The Spatial Reach of African Human Rights Treaties
Takele Soboka Bulto

Human Rights Law and Personal Identity
Jill Marshall

In Pursuit of Human Rights
NGOs, Pedagogy and Praxis in Grassroots Africa
Joanne Coysh

The Law and Practice of the European Social Committee
Francesco Seatzu and Amaya Ubeda de Torres

Human Dignity and Degrading Treatment in the European Convention on Human Rights
The Ends of Article 3 of the European Convention on Human Right
Elaine Webster

Comparative Executive Clemency
The Prerogative of Mercy in the Commonwealth
Andrew Novak

Challenging Territoriality in Human Rights Law

Building Blocks for a Plural and Diverse Duty-Bearer Regime

Edited by
Wouter Vandenhole

Routledge
Taylor & Francis Group
LONDON AND NEW YORK

EUROPEAN
SCIENCE
FOUNDATION

First published 2015
by Routledge
2 Park Square, Milton Park, Abingdon, Oxfordshire OX14 4RN

and by Routledge
711 Third Avenue, New York, NY 10017

First issued in paperback 2016

Routledge is an imprint of the Taylor & Francis Group, an informa business

British Library Cataloguing in Publication Data
A catalogue record for this book is available from the British Library

Library of Congress Cataloging-in-Publication Data
Vandenhole, Wouter, author.
Challenging territoriality in human rights law : building blocks for a plural and diverse duty-bearer regime / Wouter Vandenhole.
pages cm. -- (Routledge research in human rights law)
Includes bibliographical references and index.
ISBN 978-1-138-79945-5 (hbk : alk. paper) -- ISBN 978-1-315-75603-5 (ebk) 1. International law and human rights. 2. Human rights. 3. Globalization. I. Title.
KZ1266.V36 2015
341.4'8--dc23
2014048760

ISBN: 978-1-138-70271-4 (pbk)
ISBN: 978-1-138-79945-5 (hbk)

Typeset in 11/12 Garamond 3 LT Std by
Servis Filmsetting Ltd, Stockport, Cheshire

The work reported on in this publication has been financially supported by the European Science Foundation (ESF), in the framework of the GLOTHRO Research Networking Programme, *Beyond Territoriality: Globalisation and Transnational Human Rights Obligations*, *http://www.glothro.org*.

Contents

Contributors

Koen De Feyter is the Chair of International Law at the University of Antwerp (Belgium), Faculty of Law. He is the Convenor of the International research network on 'Localising human rights' and Chair of VLIR-UOS (Flemish Interuniversity Council – university cooperation for development). He publishes on international law, development and human rights. He is the author of *World Development Law* (Intersentia 2001) and *Human Rights: Social Justice in the Age of the Market* (Zed Books 2005). His most recent edited volumes include *The Local Relevance of Human Rights* (CUP 2011), *Globalization and Common Responsibilities of States* (Ashgate 2013) and *The Common Interest in International Law* (Intersentia 2014).

Mark Gibney is the Belk Distinguished Professor at UNC-Asheville. His most recent book projects include: *The Handbook of Human Rights* (edited volume with Anja Mihr) (Sage Publications 2014); *Watching Human Rights: The 101 Best Films* (Paradigm Publishers 2013); *The Politics of Human Rights: The Quest for Dignity* (with Sabine Carey and Steven Poe) (CUP 2010); *Universal Human Rights and Extraterritorial Obligations* (edited volume with Sigrun Skogly) (University of Pennsylvania Press 2010); and *The Global Refugee Crisis* (ABC-CLIO 2010). Since 1984, Gibney has directed the Political Terror Scale (PTS), which measures levels of physical integrity violations in more than 185 countries (*http://www.politicalterrorscale.org*).

Ashfaq Khalfan is the Researcher and Advisor on Obligations Beyond Borders at Amnesty International's International Secretariat. He is also the Chair of the Board of Governors of the Centre for International Sustainable Development Law. Relevant publications include 'Division of Responsibility' and 'Accountability Mechanisms' in M. Langford, W. Vandenhole, M. Scheinin and W. van Genugten (eds), *Global Justice, State Duties: The Extraterritorial Scope of Economic, Social, and Cultural Rights in International Law* (CUP 2013) and co-authored publications include *Sustainable Development Law: Principles, Practices and Prospects* (OUP 2004); *Manual on the Right to Water and Sanitation* (COHRE, AAAS, UN-HABITAT and SDC 2008); and *The Significance of Human Rights in*

MDG-based Policy Making on Water and Sanitation: An Application to Kenya, South Africa, Ghana, Sri Lanka and Laos (COHRE 2009). He has previously served as the Policy Coordinator on Legal Enforcement of Economic, Social and Cultural Rights at Amnesty International, directed the Right to Water Programme at the Centre on Housing Rights and Evictions, and consulted for the Office of the UN High Commissioner for Human Rights (OHCHR) and the German Technical Cooperation Agency (GTZ). He holds a doctorate in law from Oxford University and degrees in common law, civil law and political science from McGill University.

Jernej Letnar Černič is an Assistant Professor of Human Rights Law at the Graduate School of Government and European Studies, where he serves as a Vice-Dean. He graduated from University of Ljubljana with the France Prešeren award. He completed his PhD in Human Rights Law in 2009 at the University of Aberdeen. He also serves on the management board of the European Union Fundamental Rights Agency and on the steering board of the GLOTHRO project. Jernej is holder of a Jean Monnet module awarded by the European Commission and of a two-year Slovenian research grant for his research project on 'Corporate obligations under economic, social and cultural human rights'. Jernej is an Editor-in-Chief of Dignitas – Slovene Journal of Human Rights and a member of the International Human Rights Committee of the International Law Association and of the Institut international des droits de l'homme. His publications include *Making Sovereign Financing and Human Rights Work* (Hart 2014, co-edited with Juan Pablo Bohoslavsky); Jernej Letnar Černič is also a co-author of a commentary of the Constitution of the Republic of Slovenia. He has written extensively on human rights law and international law and has been active in civil society in Slovenia and beyond.

George Pavlakos is Research Professor at the Faculty of Law, University of Antwerp where he directs the Centre for Law and Cosmopolitan Values, and Professor at the School of Law, University of Glasgow. Amongst the research awards he has received are two Alexander von Humboldt Fellowships and an FWO-Odysseus grant. He is the author of *Our Knowledge of the Law* (Hart, 2007) and has recently edited *Reasons and Intentions in Law and Practical Agency* (CUP, 2015). He is general editor of the book series *Law and Practical Reason* at Hart Publishing and general co-editor of the journal *Jurisprudence* published by Routledge. During the fall of 2015 George Pavlakos will be a Fernand Braudel Senior Fellow at the EUI in Florence, working on a monograph on the philosophy of International Law.

Ian Seiderman is presently the Legal and Policy Director of the International Commission of Jurists, which he rejoined in 2008, having previously served as Legal Adviser from 2000–05. He served as Senior Legal Adviser for Amnesty International from 2005–08. He has advised both organisations on a broad range of legal and policy questions in the areas of international human rights law and international humanitarian law, including on questions of torture and detention, administration of justice and fair trial, economic, social and cultural rights, and business and human rights. Previously, he was legal adviser to the Special Rapporteur on Torture of the UN Commission on Human Rights, Sir Nigel Rodley, and served as staff attorney with the US-based Central American Refugee Center. He earned his PhD cum laude at Utrecht University in 2000 and also holds an LLM (Essex), Juris Doctorate (City University of New York at Queens College) and BA (University of Pennsylvania).

Margot E Salomon is Director of the Centre for the Study of Human Rights, London School of Economics (Acting); Director of the Laboratory for Advanced Research on the Global Economy; and Associate Professor in the Law Department. Margot specialises in international human rights law and global economic justice and has consulted and published widely on the topic. She has been a consultant to the World Bank's Nordic Trust Fund on human rights and economics (2011) and to the Office of the UN High Commissioner for Human Rights on extreme poverty and human rights (2009); Advisor to the UN High-level Task Force on the Right to Development (2004–09); and a member of the International Law Association's Committee on the Rights of Indigenous Peoples (2008–12). She is currently vice-chair of the Association of Human Rights Institutes. Recent publications include: 'Of Austerity, Human Rights and International Institutions' ELJ (2015); 'From NIEO to Now and the Unfinishable Story of Economic Justice' (2013) ICLQ; and 'Deprivation, Causation, and the Law of International Cooperation' in M. Langford, et al. (eds), *Global Justice, State Duties: The Extraterritorial Scope of Economic, Social, and Cultural Rights in International Law* (CUP 2013).

Martin Scheinin is Professor of International Law and Human Rights at the European University Institute. He was a Member of the UN Human Rights Committee and is currently the UN Special Rapporteur on the protection and promotion of human rights and fundamental freedoms while countering terrorism. Currently, he is the President of the International Association of Constitutional Law. He has published widely in the field of international, constitutional and human rights law and his books include: *The Impact of Human Rights Law on General International Law*, edited with M. Kamminga (OUP 2009); *International Protection of Human Rights: A Textbook*, edited with C Krause (Åbo Akademi University Institute for Human Rights 2009); and *Cultural Human Rights*, edited with F. Francioni (Martinus Nijhoff 2008).

Wouter Vandenhole teaches human rights and holds the UNICEF Chair in Children's Rights at the Faculty of Law of the University of Antwerp (Belgium). He chairs the Law and Development Research Group of his Faculty, and the European Research Networking Programme GLOTHRO (Beyond Territoriality: Globalization and Transnational Human Rights

Obligations). Vandenhole sits on the editorial board of *Human Rights and International Legal Discourse* and of the *Journal of Human Rights Practice*. He has researched and published widely on economic, social and cultural rights, children's rights and transnational human rights obligations. Key publications on transnational human rights obligations include: 'Extraterritorial Human Rights Obligations: Taking Stock, Looking Forward' (2013) *European Journal of Human Rights*; M. Gibney and W. Vandenhole (eds), *Litigating Transnational Human Rights Obligations: Alternative Judgments, Routledge Research in Human Rights Law* (Routedge 2014); and M. Langford, W. Vandenhole, M. Scheinin and W. van Genugten (eds), *Global Justice, State Duties. The Extraterritorial Scope of Economic, Social and Cultural Rights in International Law* (CUP 2013).

Willem van Genugten is Professor of International Law at Tilburg University, The Netherlands. In addition, he is Extraordinary Professor of International Law at the North-West University, South Africa. Some relevant publications include: *The United Nations of the Future; Globalization with a Human Face*, authored with K. Homan, N. Schrijver and P. de Waart (KIT Publishers 2006), selected by *Choice Magazine* (US) as Outstanding Academic Title 2007; and 'Protection of Indigenous Peoples on the African Continent: Concepts, Position Seeking, and the Interaction of Legal Systems' (2010) *American Journal of International Law* 29–65; *Harnessing Intellectual Property Rights for Development Objectives* (Wolf Legal Publishers 2011). He co-edited with M. Langford, W. Vandenhole and M. Scheinin *Global Justice, State Duties. The Extraterritorial Scope of Economic, Social and Cultural Rights in International Law* (CUP 2013).

Preface

When we first started our collaborative work which has led to this volume, extraterritorial human rights obligations were quite peripheral or unarticulated in human rights scholarship. Ten years down the line, the issue may appear more topical than ever. It has been expanded beyond obligations of States to also cover non-State actors, and it is increasingly seriously addressed in mainstream scholarship.

The Research Networking Programme, *Beyond Territoriality – Globalisation and Transnational Human Rights Obligations (GLOTHRO)*, has sought to deepen the understanding of human rights obligations of foreign States, ie States other than the territorial ones, and to examine the legal implications of the expansion of the realm of human rights duty-bearers beyond the State. During its life as a European Science Foundation programme, GLOTHRO organised two major conferences, no less than ten workshops, a highly successful doctoral school, provided exchange grants to young scholars, and has produced a whole line of agenda-setting publications with leading publishers. In addition, it reached out to the non-academic community, both non-governmental and governmental actors, to engage in the debate.

Beyond activities and outputs, the legacy of GLOTHRO is first and foremost that it has built a European interdisciplinary research community of junior and senior scholars. The research community on transnational human rights obligations also extends far beyond Europe to include scholars from the US, Australia, India, Kenya, South Africa and Uganda, and many other countries. This relatively small but vibrant research community will now have the task of taking the research agenda forward. That is already happening, in particular by junior researchers who study specific cases of settings in which transnational human rights questions arise, in areas such as diplomacy, digital communication and armed conflict.

Substantively, the understanding of *extraterritorial human rights obligations* has increased rather dramatically during GLOTHRO's life-span. Thanks to the commitment of the ETO (Extra-Territorial Obligations) Consortium, a wide network of human rights related civil society organisations and academics, in September 2011 the Maastricht Principles on Extraterritorial Obligations in the Area of Economic, Social and Cultural Rights (the Maastricht Principles) were adopted by 40 academic, NGO and practitioner experts. The Maastricht Principles are today the main point of reference in any debate on extraterritorial human rights obligations in the area of economic, social and cultural rights.

The increased attention over the last 15 years or so to the human rights obligations of other States than the territorial one is a discourse loaded with two foundational paradoxes. First, the position that human rights would be primarily or exclusively territorial in nature does not reflect the historical emergence of human rights as a concept of international law. Traditionally, a State could hold foreign States to account for how they treated its nationals but was not supposed to interfere in what those other States did with their own nationals. This was the paradigm of 'diplomatic protection' where a State was acknowledged as having a legitimate interest in protecting the rights of its own nationals, wherever situated. In the League of Nations era between the two World Wars, States were keeping an eye on each other as to how a foreign State treated 'national minorities' living within its borders, ie groups that had a historical, linguistic or other tie with another, often neighbouring State. Finally, the atrocities of the Nazis and of World War Two triggered the breakthrough of the concept of human rights in the United Nations Charter (1945) and the Universal Declaration of Human Rights (1948). The revolutionary significance of this step was that other States and the international community as a whole were finally acknowledged as having a legitimate interest in how a State treats its own nationals within its own territory. Previously, this would have been seen as an improper interference in the internal affairs of a sovereign State. The underlying idea was to fill a gap, not to create a regime of exclusivity. It is a sad paradox of history that the traditionally weak role that international law has had in shielding individuals against violence and oppression from their own State is now being used to deny exactly the same protection to any others than those who happen to live within the territory of a State.

It is true that some of the main human rights treaties that deal with civil and political rights – namely the UN Covenant on Civil and Political Rights and the European Convention on Human Rights – came to use the notion of 'jurisdiction' together with the word 'everyone' in pronouncing the central obligation of a State to respect and protect human rights. The consistent practice, since the very first Uruguayan cases of the early 1980s, of the Human Rights Committee acting under the first-mentioned treaty demonstrates that there is no conceptual difficulty in including extraterritorial acts of a State under that central obligation. Sadly, after the atrocious terrorist attacks of 11 September 2001 and the resulting global hunt for suspected terrorists, certain States, primarily the US and the UK, launched an articulated doctrinal attack against the idea of civil and political rights having also extraterritorial reach whenever a State violates those rights elsewhere than within its own borders. Those positions of blanket denial and the degree of understanding initially shown to them by the ECtHR in the *Bankovic* case should today be seen as a temporary overreaction which is gradually being replaced by acknowledging that a State must not do overseas what would be a human rights violation at home. This move is reflected in subsequent cases also by the ECtHR and recent statements by the US before the UN Committee Against Torture.

The second paradox is that even if treaties on economic social and cultural rights, such as the UN Covenant on those rights, do *not* contain a clause referring to the territory or jurisdiction of a ratifying State as in any way defining the scope of its human rights obligations but, rather, contain explicit clauses that pronounce an obligation of international cooperation, the denial of extraterritorial obligations has all too easily been extended from civil and political rights to State obligations in respect of economic, social and cultural rights.

Having started its work with a focus on States, in its second phase GLOTHRO broadened its work to include non-State actors. Five trajectories were initiated in parallel in order to strengthen progress in the understanding of transnational human rights obligations. They engaged with other disciplines and dealt with transversal themes of global justice, common interest, and law enforcement and migration control, and with two focal types of non-State actors (companies and international financial institutions). In particular but not unexpectedly, the work on human rights obligations of non-State actors proved more challenging. First, the whole idea of non-State actors having human rights obligations triggers hesitations of a conceptual nature. The expansion of the duty-bearer side of human rights law challenges quite fundamentally the basic design of human rights law, with its traditionally exclusive focus on the State and the vertical relationship between the omnipotent State and its 'subject', the individual. Other reasons for hesitation balance between pragmatism (the topic is politically not yet ripe) and strategic considerations (other avenues than or alongside human rights law may be more effective in achieving accountability of non-State actors). As this edited volume demonstrates, important progress has been made, not in the least in understanding much better the key questions and issues that lie ahead of us if we want to integrate foreign States and non-State actors fully in the human rights duty-bearer regime.

Gradually but surely, we may have moved from the debate *whether* or not foreign States and non-State actors have human rights obligations – or at least responsibilities – to questions on the substantive content and limits of their duties, the ways in which responsibility for human rights violations may be adequately attributed to a whole range of actors, and the mechanisms through which accountability may be established.

Second, reality necessitates us to look at the role of other actors than the domestic State in human rights realisation. Opening up the duty-bearer side of human rights law certainly holds new prospects for victims of human rights violations: it may allow them to direct complaints against other actors than their own State. Then, the question arises about where and under what legal framework those complaints are formulated: they may be international human rights claims in substance but raised before domestic courts under those legal frameworks that happen to be available there, including by arguing that some measures by private actors that result in the denial or destruction of human rights amount to *crimes* deserving penalties, or to *civil wrongs* that give rise to a compensation claim. The more duty-bearers there are, the more complex it may also become for victims to obtain redress. Therefore, the question whether actual victories towards the realisation of human rights are primarily reached through focusing on identifying new human rights duty-bearers, or through insisting on implementing and strengthening the human rights obligations of States is worth being raised from time to time. For the latter, legally binding international treaties and treaty-based mechanisms before regional human rights courts or other independent bodies already exist and can be used to transform recognised human rights into reality. For other actors, a matter of high priority is what mechanisms are available or can be created, in particular on the international level, for addressing substantive human rights claims in respect of, for instance, international organisations, such as international financial institutions, and transnational corporations.

In sum, GLOTHRO has undoubtedly taken the research agenda forward, but the work is not, and never will be, finished: old and new fundamental questions merit further scrutiny.

We would like to thank all colleagues who have contributed to the successes of GLOTHRO, in particular all Steering Committee members, those colleagues who have organised a GLOTHRO event, and all scholars who have intellectually contributed to our work. A special word of thanks goes to Arne Vandenbogaerde, who has skilfully and with enthusiasm assisted in the coordination of the programme.

We are heavily indebted to the European Science Foundation (ESF) and all the national research councils that through ESF contributed towards funding GLOTHRO, and the European University Institute and the University of Antwerp that additionally provided financial support to the programme. We are also grateful to Katie Carpenter, Annabelle Harris and Mark Sapwell (Routledge) for their professional and committed guidance in producing this edited volume.

Martin Scheinin
Florence
Willem van Genugten
Tilburg
Wouter Vandenhole
Antwerp
December 2014

List of Abbreviations

AEDPA	Antiterrorism and Effective Death Penalty Act
ASR	Articles on State Responsibility
ATS	Alien Tort Statute
BWIs	Bretton Woods Institutions
CAT	Convention Against Torture and Other Cruel, Inhuman or Degrading Treatment or Punishment
CAT Committee	Committee Against Torture
CDP	Committee for Development Policy
CESCR	Committee on Economic, Social and Cultural Rights
CEO	Chief Executive Officer
CP	Civil and Political
DARIO	Draft Articles on the Responsibility of International Organizations
DfID	Department for International Development
EBA	Everything But Arms
EC	European Communities
ECHR	European Convention on Human Rights
ECOSOC	Economic and Social Council
ECtHR	European Court of Human Rights
EMEP	European Monitoring and Evaluation Programme
ESC	Economic, Social and Cultural
ETOs	Extra-Territorial Obligations
EU	European Union
FSIA	Foreign Sovereign Immunity Act
GATT	General Agreement on Tariffs and Trade
HIV/AIDS	Human Immunodeficiency Virus infection/Acquired Immune Deficiency Syndrome
HRCommission	Human Rights Commission
GNI	Gross National Income
IBRD	International Bank for Reconstruction and Development
ICESCR	International Covenant on Economic, Social and Cultural Rights

ICCPR	International Covenant on Civil and Political Rights
ICJ	International Court of Justice
ICTY	International Criminal Tribunal for the Former Yugoslavia
IDA	International Development Association
IFI	International Financial Institution
IGO	Inter-Governmental Organisation
IL	International Law
ILC	International Law Commission
ILO	International Labour Organization
IMF	International Monetary Fund
IACtHR	Inter-American Court of Human Rights
LRTAP Convention	Convention on Long-range Transboundary Air Pollution
MDB	multilateral development bank
MNC	multi-national corporation
MSI	Multi-stakeholder initiatives
NCP	National Contact Point
NGO	Non-governmental organization
NSAs	non-State actors
OECD	Organisation for Economic Co-operation and Development
OECD-DAC	Development Assistance Committee of the Organisation for Economic Co-operation and Development
OHCHR	Office of the High Commissioner on Human Rights
OP	Optional Protocol
SCFAIT	Standing Committee on Foreign Affairs and International Trade
TNC	Transnational Corporation
TRIPS	Trade-Related Aspects of Intellectual Property Rights
UDHR	Universal Declaration of Human Rights
UK	United Kingdom
UN	United Nations
UNGPs	UN Guiding Principles on Business and Human Rights
UNCTAD	United Nations Conference on Trade and Development
UN-OHRLLS	UN Office of the High Representative for the Least Developed Countries, Landlocked Developing Countries and the Small Island Developing States
US	United States
VCLT	Vienna Convention on the Law of Treaties
VDPA	Vienna Declaration and Programme of Action

WBG	World Bank Group
WHO	World Health Organization
WTO	World Trade Organization
WW	World War

1 Introduction: an emerging multi-duty-bearer human rights regime?

Wouter Vandenhole and Willem van Genugten

Beyond territoriality[1]

Traditionally, human rights law has a strong territorial bias. Human rights obligations are in principle incumbent on the territorial State, ie the State on the territory of which a human rights violation takes place. The duties of States are confined to the residents on their territory. Obligations beyond this 'territorial space' have been viewed as either being non-existent or minimalistic at best. This territorial paradigm has achieved particular prominence in the interpretation of international human rights treaties.

However, the territorial paradigm has been increasingly challenged. In practice, the ability of States and other actors to impact human rights far from home has never been clearer. Economic globalisation has highlighted socio-economic disparities across the world. The often decentred position of the territorial State and the increased power and impact of corporations, international organisations and other non-State actors (NSAs), pose major practical and conceptual challenges to human rights law. In practice, human rights law will become less and less relevant if it fails to adapt to changing realities in which States are no longer the only leading actor. A striking example of this can be found in chapter 2 of this volume, where mention is made of 'company towns', the 'governance of which is in private hands'.[2] Conceptually, the displacement of the territorial State necessitates a fundamental re-thinking of a basic tenet of human rights law, ie that human rights obligations are primarily incumbent on the territorial State. Human rights law has to move beyond territoriality as the main criterion for assigning human rights obligations.

Considerable work has been done in recent years on human rights obligations of States acting extraterritorially or foreign States, and of eg international financial organisations and business enterprises. Scholarly work on

1 This section draws on W Vandenhole and M Gibney, 'Introduction: Transnational Human Rights Obligations' in M Gibney and W Vandenhole (eds), *Litigating Transnational Human Rights Obligations: Alternative Judgments* (Routledge 2014) 1–9.

2 D Monti, *Race, Development and the New Company Town* (NYP 1990).

extraterritorial human rights obligations gained momentum in the mid-2000s,[3] and attention was increasingly directed at defining the legal basis, nature and scope of extraterritorial human rights obligations (mainly but not exclusively in the area of economic, social and cultural rights), either by looking at it right-by-right,[4] or by investigating cross-cutting issues of causation, attribution and distribution of responsibility, and accountability and remedies.[5] There equally emerged a small but important body of work on extraterritorial human rights obligations in the area of civil and political rights,[6] sometimes with a particular focus on, for instance, migration.[7] Furthermore, the question of extraterritoriality in the area of children's rights was examined.[8] In addition, questions of accountability and amenability of extraterritorial obligations to litigation have been addressed, in particular under the OP-ICESCR.[9] Following the adoption of the Maastricht Principles on Extraterritorial Obligations in the Area of Economic, Social and Cultural Rights in 2011, recent work has road-tested the application of these Principles, either in real-life cases or in hypothetical legal opinions and judgments.[10]

Important work has equally been done on direct human rights obligations of individual non-State actors such as international (financial) organisations or

3 For a more substantive stock-taking, see eg W Vandenhole, 'Extraterritorial Human Rights Obligations: Taking Stock, Looking Forward' (2013) *European Journal of Human Rights* 804–835.

4 M Gibney and S Skogly (eds), *Universal Human Rights and Extraterritorial Obligations* (University of Pennsylvania Press 2010); M Mustaniemi-Laakso, 'The Right to Education: Instrumental Right Par Excellence', in ME Salomon, A Tostensen and W Vandenhole (eds), *Casting the Net Wider: Human Rights, Development and New Duty-Bearers* (Intersentia 2007) 331–352.

5 M Langford, W Vandenhole, M Scheinin and W van Genugten (eds), *Global Justice, State Duties. The Extraterritorial Scope of Economic, Social and Cultural Rights in International Law* (CUP 2013).

6 M Milanovic, *Extraterritorial Application of Human Rights Treaties, Law, Principles, and Policy* (OUP 2011); N Lubell, *Extraterritorial Use of Force Against Non-State Actors* (OUP 2010) 193–235; M Gondek, *The Reach of Human Rights in a Globalising World: Extraterritorial Application of Human Rights Treaties* (Intersentia 2009); F Coomans and M Kamminga, *Extraterritorial Application of Human Rights Treaties* (Intersentia 2004). The latter two pay some attention to economic, social and cultural rights too.

7 T Gammeltoft-Hansen, *Access to Asylum: International Refugee Law and the Globalisation of Migration Control* (CUP 2011); M den Heijer, *Europe and Extraterritorial Asylum* (Hart 2012).

8 C Apodaca, *Child Hunger and Human Rights: International Governance* (Routledge 2010); M Wabwile, *Legal Protection of Social and Economic Rights of Children in Developing Countries. Reassessing International Cooperation and Responsibility* (Intersentia 2010); W Vandenhole, 'Economic, Social and Cultural Rights in the CRC: Is There a Legal Obligation to Cooperate Internationally for Development?' (2009) 17 *International Journal of Children's Rights* 23–63.

9 M Sepúlveda, 'Obligations of "International Assistance and Cooperation" in an Optional Protocol to the International Covenant on Economic, Social and Cultural, Rights' (2006) 24 *Netherlands Quarterly of Human Rights* 271–303; C Courtis and M Sepúlveda, 'Are Extra-Territorial Obligations Reviewable under the Optional Protocol to the ICESCR?' (2009) 27 *Nordic Journal of Human Rights* 54–63.

10 F Coomans and R Künneman, *Cases and Concepts on Extraterritorial Obligations in the Area of Economic, Social and Cultural Rights* (Intersentia 2012); M Gibney and W Vandenhole (eds), *Litigating Transnational Human Rights Obligations: Alternative Judgments* (Routledge 2014).

companies.[11] Guiding Principles, albeit of a totally different legal and political standing, have been adopted for both types of actors: the UN Guiding Principles on Business and Human Rights in 2011; and the Tilburg Guiding Principles on the World Bank, IMF and Human Rights in 2003.

Understanding the relative strength of human rights obligations incumbent on States may help consider how the emerging regime of human rights obligations for other actors should be further developed. However, attempts to identify key concepts and principles that guide human rights obligations of States and non-State actors alike remain rare.[12] This edited volume seeks to map the State of the art across the different fields of human rights obligations of foreign States, transnational corporations and international organisations, with the purpose of identifying foundational principles for the attribution and distribution of responsibility for these actors. Contributors to this volume do not necessarily agree on how to redesign the duty-bearer side of human rights law: some seem to favour an incremental approach and want to remain as much as possible within a State-centric regime (see eg Khalfan and Seiderman), whereas others (Pavlakos, Vandenhole) argue that a more fundamental revision is warranted. For sure, progress has been slow and reluctance to redesigning the human rights duty-bearer doctrine has been persistent. That hesitation stems, inter alia, from the fact that the expansion of the duty-bearer side of human rights law fundamentally challenges the basic design of human rights law, with its exclusive focus on the State. Other reasons oscillate between pragmatism (the topic is politically not yet ripe) and strategic considerations (other avenues than human rights law may be more effective in achieving accountability of non-State actors). At the same time,

11 For international financial institutions, see inter alia GA Sarfaty, *Values in Translation. Human Rights and the Culture of the World Bank* (Stanford University Press 2012); A McBeth, *International Economic Actors and Human Rights* (Routledge 2010); DD Bradlow and DB Hunter (eds), *International Financial Institutions and International Law* (Kluwer Law International 2010); M Darrow, *Between Light and. Shadow, The World Bank, The International Monetary Fund and International Human Rights Law* (Hart Publishing 2003); S Skogly, *The Human Rights Obligations of the World Bank and the IMF* (Cavendish Publishing 2001); W van Genugten, P Hunt and S Mathews (eds), *World Bank, IMF and Human Rights* (Wolf Legal Publishers 2002). For companies, see inter alia D Augenstein and D Kinley, 'When Human Rights "Responsibilities" Become "Duties": The Extra-territorial Obligations of States that Bind Corporations', in S Deva and D Bilchitz (eds), *Human Rights Obligations of Business. Beyond the Corporate Responsibility to Respect?* (CUP 2013) 271–294; O De Schutter (ed), *Transnational Corporations and Human Rights* (Hart Publishing 2006); N Jägers, *Corporate Human Rights Obligations: In Search of Accountability* (Intersentia 2002); M Kamminga and Zia-Zarifi, *Liability of Multinational Corporations under International Law* (Kluwer International Law 2000).

12 Exceptions are P Alston (ed), *Non-State Actors and Human Rights* (OUP 2005); A Clapham, *Human Rights Obligations of Non-State Actors* (OUP 2006); see also W Vandenhole, *Emerging Normative Frameworks on Transnational Human Rights Obligations*, EUI Working Papers RSCAS 2012/17, *http://cadmus.eui.eu/bitstream/handle/1814/21874/RSCAS_2012_17.pdf?sequence=1* (12 December 2014); W Vandenhole, GE Türkelli and R Hammonds,'Reconceptualizing Human Rights Duty-Bearers', in A Mihr and M Gibney (eds), *The SAGE Handbook of Human Rights* (Sage 2014) 1031–1046.

more and more case-studies are undertaken in which the human rights obligations of a mix of actors is examined.[13] The findings of these case-studies may be instrumental in moving the theoretical debate forward.

Identifying direct human rights duty-bearers beyond the State

A key question in identifying human rights duty-bearers beyond the State is whether *any* actor can be a duty-bearer, or whether only a selection of them is eligible for inclusion. For some, any extension beyond the State is fundamentally weakening the very concept of human rights (law). In any case, the more diverse the range of duty-bearers, the higher the risk that human rights law gets diluted. Different criteria may be applied to single out human rights duty-bearers beyond the State, eg those actors who hold institutionalised power. A more functional approach focuses on effective human rights protection, ie which actors need to be brought within the purview of human rights law in order to be able to offer effective human rights protection.[14]

Vandenhole and others have argued elsewhere in favour of a combination of both, ie power and effective protection:

> In essence, human rights (law) is about correcting power, first and foremost for the protection of the most vulnerable and marginalised [reference omitted]. Given this basic mission of human rights (law), the decisive criterion for singling out actors as human rights duty-bearers is whether they exercise power or are in a position to do so. Human rights law thus becomes applicable to all actors that hold or exercise power, regardless of the identity of the power holder.[15]

Alternative options may be considered. For example, De Feyter points out how social movements define human rights duty-bearers as all those actors who adversely affect human dignity.[16] Pavlakos suggests that, rather than power, the idea of hindrance of freedom may be the guiding principle, which seems to point to the direction of effective protection again.[17] Karp advances from

13 See eg RR Gupta, 'Germany's Support of Assad: Corporate Complicity in the Creation of the Syrian Surveillance State Under the European Convention on Human Rights' (2013) 28 *American University International Law Review* 1357–1391. Whereas the author's argument is mainly constructed as one of State responsibility, the underlying case of a Western company providing technological infrastructure and maintenance services to an oppressive State does also raise the question of direct corporate human rights obligations (and ensuing responsibility for violations thereof).

14 The latter is in line with an argument often used by regional human rights courts.

15 W Vandenhole, GE Türkelli and R Hammonds, 'New Human Rights Duty-Bearers: Towards a Re-conceptualisation of the Human Rights Duty-Bearer Dimension', in A Mihr and M Gibney (eds), *The SAGE Handbook of Human Rights* (Sage 2014) 1036.

16 K De Feyter, chapter 8 in this volume, 186.

17 G Pavlakos, chapter 7 in this volume, 146.

international theory to a 'publicness' approach; in a 'publicness' approach, actors who are 'relevantly public' have human rights obligations.[18]

In this volume, we focus in particular on two non-State actors, ie companies and international financial institutions. The selection has been pragmatic, and is mainly informed by the fact that some meaningful standard-setting on their direct human rights obligations has taken place (companies), or that the debate had come to a halt and that it was felt necessary to bring human rights obligations in line with the state of the art of international human rights law (the international financial institutions). Other actors could and should be included in future research, among them non-governmental organisations and armed groups.[19]

Obligations and responsibility

There is a risk of terminological confusion due to the fact that responsibility is sometimes used in its plain sense (as a synonym for having obligations), and sometimes in its public international law sense (as responsibility for an internationally wrongful act, ie the breach of an obligation). In this volume, the notions of obligations and responsibility are used as follows, unless authors explicitly distance themselves from this understanding: the notion of 'obligations' refers to substantive human rights obligations (primary norms), responsibility refers to responsibility for human rights violations (secondary norms).

Within the obligations category, human rights obligations of foreign States are called 'extraterritorial obligations'. 'Transnational human rights obligations' is used as an overarching concept that includes extraterritorial human rights obligations as well as *direct* human rights obligations of other actors than States (NSAs).

The obligations of foreign States and NSAs can be said to be *complementary* to domestic States' obligations. Their obligations accompany but never replace domestic States' obligations. 'Complementarity' recognises that a State's extraterritorial obligations are always applicable while it simultaneously affirms that the domestic States' obligations remain the primary ones. The transnational obligations to *respect and to protect* can be said to apply simultaneously with the domestic States' obligations. On the other hand, the transnational obligation to *fulfil* is considered to be a subsidiary obligation, ie it may be triggered eg by the domestic State's inability, for reasons beyond its control, to abide by its obligation to fulfil the minimum core content of ESC rights.

18 DJ Karper, *Responsibility for Human Rights. Transnational Corporations in Imperfect States* (CUP 2014) 4.
19 For some discussion and further useful references, see eg P Alston and R Goodman, *International Human Rights* (OUP 2013) 1497–1515.

Standard-setting for non-State actors

To introduce *direct* human rights obligations of NSAs does not necessarily require international law standards in the sense of State-made binding norms agreed upon in a treaty. Alternatively, one can think of what Backer calls 'an autonomous transnational governance system' when referring to the OECD Guidelines for Multinational Enterprises and their application by National Contact Points.[20] He envisages a dynamic 'matrix of hard law, soft law, governance norms, rules applicable to States, municipal law and policy', as well as transnational custom and customary normative frameworks 'as the framework basis of behaviour' for companies, through instruments like the OECD Guidelines.[21]

Along slightly more familiar lines to lawyers, treaty-making can be envisaged, whereby the NSAs on which human rights obligations are imposed could be involved in the standard-setting procedure (as is eg the case for the International Labour Organization with its tripartite structure).

It seems difficult to maintain that whereas direct human rights obligations may be crafted for a spectrum of State and NSAs, standard-setting remains the prerogative of States. Multi-stakeholder approaches to rule-making may look like a logical consequence of extending the duty-bearer side of human rights law therefore. Moreover, NSA participation in standard-setting may also be vital to increase the legitimacy and hence the potential abidance by the rules.

Baumgärtel and others have classified global law theories into three groups: those who favour a hierarchical approach, those who accept legal pluralism but seek still coordination and those who identify conflict as the key factor in law creation. It is striking to see how much space each strand gives to the inclusion of other powerful actors than the State to be subjected to global law. The theories that favour a coordination approach seem to be most open to new and hybrid forms of norm creation. The hierarchical strand is less, given its emphasis on authoritative norm imposition. The conflictual strand is sceptical too about a multi-stakeholder approach, for fears of appropriation of the process by the more powerful actors.[22] Wolfgang Benedek considers multi-stakeholderism as potentially more inclusive provided that certain principles are respected, such as the representation of all relevant stakeholders and due account for the interests of each of them; inclusiveness and accountability.[23]

20 LC Backer, 'Rights and Accountability in Development (Raid) v. Das Air and Global Witness v. Afrimex-Small Steps towards an Autonomous Transnational Legal System for the Regulation of Multinational Corporations' (2009) 10 *Melbourne Journal of International Law* 258–307 at 283–286.

21 Ibid at 293–294.

22 M Baumgärtel, D Staes and FJ Mena Parras, 'Hierarchy, Coordination or Conflict: Global Law Theories and the Question of Human Rights Integration' (2014) *European Journal of Human Rights* 326–354.

23 W Benedek, 'Multi-Stakeholderism in the Development of International Law', in U Fastenrath,

In this volume, Letnar Černič (chapter 4, 88) approvingly quotes Backer who argues that '[w]ithin its own logic, and in the context of emerging complex non-State governance orders, a recognition of anarchy in governance might liberate norm production from State control and permit more active engagement directly by civil society elements …'.[24] De Feyter submits that '[a]s the treaty approach inevitably remains State centric, multi stakeholder initiatives may provide an interesting supplement or alternative'.[25] Khalfan and Seiderman adopt a much more traditional understanding of law making: 'It is necessarily only through State authority, whether exercised unilaterally or multilaterally, that a social norm or a moral norm, becomes a legal norm.'[26]

Introduction to the chapters

The edited volume consists of two parts. The first part focuses on the state of the art of extraterritorial human rights obligations and emerging regimes of direct human rights obligations of companies and international financial institutions. It adopts a strong forward-looking perspective as to how these currently emerging regimes may evolve in the future and inspire each other. Particular attention is paid to questions of attribution and distribution of both obligations and responsibility for violations. In addition to three actor-specific chapters, this part also contains one cross-cutting chapter, in which potential (quasi-) judicial application of transnational human rights obligations is explored.

The second part moves beyond stock-taking and the identification of promising pathways. Its first chapter suggests foundational principles on obligations and responsibility in a multi and diverse duty-bearer human rights regime. The next chapters move beyond the technicality of human rights law and open up to insights from other disciplines that give food for thought. One chapter explores the relevance of insights from legal philosophy and ethics, a second looks into lessons to be learned from the way in which the common interest in public international law is addressed. Particular attention is paid again to questions of attribution and apportioning of obligations and responsibility in a multi-duty-bearer setting. A final chapter warns of the impact of market primacy on human rights law, and serves as a strong reminder of whose interests human rights (law) is to serve.

Each chapter provides the state of the art and examines novel and forward-looking perspectives for its own field. It equally explores how the findings

R Geiger, D-E Khan, A Paulus, S von Schorlemer and C Vedder, *From Bilateralism to Community Interest. Essays in Honour of Judge Bruno Simma* (OUP 2011) 209–210.

24 LC Backer at the second UN Forum on Business and Human Rights – Reflections on Bilchitz and Deva (eds), 'Human Rights Obligations of Business: Beyond the Corporate Responsibility to Respect?', 1 December 2013, *http://lcbackerblog.blogspot.com/2013/12/at-2nd-un-forum-on-business-and-human.html*.

25 K De Feyter, chapter 8 in this volume, 167.

26 A Khalfan and I Seiderman, chapter 2 in this volume, 26.

may apply across international human rights law in a multi and diverse duty-bearer setting.

Khalfan and Seiderman in their chapter, 'Extraterritorial human rights obligations: wider implications of the Maastricht Principles and the continuing accountability challenge' look into questions of apportionment and attribution of obligations, drawing on the work done with regard to extraterritorial obligations of *States*, as reflected in the Maastricht Principles on the Extraterritorial Obligations of States in the area of Economic, Social and Cultural Rights. They tackle four areas in particular: the applicability of the Maastricht Principles to the full range of human rights, including civil and political rights; the relevance of the Principles to the apportionment of obligations to non-State actors and international organisations; and the review of existing accountability mechanisms in order to enable them to deal with multiple duty bearers. As far as human rights obligations of businesses are concerned, they see the 'optimal starting point' in a State responsibility framework: ie they propose to 'place the responsibility of businesses to respect directly *under* the State's obligation to protect'.[27] Whereas they also identify (member) State obligations with regard to international organisations, they clearly argue in favour of direct obligations incumbent on international organisations, since these are said to be much like States. Generally, they believe that the obligations set forth in the Maastricht Principles apply to international organisations, with some exceptions. When it comes to accountability mechanisms, they explicitly turn to a *multiple* duty-bearer setting. Some instances of joint responsibility notwithstanding, they mainly advocate for a system of international coordination and allocation of obligations both for States and international organisations.

Some of the introductory thoughts on human rights obligations with regard to companies and international organisations offered by Khalfan and Seiderman are further developed in two actor-specific chapters by van Genugten on international financial institutions and Letnar Černič on businesses.

In his chapter 'The World Bank Group, the IMF and human rights: about direct obligations and the attribution of unlawful conduct', van Genugten looks into the way the World Bank Group and the International Monetary Fund themselves view the intersection of their mandate with international human rights, and takes stock of what current international human rights law demands from both international financial institutions (IFIs). He makes the case for direct obligations of IFIs, and identifies those obligations that find support in hard law and in legal developments. He then explores shared responsibility in the relationship between member States and the IFIs. Van Genugten pays particular attention to the attribution of conduct. In his analysis, 'factual control' standard is a key notion in the attribution of conduct as well as the apportioning of responsibility to member States and an IFI.

27 A Khalfan and I Seiderman, chapter 2 in this volume, 26.

Letnar Černič assesses in his chapter, 'Corporate responsibility for human rights: towards a pluralist approach', the extent to which corporate human rights responsibility has been acknowledged. He submits that there is no fundamental legal problem with conceptualising direct human rights obligations incumbent on business *de lege ferenda*, and that corporations already have direct human rights obligations that derive from international law as well as national legal orders. With regard to the latter, he argues that national legislation provides an authoritative legal source for the development of direct human rights obligations for companies in international law.

Letnar Černič advances a holistic and pluralist approach that incorporates national and international law, and spans across civil, criminal and human rights law. In his view, the different types of responsibility (individual, corporate, State) and the different legal levels (national and international) are not silos but communicating vessels: they may apply concurrently and/or compensate for their respective deficiencies. He also flags the need to scrutinise whether and how the concept of complicity as a notion taken from domestic criminal law can provide guidance on the relationship between State and corporate responsibility for human rights violations in the context of international law. Useful guidance may come from the South African Truth and Reconciliation Commission, which used a typology of involvement of companies in the apartheid regime. The typology is arguably rather moral than legal, but nonetheless potentially inspiring.

Gibney makes an analysis of the extent to which litigation has so far engaged with transnational human rights obligations in his chapter 'Litigating transnational human rights obligations'. He looks into questions of establishing, assigning and resisting responsibility in a selection of judicial findings. Under establishing responsibility, he criticises the ICJ, drawing on the ASR, for having identified nearly impossible-to-meet standards and for failing to identify degrees of State responsibility with regard to the assessment of aiding/complicity of an external State. He welcomes, on the other hand, the due diligence test employed by the Court with regard to the duty to prevent. Assigning responsibility is found to often be obstructed by jurisdictional limitations. Joint and several responsibility may help to overcome these limitations, but also creates new problems, in particular that the State that is held responsible, made only a minor contribution to the violation. The need for a theory of shared responsibility is emphasised. Rather than an all-or-nothing approach on the basis of exact levels of responsibility, he argues in favour of a due diligence test that would allow for degrees of responsibility to be established. Under the sub-heading of resisting responsibility, the denial of remedy through narrow interpretation of jurisdictional scope, sovereign immunity, the unwillingness to regulate corporations and the restrictive reading of the Alien Tort Statute under a 'presumption against extraterritorial application' is discussed.

Building on all these developments in international human rights law, **Vandenhole** in his chapter 'Attributing obligations and apportioning responsibility in a multi-duty-bearer human rights regime' seeks to take a meta-view and tries to articulate some emerging or possible foundational principles on the attribution of human rights obligations and the apportioning of responsibility for violations, regardless of the type of actor. He proposes defining the scope of transnational obligations in the abstract. Parameters include the type of obligation and the degree of control or influence exercised. The distributive allocation of human rights obligations among duty-bearers may still take the primary obligation of the domestic State as its logical starting point, while other States and non-State actors can be said to have complementary obligations. As to the distributive allocation of obligations to fulfil among other actors than the domestic State, he advances a differentiated human rights obligations regime based on an abstract system of allocation. He then moves on to assigning responsibility for human rights violations in a context of a plurality and diversity of actors based on three principles: that of shared responsibility; of differentiation of responsibility along a continuum; and of liability for monetary compensation that is commensurate with the degree of responsibility.

The next three chapters explore what it would take for international human rights law to fundamentally re-design its duty-bearer side beyond the changes outlined in the previous chapters.

Pavlakos in his chapter 'Transnational legal responsibility: some preliminaries' submits that a rather radical *reconstruction* is needed of the standard perception of legal obligation that reaches beyond the limits of national sovereignty, rather than an ad hoc accommodation of new actors. Pavlakos suggests a shift from the primacy of the site of a legal obligation (ie sovereignty) to the scope of a legal relation (ie the wrongdoing and the set of agents involved), by focusing on the proto-legal relation that pertains to joint patterns of action that trigger off a constraint of permissibility. Taking the protolegal relation and obligations rather than actors (in particular States) as the starting point, it becomes possible to ground transnational obligations. Moreover, shared responsibility is promoted, since joint patterns of action generate enforceable obligations that are jointly shared by all actors involved in the scheme: plural and diverse actors can be brought jointly under the same ground of responsibility.

In his chapter, 'The common interest in international law: implications for human rights', **De Feyter** explores from the perspective of public international law the potential of a common interest approach to human rights law. Global common interest treaties draw on the responsible exercise of sovereignty and include duties for other actors, both non-territorial States and actors other than States. A distinctive characteristic of common interest regimes is also that they differentiate obligations depending on, inter alia, capacity.

De Feyter is cautious about the contribution of a global common interest approach to human rights, mainly because of the biases of the human rights treaty regime, with its focus on the individual harm and its reluctance to differentiate obligations. In a global common interest approach, the heaviest burden would remain on the jurisdictionally responsible State. If domestic capacity to realise human rights were no longer presumed, but empirically assessed, a solidarity obligation – to be agreed upon among States – to provide implementation aid would be triggered. A global common interest approach would also favour the inclusion of actors other than States.

Salomon in her chapter, 'You say you want a revolution: challenges of market primacy for the human rights project', cautions on the dangers that market primacy has for the human rights project. Rather than challenging market primacy and the regulatory regimes that create it, human rights often seek merely to soften the worst tendencies of economic globalisation. Salomon also warns that efforts to expand the duty-bearer side of human rights law are not beyond criticism: 'The shift from the national to the global arena – to transnational actors and their influence, to international organisations and their power – is of paramount significance, but the law is suspiciously selective in its application and reach.' Salomon's chapter flags the risk of co-optation of human rights law by the market. Hence, any effort to redesign the human rights regime may not only seek to expand the duty-bearer side, but will also have to take a clear position on the principles that underscore market primacy.

Part 1

Emerging frameworks for human rights obligations of new duty-bearers

2 Extraterritorial human rights obligations: wider implications of the Maastricht Principles and the continuing accountability challenge

Ashfaq Khalfan and Ian Seiderman

On 28 September 2011 a group of 40 international human rights experts adopted the Maastricht Principles on the Extraterritorial Obligations of States in the area of Economic, Social and Cultural Rights at a meeting convened by the University of Maastricht and the International Commission of Jurists.[1] The meeting culminated a two-year drafting process involving extensive research and wide-ranging consultations. The members of the six-person drafting committee who prepared the Maastricht Principles, and include the authors of this present article, subsequently published a Commentary to the 44 Articles of the Principles.[2]

The Maastricht Principles define obligations and responsibilities for the realization of human rights, particularly economic, social and cultural rights (ESC rights), in respect of the conduct of States beyond their borders. They address themselves to two distinct, but necessarily interrelated, concerns. First, there is the continuing, never extinguishable, obligation of States to respect, protect and, in some instances, even fulfil rights when their conduct has real and foreseeable effects beyond their borders. Second is the injunction under international law that States must proactively take measures, especially through international assistance and cooperation, to realize rights extraterritorially. While the Maastricht Principles tackled an ambitious range of questions in this framework, there were inevitably a number of important questions that were not fully addressed or clarified.[3]

1 Maastricht Principles on Extraterritorial Obligations of States in the area of Economic, Social and Cultural Rights (adopted 28 September 2011). See *http://www.maastrichtuniversity.nl/web/Institutes/MaastrichtCentreForHumanRights/MaastrichtETOPrinciples.htm* (accessed 26 January 2015).

2 O De Schutter, A Eide, A Khalfan, M Orellana, M Salomon and I Seiderman, 'Commentary to the Maastricht Principles on Extraterritorial Obligations of States in the Area of Economic, Social and Cultural Rights' (2012) 34 *Human Rights Quarterly* 1084–1169. Also available at *http;//www.icj.org/protecting-human-rights-beyond-borders/* (accessed 26 January 2015).

3 M Salomon and I Seiderman, 'Human Rights Norms for a Globalized World: The Maastricht Principles on Extraterritorial Obligations of States in the area of Economic, Social and Cultural Rights' (2012) 3 *Global Policy* 458–462 at 459.

In furtherance of the task of the present volume, which is to elaborate on principles and concepts that will assist in a determining how to attribute and apportion human rights responsibilities[4] in a multi-duty-bearer setting, we touch on four of these areas. In doing so, we seek to demonstrate that, while they by no means present a comprehensive solution to the overall question of apportionment and attribution, the Maastricht Principles provide more guidance than is readily evident from the text of the Principles.

The four areas addressed are: (1) The question of the applicability of the Maastricht Principles to the full range of human rights, including civil and political rights (CP rights); (2) the relevance of the Principles to the apportionment of responsibilities of non-State actors; (3) the applicability of the Principles to responsibilities of international organizations; and (4) the need to review existing accountability mechanisms, including for redress of violations, to ensure they are able to address situations in which multiple duty-bearers may be implicated in particular human rights abuse.[5]

The Maastricht Principles

A full analysis of the Maastricht Principles is available in the published commentary and we will not recount it in full here. It is worth recalling, however, some of the main elements of the Principles.[6] The Principles are ordered in accordance with the now widely invoked 'respect/protect/fulfil' framework. They recognize that general international human rights law imposes obligations on States to refrain from impairing rights beyond borders under the duty to respect (Principles 19–22). This obligation may be breached through the direct interference with the enjoyment of human rights, such as when an attacking or occupying military force unlawfully destroys homes or agricultural capacity on which persons in the besieged State depend for their livelihood.[7] It may also take the form of an indirect interference, such as when one State assists another state in carrying out violations.[8] The Principles address the specific instance of the imposition of sanctions or equivalent measures that may impair the enjoyment of human rights.[9]

Pursuant to the obligation to protect, Principles 23–27 posit that States must act to protect against the adverse conduct of third parties, such as transnational corporations and other business enterprises, other organizations and

4 The term 'responsibilities' is used here in a general descriptive sense to encompass any manner of hard or soft obligation or duty, and not exclusively as it relates to secondary legal obligations, ie rules of State responsibility.

5 The views herein are ours alone, and do not necessarily represent those of our colleagues in the Drafting Committee, the larger Expert Group that ultimately elaborated and agreed on the text of the Maastricht Principles.

6 See also Salomon and Seiderman (n 3).

7 Principle 20.

8 Principle 21.

9 Principle 22.

private persons. States have an obligation to regulate such entities as business enterprises though administrative, legislative, investigative or adjudicatory measures where they are in a position to do so.[10] Such circumstances will arise when the harm or threat of harm takes place on the State's own territory; when the non-State actor has the nationality of the State(s) concerned, such as when a malfeasant business is incorporated in the State; or when the company or its parent company has its centre of activity in the State, is registered or domiciled in the State or has substantial business activities in the State.[11] In addition, a basis of protection may be engaged 'where there is a reasonable link between the State concerned and the conduct it seeks to regulate, including where aspects of non-state actor's activities are carried out in that State's territory'.[12]

The general obligation of States to fulfil the rights of persons outside their respective territories, through international cooperation and assistance, addressed in Principle 28, arises, among other sources, from the United Nations (UN) Charter and Art 2(1) of the International Covenant on Economic, Social and Cultural Rights (ICESCR).[13] This obligation involves the requirement to establish international trade, investment, and financial and environmental arrangements conducive to the realization of human rights for all persons.[14] States are required to develop means of coordinating the allocation of responsibilities to contribute to fulfilment of rights, including through economic, technical and technological resources and influence in decision-making.[15] States requiring assistance in meeting their obligations to fulfil human rights must affirmatively seek assistance for this purpose, and those States to which a request is made must consider the request in good faith and respond in a manner consistent with their human rights obligation.[16] Fulfilling the rights of disadvantaged and marginalized people should be prioritized in the allocation of resources.[17]

Principles 36–41 address the obligation to provide for accountability and effective remedies and reparations for rights violations. Accountability entails the establishment and use of effective domestic and international judicial and non-judicial mechanisms.[18] Remedies must be prompt, effective and accessible before an independent authority, and available both in the territorial State and the State where the harm occurred. Reparations include restitution, compensation, satisfaction, rehabilitations and guarantees of non-repetition and the right to truth.[19]

10 Principle 24.
11 Principle 25.
12 Principle 25(d).
13 Charter of the United Nations (adopted 24 October 1945, entered into force 31 August 1965) 1 UNTS XVI (UN Charter) and International Covenant on Economic, Social and Cultural Rights (adopted 16 December 1966, entered into force 3 January 1976) 993 UNTS 171, Art 2(1).
14 Principle 29.
15 Principle 31.
16 Principle 34.
17 Principle 32(a).
18 Principle 36.
19 Principle 38.

All of the identified obligations are underpinned by a number of general Principles (1–18) that are to be applied commonly to the respect, protect and fulfil dimensions of Extra-Territorial Obligations (ETOs),[20] including in the areas of State responsibility and jurisdiction. The latter is a complicated and contested doctrinal area, but one which has predicated much of the debate surrounding extra-territorial obligations and bedevilled attempts to ensure their viability. Looking to the rapidly evolving jurisprudence and practice, the Principles take note that the classic doctrine under general international law holding that jurisdiction is presumptively territorial has been steadily eroding, especially in the area of human rights law.[21] Principle 9 affirms the now generally accepted premise that a State will be acting within its jurisdiction where it has effective control over foreign territory or persons on that territory. But it also holds that a State will be considered to be acting within its jurisdiction where, through its conduct, it has brought about foreseeable effects on the exercise of rights outside its territory; for example, impairing access to clean water by public works that divert the trajectory of water sources in a neighbouring country, thus violating the right to water.[22] Finally, it recognizes the situations where jurisdiction is engaged when the State is under an international obligation to take measures actively to support the realization of rights outside its territory.

Can the Maastricht Principles be applied to all human rights, including civil and political rights?

As a means of contributing to address the question of apportionment of human rights duties and attribution of responsibility of violations, the Maastricht Principles are of somewhat limited utility if their scope is confined only to those rights classed as economic, social and cultural rights. We propose that, notwithstanding their stated ambit, the Principles, subject to the quite limited exceptions discussed below, should be invoked to cover wider ground.

The Principles themselves expressly anticipate a potential broader scope of application. Maastricht Principle 3 affirms that '[a]ll States have obligations to respect, protect and fulfil human rights, including civil, cultural, economic, political and social rights, both within their territories and extraterritorially'.[23] The Commentary to this Principle locates these obligations in general international law, the UN Charter and the Universal Declaration of Human Rights (UDHR), applying to all rights. It also points to particular commitments towards international cooperation contained in specialized treaties such as the ICESCR, the Convention on the Rights of Persons with Disabilities, and the Convention against Torture and Other Cruel, Inhuman or Degrading Treatment or Punishment (CAT).

20 A definition of Extra-Territorial Obligations (ETOs) is provided in Principle 8.

21 De Schutter, Eide, Khalfan, Orellana, Salomon and Seiderman (n 2), 1104–1109.

22 Principle 9.

23 Principle 3

Maastricht Principle 5 states: 'All human rights are universal, indivisible, interdependent, interrelated and of equal importance. The present Principles elaborate extraterritorial obligations in relation to economic, social and cultural rights, without excluding their applicability to other human rights, including civil and political rights.'[24] The Commentary notes that 'the legal bases of extraterritorial obligations are broadly similar' for both sets of rights, but that the nature of extraterritorial obligations flowing from international cooperation in respect of ESC rights has been most developed.[25]

Although not evident from the Commentary, the experts drafting the Principles decided to avoid a direct endorsement of the broader application of the principles based on the common ground assumption that addressing civil and political rights might exceed the understood parameters of the project. It should be noted that the Maastricht Principles had its genesis in the fusion of two streams of work directly focused on economic, social and cultural rights. One was that of the ETO Consortium, a network of more than 80 civil society organizations and academics working specifically in the area of ESC rights.[26] Second was the collaboration between the International Commission of Jurists and the University of Maastricht that had produced the companion ESC standards: The Limburg Principles on the Implementation of the International Covenant on Economic, Social and Cultural Rights (1986)[27] and the Maastricht Guidelines on Violations of Economic, Social and Cultural Rights (1997).[28]

A common understanding did emerge that at least a substantial portion of the Maastricht Principles would indeed fit comfortably as CP rights constructs. The General Principles, notably in respect of 'jurisdiction'; state responsibility; the areas of 'respect' and 'protect', and remedy and reparation, were not only deemed apposite, but they also ultimately relied in significant measure more on authority from CP rights than ESC rights sources, as is evident from the Maastricht Commentary.[29] However, in the area of 'fulfil' (Principles 28–35), the question arose as to whether international cooperation is a principle uniquely at the core of ESC rights, as evidenced by its express placement as part of the general obligation in Art 2(1) of the International Covenant on Economic, Social and Cultural Rights (ICESCR) in contradistinction to its loud omission from the International Covenant on Civil and Political Rights (ICCPR). The question then is whether any divergence

24 Principle 5.

25 De Schutter, Eide, Khalfan, Orellana, Salomon and Seiderman (n 2), 1098.

26 ETO Consortium, *http://www.etoconsortium.org/* (accessed 7 May 2014).

27 The Limburg Principles on the Implementation of the International Covenant on Economic, Social and Cultural Rights, UN Doc E/CN.4/1987/17 and (1987) 9 *Human Rights Quarterly* 122–135.

28 The Maastricht Guidelines on Violations of Economic, Social and Cultural Rights (1998) 20 *Human Rights Quarterly* 691–704.

29 De Schutter, Eide, Khalfan, Orellana, Salomon and Seiderman (n 2), 1104–1112, 1126–1145, 1159–1165.

between the sets of rights goes to the nature of the extraterritorial obligation to fulfil, or only to its scope.

We consider that the Maastricht Principles, at least in very large measure, can and should be applied to CP rights as they stand. Human rights advocates should feel comfortable in invoking them, or at least their legal and normative underpinnings, when considering questions of extraterritoriality in relation to CP rights.

From a juridical perspective, it seems clear enough that not only does the obligation to respect and protect international CP rights under international law have a solid foundational basis, but that CP rights standards and jurisprudence have helped form the basis for the application to ESC rights. To begin with, the basic tripartite framework of 'respect/protect/fulfil', which is widely, albeit not universally, embraced, is applicable to both sets of rights. The 1997 Maastricht Guidelines on ESC violations, underscore that '*[l]ike civil and political rights*, economic, social and cultural rights impose three different types of obligations on States: the obligations to respect, protect and fulfil'.[30] When the Committee on Economic, Social and Cultural Rights first applied the typology in its General Comment 12 on the Right to Food, it stressed: 'The right to adequate food, *like any other human right*, imposes three types or levels of obligations on States parties: the obligations to *respect*, to *protect* and to *fulfil*.'[31]

Although the UN Human Rights Committee, in its consideration of the scope of obligations arising under the ICCPR, does not typically invoke 'respect/protect/fulfil' *stricto sensu*, it does apply an alternative terminological, but ultimately similar, conception. The ICCPR, under Art 2(3) imposes an obligation for states 'to respect *and to ensure* to individuals' the rights in the Covenant.[32] The Human Rights Committee, in its General Comment No 31 on the Nature of the General Legal Obligation on States Parties to the Covenant, made clear that 'ensure' includes elements of 'protect' and 'fulfil', as understood in the tripartite typology.[33] Certain critical components of CP rights duties can best be described as 'fulfil' obligations, for example the obligation in the ICCPR to register a child immediately after birth,[34] the obligation to take positive measures to protect the right to life, for example in adopting measures to eliminate malnutrition and epidemics,[35] the obliga-

30 The Maastricht Guidelines on Violations of Economic, Social and Cultural Rights (1998) 20 *Human Rights Quarterly* 691, Guideline 6 (emphasis added).

31 UN Committee on Economic, Social and Cultural Rights, 'General Recommendation 12, The Right to Adequate Food' (12 May 1999) UN Doc E/C.12/1999/5, para 15 (emphasis added to '*like any other human right*').

32 International Covenant on Civil and Political Rights (adopted 16 December 1966, entered into force 23 March 1976) 999 UNTS 171 (ICCPR), Art 2(3) (emphasis added).

33 Human Rights Committee, 'General Comment No 31, Nature of the General Legal Obligation on States Parties to the Covenant' (29 March 2004) UN Doc CCPR/C/21/Rev.1/Add.13, para 8.

34 ICCPR (n 32), Art 24(2).

35 Human Rights Committee, 'General Comment no 6, The Right to Life' (30 July 1982) UN Doc A/37/40, para 5.

tion to provide for humane conditions of detention[36] and the obligation to establish the infrastructure and conditions required to ensure the right to a fair trial.[37]

Indeed, in regard to the extraterritorial obligations to respect and protect, there is actually a deficit of international authority in the ESC rights area, in part because these levels of obligation have attracted less scrutiny and treatment at the international level than has the obligation to fulfil. With respect to the question of 'fulfilling' rights, we do note the special place given to the role of international cooperation and assistance in Art 2(1) of the ICESCR.[38] However, notwithstanding the absence of a parallel provision in the ICCPR, human rights law in general, including in respect of CP rights, contains an abundance of obligations to engage in international cooperation. Indeed UN Charter Arts 55 and 56 are clear in this regard: 'All members pledge themselves to take joint and separate action in cooperation with the [UN] for the achievement of the purposes set out in article 55', which includes 'universal respect for, and observance of, human rights and fundamental freedoms for all without distinction as to race, sex, language, or religion'.[39] It is against this backdrop that Limburg Principle 29 states that 'International co-operation and assistance pursuant to the Charter of the United Nations (arts. 55 and 56) and the [ICESCR] shall have in view as a matter of priority the realization of all human rights and fundamental freedoms, economic, social and cultural *as well as civil and political.*'[40] In advance of this objective, Art 28 of the UDHR provides that 'everybody is entitled to a social and international order in which rights and freedoms set forth in this Declaration can be fully realized'.[41] The UDHR of course contains both ESC and CP rights.

Many international instruments covering CP rights are replete with references to forms of international cooperation. Examples include CAT (Art 9(1));[42] the International Convention for the Protection of All Persons from Enforced Disappearance (Art 15);[43] the Convention on the Rights of Persons

36 Human Rights Committee, 'General Comment no 21, Humane Treatment of Persons Deprived of Their Liberty' (10 April 1992) UN Doc HRI/GEN/1/Rev.1.

37 Human Rights Committee, 'General Comment no 13, Administration of Justice, Equality before the Courts and the Right to a Fair and Public Hearing by an Independent Court (13 April 1984) UN Doc HRI/GEN/1/Rev.1.

38 International Covenant on Economic, Social and Cultural Rights (adopted 16 December 1966, entered into force 3 January 1976), 999 UNTS 171 (ICESCR), Art 2(1).

39 Charter of the United Nations (adopted 24 October 1945, entered into force 31 August 1965), 1 UNTS XVI (UN Charter), Arts 55 and 56.

40 UNCHR, 'Note Verbale dated 86/12/05 from the Permanent Mission of the Netherlands to the United Nations Office at Geneva addressed to the Centre for Human Rights' ('Limburg Principles') (8 January 1987), E/CN,4/1987/17, Principle 29 (emphasis added).

41 Universal Declaration of Human Rights (10 December 1948), 217 A (III), Art 28.

42 Convention Against Torture and Other Cruel, Inhuman or Degrading Treatment or Punishment (adopted 10 December 1984, entered into force 26 June 1987), 1465 UNTS 85.

43 UNGA Res 61/177 (12 January 2007) 'International Convention for the Protection of All Persons from Enforced Disappearance', *http://www.refworld.org/docid/47fdfaeb0.html* (accessed 7 May 2014).

with Disabilities (Art 32);[44] the Convention on the Rights of the Child (CRC, Arts 23(4), 28(3));[45] the Optional Protocol (OP) to the CRC on the sale of children, child prostitution and child pornography (Preambular paras 6 and 9, OP 10);[46] and the Optional Protocol to the CRC on involvement of children in armed conflict (Preambular para 17, Art 7(1)).[47] The Rome Statute of the International Criminal Court devotes an entire part to international cooperation and judicial assistance in Arts 86–102.[48] Moreover, international cooperation is frequently referenced in resolutions of the General Assembly and UN Human Rights Council when calling on states to implement CP rights obligations. For example, the Council's general resolution on Enhancement of International Cooperation in the field of Human Rights contained not a single reference to 'economic, social and cultural rights' as such, but rather references to 'all human rights' or 'all human rights and fundamental freedoms'.[49]

There are certainly elements in the Maastricht Principles that are tailored particularly for ESC rights. Principle 32(b) and (d), addressing priorities in international cooperation, is framed in accordance with two particular obligations flowing from the ICESCR, as understood through the jurisprudence of the CESCR and the Limburg Principles: (1) the duty to prioritize core obligations to realize minimum essential levels of ESC rights; and (2) the duty to avoid retrogressive measures. These are details of prioritization which may well have included additional elements had CP rights been taken into account, and their inclusion does not undermine the wider point that the principles have wider applicability.

The case is equally forceful for inclusion of CP rights at the policy level. If the objective is the optimal realization of all human rights, there is good reason to move towards minimizing, if not entirely obliterating the unfortunate historical distinction between CP and ESC rights. This distinction has carried the consequence of effectively casting ESC rights into a second-class status, one in which human rights development is only recently retrenching.

44 Convention on the Rights of Persons with Disabilities (adopted 24 January 2007), A/RES/61/106.

45 Convention on the Rights of the Child (adopted 20 November 1989, entered into force 2 September 1990) 1577 UNTS 3.

46 Optional Protocol to the Convention on the Rights of the Child on the Sale of Children, Child Prostitution and Child Pornography (adopted 16 March 2001), A/RES/54/263.

47 Optional Protocol to the Convention on the Rights of the Child on Involvement of Children in Armed Conflict (adopted 25 May 2000), A/RES/54/263.

48 Rome Statute of the International Criminal Court (adopted 17 July 1998, entered into force 1 July 2002, corrected by procès-verbaux of 10 November 1998, 12 July 1999, 30 November 1999, 8 May 2000, 17 January 2001 and 16 January 2002), A/CONF.183/9, 2187 UNTS.

49 Human Rights Council Resolution 23/3, 'Enhancement of International Cooperation of Human Rights' (6 June 2013), A/HRC/23/L.6, paras 8, 17, 20. For other examples, see Human Rights Council Resolution 19/31, 'Integrity of the Judicial System' (18 April 2012), A/HRC/19/L.5/Rev.1, para 9, General Assembly Resolution 19/18, 'Human Rights, Democracy, and the Rule of Law' (10 April 2012), A/HRC/RES/19/36, paras 18, 21 and 25.

As is by now well-rehearsed, the traditional division into sets of rights was largely a product of cold war political posturing.[50] The consensus reached in 1993, as reflected in the Vienna Declaration and Programme of Action (VDPA), was clear as to the equal importance and non-hierarchical relation between the sets of rights, providing the now well-entrenched principle that '[a]ll human rights are universal, indivisible and interdependent and interrelated. The international community must treat human rights globally in a fair and equal manner, on the same footing, and with the same emphasis'.[51] Thus, the 2013 Vienna Plus 20 outcome document, adopted by leading human rights experts, recommended that States both '[a]fford the same level of protection to economic, social and cultural rights, and civil and political rights' and 'recognise the extraterritorial nature of human rights obligations'.[52]

The UN Office of the High Commissioner on Human Rights (OHCHR) has taken a clear position in favour of discarding the distinction between the two sets of rights. In its fact sheet on ESC rights, the OHCHR unequivocally states that economic, social and cultural rights are not fundamentally different from civil and political rights:

> In the past, there has been a tendency to speak of economic, social and cultural rights as if they were fundamentally different from civil and political rights. However, this categorization is artificial and even self-defeating [...] when closely scrutinised, categories of rights such as 'civil and political rights' or 'economic, social and cultural rights' make little sense. For this reason, it is increasingly common to refer to civil, cultural, economic, political and social rights.[53]

But perhaps the greatest reason to eradicate the distinction is a very practical one, relating to the very real means that rights obligations are actually discharged and for which violations are accounted. Many scenarios involving violations actually implicate multiple rights areas, some of which may relate to political and civil rights, and others to economic, social and cultural rights. The violations will often arise out of the same situation, rendering it absurd to try and tailor a distinct scope and nature of obligation for certain rights as opposed to others. On the extraterritorial 'respect and protect' levels, for

50 See, inter alia, L Henkin, G Neuman, D Orentlicher and D Leebron, *Human Rights* (1st edn, University Casebook Series, 1999), 1106.

51 Vienna Declaration and Programme of Action, A/CONF.157/23, adopted by the World Conference on Human Rights in Vienna on 25 June 1993 or UNGA Res 48/121 (20 December 1993), para 5.

52 International Expert Conference paper 'Vienna+20: Advancing the Projection of Human Rights; Achievements, Challenges and Perspectives 20 Years after the World Conference' (28 June 2013), *http://www.bmeia.gv.at/fileadmin/user_upload/bmeia/media/2-Aussenpolitik_Zentrale/Menschenrechte/Conference_Report_-_Vienna___20.pdf* (accessed 7 May 2014).

53 OHCHR, 'Fact Sheet Number 33: Frequently asked Questions on Economic, Social and Cultural Rights' (December 2008), *http://www.ohchr.org/Documents/Publications/FactSheet33en.pdf* (accessed 7 May 2014).

instance, an armed assault by a foreign military force on a human settlement may involve both violations of the right to life and right to be free from ill-treatment. Concomitantly, they may involve unlawful attacks on civilian infrastructure, involving forced evictions in violation of the right to housing, and damage to water supplies and agriculture, violating the right to food or damage to school facilities undermining the right to education. The division of rights on the fulfil level is no less coherent, for example where a donor State or international organization may seek to direct assistance for the realization of multiple rights, or towards a broader objective that impacts a range of rights, for example the reform of the justice sector which will better allow for access to justice to effectively remedy rights violations.

The Maastricht Principles and the responsibilities of private actors

The project of the Maastricht Principles has aimed exclusively at the obligations of States. However, it is an ever burgeoning challenge in a globalized world to ensure that the legal responsibility of a range of private actors is also appropriately engaged, as is accountability for their conduct, which no doubt may have an enormous impact on human rights.

Without entering into a wider discussion on the long simmering conceptual dispute as to whether private actors have (or should have) human rights duties under international law, we consider that optimal starting point by which the responsibility of transnational corporations and other business enterprises should be engaged is through a State responsibility framework. This is the approach taken by the Maastricht Principles, particularly in Principles 23–27. By adopting the widely accepted, although not uncontested, typology of 'respect, protect, and fulfil' to describe State obligations, the Principles may effectively be called upon to address significant aspects of corporate responsibility.

It should be noted that the Maastricht Principles do address the conduct of private non-State actors, including business enterprises, in respect of situations where State responsibility is engaged for such conduct. Partly tracking the language of the International Law Commission's articles on State Responsibility, Principle 12 underlines that State responsibility extends to the conduct of 'non-State actors acting on the instructions or under the direction or control of the State'; as well as to non-State actors 'empowered by the State to exercise elements of governmental authority'.[54] As the Maastricht Commentary explains, the latter instance encompasses private companies that perform regulatory or other public functions, such as in the case of private military and security companies and public water and electricity utilities.[55] The fact that in many such situations the conduct of the company may be

54 Principle 12.

55 De Schutter, Eide, Khalfan, Orellana, Salomon and Seiderman (n 2), 1111.

attributed to the State itself, gives rise to a heightened expression of the more general obligation to protect.

Regarding, more generally, the question of human rights responsibilities of non-State actors, it is informative to take account of the present state of play of international standard-setting and normative development in the area of business and human rights.[56] The UN Guiding Principles on Business and Human Rights,[57] prepared by the Special Representative of the UN Secretary General on Business and Human Rights, John Ruggie, prescribe a tripartite 'protect, respect and remedy' framework.[58] The Guiding Principles purport to establish a baseline for the conduct of States and businesses, without creating new international law obligations or undermining existing ones,[59] consisting of (1) the State obligation to protect against human rights abuses by third parties within their territory and/or jurisdiction; (2) the responsibility of business enterprises to respect human rights; and (3) the responsibility of both to provide access to remedies.[60]

The Guiding Principles, while endorsed in a consensus resolution by the UN Human Rights Council, have not been received without criticism or controversy, both in the process of their elaboration and many aspects of their content.[61] Indeed, it bears mentioning that the Council resolution '[r]ecognises the role of the Guiding Principles for the implementation of the Framework, *on which further progress can be made ...*'.[62] The latter clause replaced a previous draft version, which '[r]ecognizes the role of the Guiding Principles on Business and Human Rights in providing comprehensive recommendations for the implementation of the United Nations Protect, Respect and Remedy Framework ...'.[63]

The Guiding Principles provide a dubious basis for legal corporate accountability, not least because the entire pillar of the business responsibility to respect human rights is not founded upon any firm legal duty, but rather on 'the basic expectation society has of business'[64] or, as Special Representative Ruggie's Commentary to Principle 11 says, 'a global standard of expected conduct'.[65] The State obligation to protect under the Guiding Principles, by contrast, is predicated – at least in part – on legal foundations, as the

56 See also Černič, chapter 4 in this volume.

57 Report of the Special Representative of the Secretary-General on the issue of human rights and transnational corporations and other business enterprises (2011), Annex, 'Guiding Principles on Business and Human Rights, implementing the United Nations "Protect, Respect and Remedy" Framework', UN Doc A/HRC/17/31.

58 Human Rights Council Res 8/7 (2008), UN Doc A/HRC/RES/8/7.

59 UNGPs (n 57), para 13.

60 Guiding Principles on Business and Human Rights (n 57), para 6.

61 See, for instance, S Deva and D Bilchitz (eds), *Human Rights Obligations of Business, Beyond the Corporate Responsibility to Respect?* (CUP 2013).

62 Human Rights Council Res 17/4 (2011), UN Doc A/HRC/17/4, para 4 (emphasis added).

63 Human Rights Council Res 17/L.17 (2011), UN Doc A/HRC/17/L.17/Rev.1, para 4.

64 Guiding Principles on Business and Human Rights (n 57), para 6.

65 Guiding Principles on Business and Human Rights (n 57), commentary to Principles 11, 13.

Commentary affirms the duty of States under international law to protect against human rights abuses by third parties.[66] The implication of this weak normative foundation of the responsibility to respect is that there is a distortion in the apportionment of responsibility as between States and businesses enterprises, with the latter ascribed only soft, quasi-voluntary duties.

This deficiency in the Guiding Principles really arises from the original typological framework. The model situates the State obligation to protect and the responsibility of businesses to respect as two distinct and self-standing pillars. An alternative and, in our view, more legally coherent approach, might have been to place the responsibility of businesses to respect directly *under* the State's obligation to protect, rather than as a separate pillar; that is, to acknowledge that businesses are obliged to respect rights first and foremost because States must, as a legal obligation as part of the duty to protect, make them respect human rights and hold them accountable for any dereliction. It is necessarily only through State authority, whether exercised unilaterally or multilaterally, that a social norm or a moral norm, becomes a legal norm. By predicating the responsibility of businesses to respect human rights on social expectations, rather than legal standards, the Guiding Principles were forced to rely effectively on the voluntary good will of those businesses to self-regulate.

The 'protect' function, however, itself cannot be comprehended only in the narrow terms of the Guiding principles. The obligation to protect concerns a broad array of what States do singly and jointly, bilaterally and through international cooperation. As recognized in Guiding Principle 3, States must protect through adequate regulation at home. Under Guiding Principle 4, they must take protective measures in respect of State enterprises and export credit agencies and official investment and guarantee agencies, although this injunction is greatly weakened by the qualifier, 'where appropriate, by ensuring human rights due diligence'.[67] But States also have protective obligations when acting multilaterally through international organizations, such as the World Bank, IMF and WTO. Guiding Principle 10, addressing this area, falls back on voluntary commitments, where States are only to 'encourage' such organizations to be human rights compliant, promote a shared understanding and advance international cooperation in managing business and human rights challenges.[68]

Another stark deficiency in the Guiding Principles regarding what companies are 'expected' to do is that the responsibility of businesses in many situations is engaged beyond the level of 'respect'. It cannot simply be that businesses should do no harm and not interfere in the enjoyment of rights. There are many types of situations where the duty to protect and fulfil will arise, such as when a company performs a public function. State responsibility

66 UNGPs (n 57), commentary to Principles 1, 6.
67 Guiding Principle 4.
68 Guiding Principle 10.

may in this respect be engaged for the conduct of such companies beyond the level of respect obligations. Privatized water companies, for example, are necessarily fulfilling, and not merely respecting the right to water. A private prison contractor must respect, protect and fulfil the entire range of rights within the prison it administers. There may, indeed, be situations where a company may not be exercising a public function delegated to it by a State, but where it has effective control over the rights of individuals, for example situations where entire municipalities are 'company towns', the entire governance of which is in private hands.[69] In these and similarly pertinent circumstances, to avoid protection gaps, States should impose firm legal duties upon private companies, over whom they exercise jurisdiction, to protect and fulfil human rights.

The Maastricht Principles, therefore, do not consider the direct responsibilities of companies, but rather aim to reflect and further an expansive conception of the State obligation to protect. Were the obligations, as contemplated by the Principles, substantially discharged, companies would necessarily incur a wide range of legal duties, some possibility without much active State involvement. Principle 25 sets out five types of circumstances, pursuant to which States are required to take measures to protect, including through regulation pursuant to Principle 24:

(a) the harm or threat of harm originates or occurs on its territory;
(b) where the non-State actor has the nationality of the State concerned;
(c) as regards business enterprises, where the corporation, or its parent or controlling company, has its centre of activity, is registered or domiciled, or has its main place of business or substantial business activities, in the State concerned;
(d) where there is a reasonable link between the State concerned and the conduct it seeks to regulate, including where relevant aspects of a non-State actor's activities are carried out in that State's territory;
(e) where any conduct impairing economic, social and cultural rights constitutes a violation of a peremptory norm of international law. Where such a violation also constitutes a crime under international law, States must exercise universal jurisdiction over those bearing responsibility or lawfully transfer them to an appropriate jurisdiction.[70]

Principle 26 makes clear, as do the General Principles, that the obligation to protect is to be discharged not only unilaterally, but also by States jointly, through international cooperation. Effective cooperation in this regard, particularly at the multilateral level, requires action by international organizations, a question addressed in the following section.

69 For more information on the phenomenon of company towns, see, for instance, D Monti, *Race, Development and the New Company Town* (NYP 1990).
70 Principle 25.

One manner in which this function may discharged in the future is through an international treaty that could set out, for example, uniform regulatory standards for States to impose on business enterprises as well as the bases for establishing jurisdiction over such businesses. It could also provide for obligations to share information and evidence that a State may have on corporate human rights abuses with concerned States. Progress was made towards this end in June 2014, when the UN Human Rights Council adopted a resolution to establish an intergovernmental working group to elaborate a legally binding legal instrument on business and human rights.[71] However, the decision to proceed with this initiative was highly contentious, and the resolution was adopted on a vote that was sharply divided, largely along 'North/South' lines. Given the divisions, the prospects for a speedy drafting process are at best uncertain.

The Maastricht Principles and international organizations

The Maastricht Principles devote significant attention to the responsibility of States for their conduct in regard to those international organizations of which they are members. They did not elaborate the direct legal obligations of international organizations because the experts determined that this issue deserved separate scrutiny. Standards elaborating 'extra-territorial' obligations could hardly do justice to the general area of obligations of international organizations, for which governance and the administration of territory is the exception rather than the rule. However, the Principles, somewhat coyly, state that the Maastricht Principles apply to States 'without excluding their applicability to the human rights obligations of international organizations under, inter alia, general international law and international agreements to which they are parties'.[72] This section therefore addresses, first, the obligations of States as members of international organizations, and, second, the obligations of international organizations.

Obligations of States

Maastricht Principle 15 requires that a State 'take all reasonable steps to ensure that, in its decision-making processes, the international organization acts in accordance with the pre-existing human rights obligations of the state concerned'.[73] This obligation attaches whether or not the international organization concerned itself bears any such obligations. For the reasons described above, it would be inconceivable to conclude that States have such obligations only in respect of ESC rights and not also in respect of CP rights.

71 Office of the High Commissioner on Human Rights, *http://www.ohchr.org/EN/NewsEvents/Pages/DisplayNews.aspx?NewsID=14785&LangID=E* (accessed 27 June 2014).

72 Principle 16.

73 Principle 15.

Article 61 of the International Law Commission's (ILC) Draft Articles on the responsibility of international organizations (DARIO) stipulates:

> A State member of an international organization incurs international responsibility if, by taking advantage of the fact that the organization has competence in relation to the subject-matter of one of the State's international obligations, it circumvents that obligation by causing the organization to commit an act that, if committed by the State, would have constituted a breach of the obligation.[74]

For this rule to apply, it is necessary that the State has intended to avoid compliance with its obligations; it does not apply when the act of the organization is an unintended result of the State's conduct.[75] Furthermore, 'there must be a significant link between the conduct of the circumventing member State and that of the international organization. The act of the international organization has to be caused by the member State'.[76] The ILC's Commentary to Art 61 draws on the jurisprudence of the ECtHR, which 'holds States responsible when they fail to ensure compliance with their obligations under the European Convention on Human Rights in a field where they have attributed competence to an international organization'.[77] The ILC does not specify a threshold or test for establishing when a State has caused the conduct in question. It is therefore submitted that where a State expressly approves of a particular course of action, such as by adopting a decision requiring it, this conduct would constitute a significant link between the State's conduct and that of the international organization.

The requirement to ensure that international organizations conduct themselves in conformity with the human rights obligations of their member States is usefully explored under the tripartite typology of rights. In regard to the obligation to respect, the State obligation to ensure that its own conduct within an international organization complies with its general human rights obligations, including its obligation to refrain from direct or indirect interferences with human rights, means that it must refrain from taking positive steps to induce conduct by an international organization which would foreseeably lead to human rights abuses.[78] That obligation also arises under the

74 This rule applies whether or not the act is internationally wrongful for the international organization, as clarified in Art 61(2). The ILC concluded its work on the topic with the adoption of these articles. It considers that as practice and evidence related to the responsibility of international organizations is limited, these articles tend more towards progressive development of the law than codification, in contrast to the Articles on State Responsibility. See ILC, 'Draft Articles on Responsibility of International Organizations with Commentaries' in 'Report of the International Law Commission on the Work of its 63rd session' (2011) UN Doc A/66/10, Art 61(1) and Commentary to Art 61, para 5.

75 Ibid, Commentary to Art 61, para 2.

76 Ibid para 7.

77 Ibid, paras 3–5.

78 We use the term 'abuse' rather than 'violation' as there may be some limited instances where

secondary rules of state responsibility, in circumstances in which responsibility for human rights abuses caused or facilitated by an international organization may be attributed to a State member.

If an international organization carries out a programme or activity that would foreseeably impair the enjoyment of a human right, a State would be responsible for such impairment if it: (1) voted, or was party to a decision adopted without a vote,[79] to approve that programme; (2) requested staff of an international organization to carry out that programme, or to modify it in a manner which foreseeably caused an impairment to a human right.

Generally, in the absence of an express international obligation providing for strict liability, a State will only be responsible for harm that is a foreseeable result of its conduct.[80] Where an impact has not been 'foreseen nor of an easily foreseeable kind', the State cannot be held responsible on the grounds that this is *force majeure*.[81] However, once the impact of its conduct on human rights is manifest, the State is bound to take steps to minimize that impact and to cease further actions that could exacerbate that harm.

The obligation to ensure that an international organization conforms to the human rights obligations of its member States is *analogous* to the obligation to *protect* human rights, as it requires a State to prevent another actor from impairing the enjoyment of those rights.[82] It implies the following protective duties for each Member State:

- opposing within the organization any policies and programmes that may foreseeably impair the enjoyment of human rights;
- proposing due diligence measures to prevent such interference – for example, instructing the staff of the organization that all policies recommended to governments are to be consistent with international human rights standards; and

international organizations are not directly bound by certain human rights obligations, particularly where they pertain to newer human rights standards.

79 In some cases, as with the World Bank, a State may share its representative to the international organization with other countries. In that case, the State would be responsible for its instructions (or lack thereof) to – but not necessarily for the actions of – that representative.

80 Principle 13.

81 ILC, 'Draft Articles on Responsibility of International Organizations with Commentaries' in 'Report of the International Law Commission on the Work of its 63rd session' (2011) UN Doc A/66/10, Art 23 and Commentary to Art 23, para 2.

82 We use the expression 'analogous to the obligation to protect human rights' because the treaty body that has most consistently dealt with State obligations within international organizations, the CESCR, does not link its references to these obligations to those it has defined under the obligation to protect. Furthermore, in the context of the obligation to protect, the CESCR has defined 'third parties' that a State is required to prevent from harming ESC rights as including: 'individuals, groups, corporations and other entities as well as agents acting under their authority'. That definition of the obligation to protect appears to refer only to non-State actors. See CESCR, 'General Comment 15: The Right to Water' (2002) UN Doc E/C.12/2002/11, para 23 and CESCR, 'General Comment 19: The Right to Social Security' (2008) UN Doc E/C.12/GC/19, para 45.

- developing or revising relevant performance standards, to ensure that the organization only supports projects that comply with human rights standards.

In the event of a foreseeable impairment of the enjoyment of a human right, responsibility would be jointly attributed to the States that did not support reasonable steps to prevent it.

In regard to the obligation to *fulfil*, when the mandate or primary activity of an international organization substantially addresses human rights areas, member States are typically required to take steps to propose and support actions by the organization to fulfil these rights within the resources available to that organization. Thus, member States of organizations focusing on development issues, such as the World Bank, must promote and support a requirement that such organizations contribute to the fulfilment of human rights – for example, by prioritizing the realization of the minimum essential level of ESC rights in development aid.

Article 61 of the DARIO applies most clearly to the obligation to respect human rights, but is also relevant to obligations of States to ensure that the organization takes feasible steps to protect and fulfil these rights. However, human rights standards, as reflected in the Maastricht Principles, apply even to situations where the DARIO is silent.[83] One example is a situation in which a State may not intend to be non-compliant, but fails to take steps to prevent foreseeable non-compliance such as by establishing adequate policies and safeguards.

A State is not necessarily responsible for the conduct of an international organization simply by being a member,[84] even if it is clearly responsible for its own conduct related to decision-making within that organization. Furthermore, a State's provision of non-earmarked funds to the general budget of that organization would not necessarily render that State responsible for aiding and assisting any infringements of human rights caused or supported by the organization. In regard to the issue of aid and assistance addressed in Art 58 of the DARIO, the ILC stipulates that: 'An act by a State member of an international organization done in accordance with the rules of the organization does not *as such* engage the international responsibility of that State …'.[85] However, the ILC is careful to state that 'the possibility that aid or assistance could result from conduct taken by the State within the framework of the organization cannot be totally excluded'.[86] The ILC indicates that

83 The ILC articles do not apply if, and to the extent that, special rules of international law determine whether a State's act in connection with the conduct of an international organization is internationally wrongful. See ILC, 'Draft Articles on Responsibility of International Organizations with Commentaries' in 'Report of the International Law Commission on the Work of its 63rd session' (2011) UN Doc A/66/10, Art 64.

84 Ibid, Commentary to Art 62, para 2.

85 Ibid, Art 58(2), emphasis added.

86 Ibid, Commentary to Art 58, para 4.

such responsibility could be found 'in borderline cases' in which '[t]he factual context such as the size of membership and the nature of the involvement will probably be decisive'.[87]

It is submitted that if a State voluntarily provides funds to a particular programme or project, apart from its standard contributions to the general budget of the organization, it would or should have considered the purposes and operational aspects of that particular programme and would therefore be responsible for its contribution to any foreseeable consequences. This responsibility would then be based on either Art 58 or Art 61 of the DARIO.

Maastricht Principle 15 indicates that States must take reasonable steps, in any transfer of competences to an international organization, to ensure that the organization acts consistently with the international human rights obligations of that State. This duty logically flows from the State obligation to ensure that human rights are taken into account in the conclusion, interpretation and implementation of existing and new international agreements,[88] as well as from the obligation set out in Art 61 of the DARIO. The commentary to the Maastricht Principles indicates possible steps in this context; ensuring that each State has veto power over some of the decisions of the organization that may affect human rights, and ensuring that those affected by measures adopted by the organization will have access to a court empowered to adjudicate human rights claims.[89]

Obligations of international organizations

In contrast to our approach to private actors, where we focus on State obligations to protect rights, we do consider it essential to address the direct legal obligations of international organizations. International organizations are composed of States that carry their obligations with them and therefore must be governed under a distinctive legal regime. International organizations are bound by some components of international human rights law. The commentary to the Maastricht Principles indicates four ways in which this may be so. First, an international organization is bound by customary international law in respect of human rights that may be considered part of customary law; second, by any treaties to which such an organization is party, for example in respect of the European Union's accession to the Disabilities Convention and its possible accession to the ECHR; third, through any human rights related provision in its constitutions, a consideration particularly important in respect of the United Nations specialized agencies, as they are bound by the UN Charter; and fourth, by general principles of law.[90] In regard to customary international law and general principles, there is a strong case that at the

87 Ibid.

88 This obligation is set out in relation to ESC rights in Maastricht Principle 17.

89 De Schutter, Eide, Khalfan, Orellana, Salomon and Seiderman (n 2), 1120.

90 De Schutter, Eide, Khalfan, Orellana, Salomon and Seiderman (n 2), 1121.

very least the UDHR binds international organizations as general international law, and/or in the case of UN specialized agencies, as an authoritative interpretation of the UN Charter.[91]

To the extent that human rights standards are binding on international organizations, which elements of the Maastricht Principles might be also applicable? The Maastricht Principles elaborate the human rights obligations of States in circumstances where their conduct (including omissions to act on positive obligations) has effects beyond their borders. The same obligations are relevant to international organizations since such organizations, by definition, are designed to operate in a transnational, albeit not necessarily universal, context. We would submit that the obligations set forth in the Maastricht Principles apply to international organizations, with the exception of those elements that are specifically designed to allocate responsibilities among States. Specifically, those obligations premised on control over territory, nationality and/or the ability to exercise enforcement jurisdiction apply only to actors that have the competency and capacity to implement them, ie States and only in exceptional circumstances, international organizations (for example, transitional administrations established by the United Nations following conflict).

The implications can be discussed with regard to the tripartite typology of rights. To illustrate, Maastricht Principles 19–22, which address the obligations to *respect* rights, apply directly to international organizations. For example, international organizations are prohibited from establishing conditions for funding to States or other actors that would lead to human rights abuse, or providing funding for purposes that foreseeably would lead to human rights abuse. They are also required to ensure that those acting on their behalf refrain from human rights abuse, for example peacekeepers seconded to them by a State, or companies they have contracted to provide goods and services.[92]

In contrast, obligations to *protect* rights, developed in Maastricht Principles 23–27 would not all apply to international organizations. Of the five bases for regulation set out in Principle 25,[93] the first four – territory, nationality, registration of a company and reasonable link between the State concerned and the conduct in question – are relevant to international organizations only where they have been granted regulatory functions by their members over territories, persons or companies.

International organizations possibly also have an obligation to act in situations considered in Principle 25(e), where any conduct impairing economic, social and cultural rights constitutes a violation of a peremptory norm of

91 B Simma and P Alston, 'The Sources of Human Rights Law: Custom, Jus Cogens, and General Principles' (1988–89) 12 *Australian Yearbook of International Law* 82–108, 100–102. See also van Genugten, chapter 3 in this volume, for detailed analysis of the legal obligations of international organizations.

92 ILC Articles on Responsibility of International Organizations (n 83), arts 6–9.

93 Discussed in Section III above, in the text corresponding to n 70.

international law.[94] They would have this obligation only to the extent their constitutions give them the discretion to act and only utilizing those powers that States have granted them.

The Maastricht Principles adopt a broad definition of the term 'regulation'. Principle 24 refers to obligations to regulate by taking the necessary administrative, legislative, investigative, adjudicatory and other measures to protect rights.[95] Some of these means are open to international organizations, in particular administrative measures, whereas others may require cooperation with relevant national authorities. The obligation to engage in international cooperation to ensure protection of rights, as set out in Principle 27, is therefore directly relevant to international organizations. Furthermore, the obligation described in Principle 24 to refrain from nullifying or impairing a State's duty to protect rights is equally applicable to international organizations, whether or not they have been ascribed regulatory functions by their Members. It would preclude an international organization from relying on its immunities under international law to shield its staff or others acting on its instructions from accountability for human rights abuse.[96] Furthermore, Principle 26 calls upon States to protect rights by influencing the conduct of non-State actors wherever possible, even if they are not in a position to regulate them, such as through their procurement system or international diplomacy. Such a duty would also be potentially applicable to international organizations.

Maastricht Principles 28–33 and Principle 35, addressing obligations to *fulfil* rights, apply directly to international organizations, with the exception of references to State obligations to fulfil rights within their own territory.[97] The references to availability of resources of course have implications for international organizations distinct from those in respect of States. International organizations are bound to fulfil rights only to the extent that a particular right and aspect of its realization may lie within their particular mandate and competency and to the extent that resources for such purposes are available to them. In other words, international organizations have an obligation to fulfil rights if and to the extent that their member States either impose such obligations upon them or give them the discretion to fulfil such obligations. International organizations, unlike States, have limited options for acquiring resources, relying on contributions from their members and voluntary donations from other sources. Furthermore, in regard to the elaboration of international agreements, as referred to in Maastricht Principles 17, 29 and 31, international organizations may only be able to positively influence

94 Principle 25(e).

95 Principle 24.

96 The resulting obligation would not alter the existing scope of an international organization's immunities, but rather would require that the international organization take the necessary steps to ensure remedies for human rights abuse carried out by those acting under its instructions.

97 That obligation is described in the first sentence of Principle 31. Principle 34 is not relevant to international organizations as it addresses a related obligation of a State to seek assistance from other actors when it is necessary to fulfil rights within its territory.

international standards to the extent that States mandate or at least authorize them to take positions on such matters. International organizations, however, are always obliged to interpret international standards in conformity with human rights obligations.

In regard to accountability and remedies, Principles 36–41 are applicable to international organizations, save for the fact that those Principles addressed institutions designed to monitor State conduct. Thus, the references to obligations to cooperate with periodic reporting and inquiry procedures of treaty bodies and with peer review mechanisms do not apply to international organizations. However, international organizations and their member States are required to implement their substantive obligation to ensure a remedy for human rights abuse in any circumstance in which the international organization is involved. Such an obligation requires States to reform international human rights mechanisms to permit international organizations to accede to human rights treaties and their associated complaints and inquiry procedures, where they cannot already do so. States represented on the governing authorities of these international organizations should ensure that international organizations take the necessary accession and compliance steps.

Finally, Maastricht General Principles 1–14 are also applicable to the obligations of international organizations. There may be a concern that references to jurisdiction in Principle 9 are inapplicable to international organizations. In this regard, it should be recalled that the Maastricht Principles commentary specifies that

> [w]hen used to refer to the scope of application of human rights and comparable treaties, the term 'jurisdiction' refers to the territory and people over which a state has factual control, power, or authority. It should not be confused with the limits imposed under international law on the ability of a state to exercise prescriptive (or legislative) and enforcement jurisdiction.[98]

Principle 9 refers to *situations* over which a State has authority, control or influence – and it requires no leap in logic to apply the same criteria in determining the scope of human rights obligations of international organizations, although the extent of the obligations to protect and fulfil human rights borne by these organizations will be limited to those that can be implemented within the powers given to international organizations by member States. Finally, Principle 18, addressing situations of belligerent occupation, reflects the requirement of States to respect, protect and fulfil rights even where they have control over territory that is not sovereign territory and when they have control over people who are neither nationals of that State nor residents therein. The same obligations are applicable to situations in which international organizations have such forms of control over territory or people.

98 De Schutter, Eide, Khalfan, Orellana, Salomon and Seiderman (n 2), 1102.

The accountability challenge in situations of multiple duty-bearers

Having considered the conceptual framework for determining the basis and extent of extraterritorial obligations of States, international organizations and private actors, we now turn to the issue of the accountability challenge. Most existing accountability mechanisms competent to address extraterritorial obligations are designed to address the accountability of a single State or of a single international organization, rather than situations in which there are multiple duty-bearers. This suggests that guaranteeing a remedy for human rights abuses may require very significant reforms to overall global governance arrangements. This challenge is particularly important for this book, which seeks to examine the consequences of expanding the set of duty-bearers beyond States – and thereby, at first glance, compounding the difficulty of ensuring accountability of duty-bearers. States do already have the legal competency to establish regimes to govern the accountability of private actors and international organizations. The challenge however, rests in allocating responsibility amongst States for the discharge of this function.

By accountability mechanisms, this section considers institutions that (1) receive and adjudicate complaints and provide for access to effective remedies to victims, (2) impose criminal, civil or administrative sanctions on officials responsible for conduct leading to human rights violations, and/or (3) independently monitor the extent to which a State has implemented its obligations and require or encourage a State to take the necessary steps to meet its obligations. There is a wide range of mechanisms and processes capable of making States accountable for breaches of extraterritorial obligations related to human rights.[99] These include universal and regional human rights treaty bodies, the International Court of Justice (ICJ), the Universal Periodic Review (UPR) system of the UN Human Rights Council, the Special Procedures appointed by the Human Rights Council to examine in an independent capacity, a particular right, country situation or theme, and the International Criminal Court, which can ensure individual criminal responsibility where a violation is also a crime under the Rome Statute.[100] Aspects of some extraterritorial obligations correspond to the requirements of international financial institutions for the provision of financial support by

99 For a survey of such mechanisms relevant to ESC rights, see A Khalfan, 'Accountability Mechanisms', in M Langford, W Vandenhole, M Scheinin and W van Genugten (eds), *Global Justice, State Duties: The Extraterritorial Scope of Economic, Social, and Cultural Rights in International Law* (CUP 2013), 391–416.

100 Another possible mechanism is the peer review system of Development Assistance Committee of the Organisation for Economic Co-operation and Development (OECD-DAC) which is designed to assess international aid programmes and can take into account human rights obligations. See OECD-DAC, 'Action-Oriented Policy Paper on Human Rights and Development' (2007) OECD Doc DDC/DAC 5/FINAL 17.

those institutions – for example those contained in the World Bank Policy on Involuntary Resettlement.[101]

A State's compliance with its extraterritorial obligations could and should be reviewed by national mechanisms. These might include, for example, reviews of executive action by national judiciaries or national human rights institutions, particularly when the latter has the competency to issue binding decisions which are then subject to judicial review. National review will be most effective where international human rights treaties are treated as part of domestic law, where human rights treaties have been incorporated into domestic law, or where such law already effectively incorporates State duties corresponding to particular extraterritorial human rights obligations.[102]

Significant progress is required to render these mechanisms fully effective to ensure accountability for extraterritorial obligations. Legislative change and development of jurisprudence are required in many jurisdictions to give full effect to the approach set out in the Maastricht Principles. As prescribed in Maastricht Principle 37(e), all States should adhere to the complaints mechanisms established under the treaty bodies, including their inquiry and inter-State complaints mechanisms, and to accept the compulsory jurisdiction of the ICJ. We do not propose to evaluate here the changes that might be necessary to each type of institution. Rather, we focus on a common challenge that such mechanisms would face in dealing with situations in which there are multiple duty-bearers in regard to the rights of particular persons.

Human rights accountability mechanisms are generally designed to deal with the conduct of a single State, irrespective of whether the mechanisms in question operate through periodic reporting, consideration of complaints or peer review. Those mechanisms that are designed to adjudicate rights and duties as between States can be activated only by States, and even then only by consent of all relevant States (expressed in advance, via a treaty or at the time of the dispute). The consent hurdle can only be surmounted by requests for Advisory Opinions, in particular in regard to the ICJ. Accountability provided by a State's own judiciary or other national monitoring bodies can only appropriately deal with the conduct of that State alone, rather than other States.

International accountability mechanisms can (and sometimes do) address failures to implement extraterritorial obligations in situations in which a single State's conduct has a foreseeable adverse impact on the human rights of people in another State, or where that State influences the conduct of another State in carrying out violations. However, there is a range of important situations in which allocating responsibility is so complex that accountability and the right to a remedy may be significantly limited. Four such circumstances

101 World Bank, 'Operational Policy 4.12: Involuntary Resettlement' (revised April 2013), *http://go.worldbank.org/XTKMH8TNP0* (accessed 26 January 2015).

102 For example, *R v Secretary of State for Foreign Affairs, ex p World Development Movement Ltd* [1995] 1 All ER 611 (QB) 615, 626.

are addressed here: (i) State conduct within international organizations; (ii) international regulations which may serve to infringe human rights or make inadequate provision for the advancement and protection of human rights; (iii) situations in which each State's conduct, which individually may not cause harm, incrementally contributes to significant harm to the enjoyment of human rights in other States; and (iv) gaps in provision of international cooperation and assistance for the realization of rights.

In regard to the first and second circumstances, the extent to which a State attempts to influence the conduct of an international organization or the design of international regulations could, in principle, be monitored and assessed by an accountability mechanism, if the relevant evidence, including documentary records, of decision-making are available to that mechanism. However, a State's ability to ensure compliance with human rights by the international organization or in the design of the regulation almost always depends on the concurrence of at least a significant number of other members. The third circumstance above is best illustrated by trans-boundary environmental harm, in particular climate change. A State's failure to limit greenhouse gas emissions contributes, but is not the sole cause, of harm to the enjoyment of human rights. It is the cumulative failures of several States that leads to a violation.

In regard to the fourth circumstance, the general obligation to contribute to the fulfilment of rights extraterritorially does not, thus far, require States to provide cooperation and assistance to particular countries and persons. The requirements to prioritize the realization of minimum essential levels of rights as well as the rights of disadvantaged, marginalized and vulnerable persons, as reflected in Maastricht Principle 32, do limit States' discretion in this regard.[103] Nevertheless, any State engaging in international cooperation and assistance will have to make difficult choices as to whom it should provide its assistance from amongst the wide range of populations lacking basic levels of human rights. It has been argued that a State may have a *prima facie* obligation towards a particular population in another country when it is the only State able to assist (for example, due to geographic location),[104] or when it has effective control over a person's rights in another country.[105]

103 See also W Vandenhole and W Benedek, 'Extraterritorial Human Rights Obligations and the North-South Divide', in M Langford, W Vandenhole, M Scheinin and W van Genugten (eds), *Global Justice, State Duties: The Extraterritorial Scope of Economic, Social, and Cultural Rights in International Law* (CUP 2013), 332–363, at 349.

104 These are discussed in more detail at A Khalfan, 'Division of Responsibility amongst States', in M Langford, W Vandenhole, M Scheinin and W van Genugten (eds), *Global Justice, State Duties: The Extraterritorial Scope of Economic, Social, and Cultural Rights in International Law* (CUP 2013), 299–331 at 322–323.

105 See eg the complaint by Senegalese former soldiers in the French army, residing in Senegal, who faced discrimination in their pension rights on the basis that they were not French nationals. The HRC held that the complainants fell under France's jurisdiction for the purposes of the ICCPR as the authors relied on French legislation in relation to the amount of their pension rights, *Gueye et al v France* (1989) Communication 196/1985, UN Doc CCPR/C/35/D/196/1985, para 9.4.

Such cases, however, are exceptional and do not solve the broader challenge: Persons for whom certain rights have not been fulfilled by their State (due to either inability or unwillingness), such as where it fails to ensure their access to essential goods or services, may find that other States in position to assist are focusing their available resources and capacity on other countries, persons or rights.

Some situations in which several States breach their obligations in concert may be dealt with under the principle of joint responsibility. Applying the ILC's Articles on State Responsibility, any State party to a human rights treaty, or any State, in the case of human rights recognized under general international law, may invoke the responsibility of a collectivity of States (including, for example, the members of an international organization) for infringing the rights of any individual. This is because human rights obligations are *erga omnes*. States may seek remedies including: cessation of the internationally wrongful act, guarantees of non-repetition and reparation in the interest of the affected persons.[106] Each of the States that carried out the relevant conduct would be separately liable for the wrongful act as a whole.[107] The ILC Articles on State Responsibility do not address the *invocation* of State responsibility by non-State entities,[108] and therefore Parts II and III of the Articles (Arts 28–54) would not apply in the event that an individual claim was heard by a review mechanism.[109] It is possible, however, that an accountability mechanism would be influenced by those Parts in its determination of the claim.

Joint responsibility may create an incentive for States to cooperate to ensure protection of rights. It is not applicable, however, in situations in which the States concerned separately carry out internationally wrongful conduct that coincidentally contributes to causing the same damage. In such cases, 'the responsibility of each participating State is determined individually, on the basis of its own conduct and by reference to its own international obligations'.[110] Thus State conduct could be evaluated to assess whether a State has taken all reasonable steps to secure human rights in its conduct that has effects beyond its borders. However, some rights claims may raise complex issues of allocation of liability and resources amongst States, which international human rights mechanisms and judicial and dispute settlement bodies

106 ILC, 'Draft Articles on Responsibility of States for Internationally Wrongful Acts' (November 2001), Supplement No 10 (A/56/10), ch IV.E.1, Arts 47, 48 and Commentary to Art 48, paras 7–8.

107 Ibid, Art 47(1). The Commentary to Art 47, para 2, gives an example of a situation where two States act through a joint organ that carries out a wrongful act.

108 Ibid, Commentary to Art 33, para 4.

109 However, the general principles of State responsibility, defined in Part I of the Articles (ie Arts 1–27) extend to 'human rights violations and other breaches of international law where the primary beneficiary of the obligation breached is not a State'. See ILC, 'Draft Articles on Responsibility of States for Internationally Wrongful Acts' (November 2001), Supplement No 10 (A/56/10), ch IV.E.1, Commentary to Art 28, para 3.

110 Ibid, Commentary to Art 47, para 8.

may not consider themselves equipped or adequately mandated to address. A decision by such accountability mechanisms requiring or recommending that the States concerned negotiate an appropriate allocation amongst themselves may be futile. Some of the difficult issues in this regard would include trans-boundary environmental pollution, in particular that leading to climate change, burden-sharing in accepting refugees, commitments towards peace-keeping, the provision of military force to prevent genocide, the allocation of development aid and decisions on terms of internationally agreed intellectual property rights.

To address this challenge, Maastricht Principle 30 proposes:

> States should coordinate with each other, including in the allocation of responsibilities, in order to cooperate effectively in the universal fulfilment of economic, social and cultural rights. The lack of such coordination does not exonerate a State from giving effect to its separate extraterritorial obligations.

It was the intent of the drafters of the Maastricht Principles to adopt the formulation 'should' to refer to duties, such as those contained in Principle 30, that are considered as strongly recommended. The commentary to Principle 30 notes that human rights law does not at present determine with precision a system of international coordination and allocation to facilitate the discharge of obligations to fulfil ESC rights globally. It states that the Principle 'affirms a procedural obligation that should be seen as complementary to the substantive obligation to cooperate internationally' to fulfil rights.[111] The Principle aims to reflect conduct that is arguably essential to implement the obligations reflected in Arts 55 and 56 of the UN Charter and Art 2(1) of the ICESCR. The Principle, therefore, should be seen as applicable not only to the extraterritorial obligation to fulfil rights, but also to respect and protect rights.

Even if the conduct set out in Principle 30 were strictly obligatory, it would not specifically require States to establish any particular institution, mechanism or process to authoritatively allocate responsibilities amongst them nor would it require them to designate an international organization with the authority to respond to and provide remedy for extraterritorial claims. Without a threat of an imposed settlement by a third party, a State's obligation to negotiate with other States to achieve an appropriate outcome is weak and is difficult to monitor and enforce. Thus, the implementation of States' extraterritorial obligations would in some cases be frustrated – not only by the potential unwillingness of States to act – but also by the real difficulties of coming to inter-State agreement on the allocation of obligations among them, in order to work in concert for the realization of these rights. National accountability mechanisms typically do not provide a clear model that could be applied by analogy to the international level in order to

111 De Schutter, Eide, Khalfan, Orellana, Salomon and Seiderman (n 2), 1149–1150.

address this challenge. Where government action is required that is beyond the capacity of sub-State governments, such as municipalities or regions, this challenge is generally dealt with by transferring responsibility to the national government, rather than by requiring sub-State governments to coordinate their efforts to ensure an adequate outcome for all their constituents.

Human rights, and the necessary trans-boundary State obligations, can only fully be guaranteed if there is an international mechanism that can require States to take up and allocate amongst themselves obligations to ensure human rights extra-territorially, and if they fail, to step in to impose such a division of responsibility if required. One potential mechanism is a world court of human rights,[112] which was seriously considered by the UN as far back as 1947 and has gained some recent traction, if accompanied by some formal commitment from States to enforce its decisions. There may be issues as to whether a court would be sufficient for this purpose – for example, would it be able to do more than simply require States to negotiate in good faith towards establishing an appropriate regime to allocate responsibilities?[113]

Consideration would also need to be given to transferring greater powers and responsibilities to the UN's political bodies and international organizations. The States negotiating an early instrument that would eventually lead to the ICESCR did not take up text proposed by Pakistan and Sweden that might have helped resolve this problem – at least in regard to ESC rights. That text, presented in 1951 before the substantive Articles describing the rights in question had been drafted, stated the following:

> Recognizing
> (a) That responsibility for the coordination of appropriate international action to promote the general observance of economic, social and cultural rights set out in Articles __ to __ rests with the United Nations;
> (b) That the responsibility for appropriate international action, in respect of rights within their competence and insofar as their States Members are concerned, rests with the Specialised Agencies as provided by their constitutions and the terms of their agreements with the United Nations;
> . . .[114]

112 International Commission of Jurists, 'Towards a World Court on Human Rights: Questions and Answers' (December 2011), *http://icj.wpengine.netdna-cdn.com/wp-content/uploads/2013/07/World-court-final-23.12-pdf1.pdf* (accessed 7 May 2014); and J Kozma, M Nowak and M Scheinin, *A World Court of Human Rights – Consolidated Statute and Commentary* (Neuer Wissenshäftlicher Verlag 2011).

113 See the International Court of Justice's decision in *Legality of the Threat or Use of Nuclear Weapons* (Advisory Opinion) [1986] ICJ Rep 226, para 105(F). In fairness to the Court, its response in the event of a contentious case on such matters remains to be seen.

114 UNCHR, 'Pakistan and Sweden: Draft Articles on Implementation of the Economic, Social and Cultural Rights' (14 May 1951) UN Doc E/CN.4/622. The official records of the Commission do not reflect any discussion of the text quoted above.

The proposed provisions would have significantly increased the responsibility and power of the UN and its agencies over States' international cooperation policies. Presumably, that was a step too far for other States to even contemplate at the time.

Such a provision could provide a means for claimants to focus their extra-territorial claims towards a sole duty-bearer – the UN agency responsible for the right in question – that would then have the responsibility of coordinating measures to ensure remedy to the affected individuals. This would be particularly effective if international organizations adhere to international human rights treaty complaints and inquiry mechanisms.

Under such a system, rights-holders would be able to hold international organizations accountable for taking steps within their power to ensure the respect, protection and fulfilment of human rights. Although ultimate authority over the international organization would continue to rest with its member States, the international organization's staff could be required, following a process of meaningful research and consultation, to present its members with options and strategies for compliance of the international organization, and its members, with their respective human rights obligations. In other words, international organizations would have a critical agenda-setting responsibility to address trans-boundary human rights issues.

We recognize that the necessary reforms, implying a significant shift of political power to international organizations, are unlikely to occur in the near-term. The objective of this analysis is to show that the full guarantee of human rights requires not only a change in State policy and practice, but also to global institutional structures. In this regard, human rights are only one of several collective international legal obligations whose realization is hindered by the absence of a clear allocation of labour among States. Other examples include the obligations to ensure respect for the Geneva Conventions,[115] to provide substantial financial and technical assistance to anti-desertification programmes,[116] and to cooperate in repressing piracy in places outside the jurisdiction of any State.[117] Generality in such obligations can be useful as they allow obligations to become concretized based on context, but they leave protection gaps and therefore need to be defined more tightly. In discussing transnational human rights obligations, it would be useful to carry out dialogue with experts in other international fields of international cooperation.

115 Common Art 1 of the Geneva Conventions, for example. See Geneva Convention Relative to the Protection of Civilian Persons in Time of War (adopted 12 August 1949, entered into force 21 October 1950) 75 UNTS 287.

116 United Nations Convention to Combat Desertification in those Countries Experiencing Serious Drought and/or Desertification, Particularly in Africa (adopted 14 October 1994, entered into force 26 December 1996) 1954 UNTS 3, Regional Implementation Annex for Africa, Art 20(2).

117 United Nations Convention on the Law of the Sea (adopted 10 December 1982, entered into force 16 November 1994) 1833 UNTS 397, Art 100.

Ultimately, the realization of human rights is inseparable from broader issues of adequate global governance.

Conclusion

The Maastricht Principles project, through a consolidation and explication of standards and jurisprudence that have emerged since adoption of the UN Charter and the UDHR, aimed to give cohesion and clarity to the nature and scope of extra-territorial human rights obligations. The Principles are a significant contribution towards the overall project of ensuring that international human rights law is fit for purpose in an increasingly globalized world. However, read in isolation, they do not entirely complete the picture. In this chapter, we have suggested ways in which the Principles are applicable to certain areas that the Maastricht Principles project had not expressly addressed.

First, regarding the material scope of rights (*ratione materiae*), it is conceptually incoherent and practically unworkable to confine the Principles to the area of ESC rights. The international trend has been to move away from the artificial division into rights groups, and in the real world many single situations engage obligations or give rise to violations of rights from both rights areas. Second, while the Principles clearly are directed to State obligations, they underscore that the inevitable consequence of discharging State obligations, particularly in the area of obligations to protect, will be to impose human rights duties on private actors, especially business enterprises. The imposition of such legal duties necessarily involves State action, and so is comfortably situated within the framework of Maastricht Principle 25 and correlative standards.

Third, in recognition of the critical role that certain international organizations play in the fulfilment of human rights, as well as their capacity to impair rights through failures to respect and protect, we look to see whether and the extent to which the Principles can be made applicable to such organizations. We conclude that by and large they can; unlike private actors, international organizations are composed of States that carry to these organizations their human rights obligations and, in some critical respects, international organizations more closely resemble States than other non-State actors. Finally, in recognition of the fact that obligations, particularly in respect of remedy and accountability, may be rendered illusory without effective implementation and enforcement mechanisms, we consider such mechanisms in light of the Maastricht Principles. Current accountability mechanisms are generally not able to properly ensure remedy in situations where multiple duty-bearers are linked to an abuse of a particular person's rights. Fully resolving this deficit will require significant institutional developments, which might include a world court of human rights and increased powers of international organizations to allocate responsibilities amongst States for realization of extraterritorial obligations.

3 The World Bank Group, the IMF and human rights: about direct obligations and the attribution of unlawful conduct

Willem van Genugten[1]

Introduction

Are the World Bank Group (WBG) and the International Monetary Fund (IMF) bound to live up to international human rights law? For some, amongst them former UN Secretary-General Kofi Annan, it is clear: 'The promotion of human rights must not be treated as something separate from ... other activities [conducted by the UN]. Rather, it is the common thread running through all of them ...'.[2] This is the 'mainstreaming of human rights'. In this approach, the concept of human rights is used as a bridge or as a 'lynch-pin' in the fight against the (over) fragmentation of international law and as one of the, if not *the*, 'lode star(s)' for the composite and complex organization called United Nations (UN). This approach would include the main organs of the UN and all the international organizations and specialized bodies linked to the organization, such as, in the context of the present publication, the WBG and the IMF. Others, however, argue that the charters and other constitutive documents of both International Financial Institutions (IFIs) have to be honoured and that one has to respect their specializations. The consequence thereof would be that such charters could/should be placed above or, at least, alongside other international obligations which the IFIs do have by virtue of their links to the 'UN family'.[3] Both views keep coming back in numerous discussions on the questions why and to what extent the WBG and the IMF would be legally bound by human rights standards. The key aim of this chapter is to make clear by what norms of international human rights law the WBG and the IMF are bound, and to further identify and specify points for

1 The chapter is part of a larger project and bears fruit from the intense cooperation with a range of people, especially Wolfgang Benedek, Josh Curtis, Charline Daelman, Asbjørn Eide, Mary Footer, Ana Sofia Freitas de Barros, Tara van Ho, Yannick Radi, Cedric Ryngaert, Arne Vandenbogaerde and Wouter Vandenhole. A more extensive text, including large sections on accountability and redress, and Guiding Principles on the WBG, IMF and Human Rights has been published in a separate book, W van Genugten, *The World Bank Group, the IMF and Human Rights: A Contextualised Way Forward* (Inttersentia 2015).

2 United Nations, New York, *Report of the Secretary-General on the Work of the Organization* (1998), 23.

3 J Oloka-Onyango and Deepika Udagama, UN Doc E/CN.4/Sub.2/1999/11, 14.

coining their responsibility for the violations of such norms. As to the latter, the focus is on principles and concepts that can help to attribute unlawful conduct and apportion the corresponding responsibility, including the responsibility shared with their member States.[4]

This chapter first addresses the way both the WBG and the IMF identify the overlap between their respective fields of operation and human rights issues. Next, it elaborates upon the human rights obligations of both IFIs and their member States. The following section discusses the responsibility for human rights violations by the IFIs and their member States. The final section provides for some concluding remarks.

The IFIs positioning themselves in the human rights field

Before addressing the requirements following from existing international human rights law for the WBG and the IMF, this part of the chapter illustrates how both IFIs present themselves today in relation to the links between their respective mandates and international human rights issues. This is done in order to make clear that discussing the obligations following from existing human rights law and the attribution of conduct that violates these norms, in the latter sections of this chapter, is not a matter of 'imposing something externally' upon them only, but links to discussions underway in both IFIs.

The official World Bank Group position

The WBG underlines in its own recent policy statements that internal developments have shown 'growing recognition of the need for the Bank to address human rights in a more explicit fashion' and that there 'have been significant advances in the Bank's thinking on this issue'.[5] In addition, the Bank explicitly states that 'there are wide areas of overlap between substantive

4 As to terminology used in this chapter: The 2001 'Draft Articles on the Responsibility of States for Internationally Wrongful Acts' do use the terms 'attribution of conduct' to a State (Art 2, the header of Chapter II, and the Arts 10 and 11). The 2011 'Draft Articles on the Responsibility of International Organizations' do the same in relation to international organizations (Art 4, the header of Chapter II, and Art 9). The 2012 Maastricht ETO Principles, on the other hand, speak about 'the attribution of State responsibility for the conduct of …' (header Principle 12), while Principle 11 states that 'State responsibility is engaged as a result of conduct attributable to a state …'. My approach is: the facts have to be established first; the next step is to see whether or not the facts reveal human rights violations, and if yes: which one(s) specifically; the third step is to establish who bears the responsibility for these violations and would have to accept the consequences thereof. For these reasons I use wordings such as 'concepts that can help to attribute unlawful conduct and apportion the corresponding responsibility' or 'the attribution of unlawful conduct and the establishment of the corresponding responsibility'.

5 See *http://web.worldbank.org/WBSITE/EXTERNAL/EXTSITETOOLS/0,,contentMDK:20749693~pagePK:98400~piPK:98424~theSitePK:95474,00.html#1* (accessed 27 January 2015). The website refers to underlying publications, some of which will be referred to throughout this chapter.

areas covered by core human rights treaties and those areas in which the Bank operates'.[6] And while reflecting on 'the way forward', the Bank speaks of 'recognizing the role of human rights as legal principles, which may inform a broad range of policies and activities'.[7] Even more directly, the Bank speaks of 'understanding human rights as actionable legal obligations'.[8] This terminology approaches the legal terminology used in the latter parts of the present chapter, and overlaps with the beginning of the legal reasoning developed those parts. The Bank goes even further by stating that 'our partners in the broader UN family have *a comparative advantage* in this area. Unlike the WBG, many of them have mandates that contain an explicit commitment to human rights, including, in some cases, monitoring and enforcement capabilities'[9] (emphasis added). In other words, the WBG seems, in some way, to 'regret' that in the past its mandate has not been explicitly linked to human rights, a fact that would have made its current work 'easier' ('comparative advantage') in a sense.

Formulating its position this way, the Bank shows its (not contested) openness to the human rights domain and even acknowledges the practical utility of being linked to human rights norms and even human rights enforcement mechanisms. It should be added, however, that the quotes presented are still rather 'empty' from a legal point of view, despite the terminology chosen. In that sense they do reflect a paper reality that will have to be filled in. The same would go for the link between the words chosen and reality. The latter, however, is not the focus of the present chapter. The way the WBG presents itself to the outside world will be used to further confront the WBG with its human rights obligations and the legal consequences thereof.

The official IMF position

Many issues the IMF is dealing with are directly related to human rights as well. However, it is well-known that, compared to the WBG, the IMF is even less pronounced on linking such activities to obligations stemming from international human rights law. Whether that position is tenable will also be discussed below. For now, the focus is on wordings chosen by the IMF itself in order to illustrate the overlap in substance between its mandate and the domain of human rights (law).

In quite a number of IMF publications over the last decade, one can find references to a variety of human rights. Let me take just one illustration: a speech delivered by Christine Lagarde, Managing Director of the IMF, during a visit to Malawi in early 2013. While discussing the 'Global and regional economic context', she observes, *inter alia*, that one should 'not forget the

6 Ibid.
7 Ibid.
8 Ibid.
9 Ibid.

threat from food prices and food scarcity. So far, rising global food price pressures are concentrated in a few crops like maize, soybeans, and wheat. But drought and crop failure are becoming ever-present dangers in some areas, with grave consequences for livelihoods and even lives.'[10] Other remarks made by Lagarde in this particular speech relate to looking at 'improving human development' by seeing economic growth as 'a means to a higher end: creating the conditions for the flourishing of human potential'. In that context, she quotes Malawi President Banda:

> Growth is not merely GDP growth. Growth is about wealth and prosperity for all, opportunity for all, happiness for all, political and economic freedom for all. Growth is also about growing the number of children in school, and young people in jobs. Growth is about increasing the number of mothers who give safe birth in a hospital, and growing the number of families who have plenty of food.[11]

The links to human rights are extremely clear, from political freedom to the right to education, from the right to adequate healthcare to the right to food. The quotes taken from the speech would not be misplaced in a document devoted to the key social goal behind human rights law: how to realize a life in human dignity for all human beings worldwide, more particularly in the context of the present chapter, for those human beings living in the States with which the IMF has a working relation. It should be clear, however, that the IMF does not draw the legal consequences of all that. In addition, it must be observed that even speeches given by the IMF General Director are not necessarily reflecting the mainstream view of the organization. Nevertheless, it is reasonable to assume that the quotes at least reflect an ongoing debate of direct relevance to the role of human rights within the work of the IMF. As observed in relation to the WBG: the IMF cannot afford to use such words without accepting a range of consequences attached to them, as will become clear in the remainder of this chapter.

Applicable human rights obligations

Introduction

As subjects of international law and as international legal personalities, the WBG and the IMF are capable of possessing rights and duties under their constituent instruments, general rules of international law and the treaties to which they have acceded. This includes obligations in the domain of

10 C Lagarde, 'Malawi – Economic Rebirth, Renewed Partnerships' (speech, 5 January 2013), Lilongwe, Malawi, available at *https://www.imf.org/external/np/speeches/2013/010513.htm* (accessed 27 January 2015).

11 Ibid.

human rights, to be exercised separately from or jointly with their member States. This 'opening statement' will be further substantiated in this section by addressing five issues: a further scrutiny of the links between the IFI mandates and international human rights law; the incorporation of the IFIs in the domain of international human rights law; the 'political prohibition'; human rights obligations of States, acting in the context of the IFIs; and obligations following from (legal) relationships between the IFIs and private subcontractors.

Deepening the links between the IFI mandates and international human rights law

As shown above, the WBG has chosen not to interpret its mandate in separation from developments taking place in the human rights domain, while touching sometimes upon legal terminology. Also, the IMF 'plays' with human rights terminology, be it in a different way. The question now is what more specific human rights obligations can be linked to the mandates, and on what grounds. Let me first borrow the enlightening words of Mac Darrow – a decade ago the author of a seminal book on the issue[12] – used by him in a piece written in 2009 for the *Encyclopaedia of Human Rights*[13]:

> The UN Charter is perhaps the most important source of human rights duties for members of the extended UN family; the UN Charter binds the bank and the IMF equally. The IBRD [International Bank for Reconstruction and Development], IDA [International Development Association], and IMF have all entered into formal relationship agreements with the UN. The promotion of human rights is at the heart of the UN system's purposes, as provided in articles 1(3) and 55 of the UN Charter, although specific obligations are not well-defined. However, the Universal Declaration of Human Rights (1948), and to some extent subsequent international human rights treaties enjoying broad acceptance and are viewed by many as an elaboration or authoritative interpretation of the brief human rights references in the UN Charter. Taking the relevant provisions of the UN Charter as a whole, it is strongly arguable that cooperation between the BWIs [Bretton Woods Institutions] and the UN in the economic and social fields should be based, at least in part, on the UN Charter's human rights principles.[14]

This links to, and further specifies, what has already been stated above on 'human rights in general'. Darrow adds in the same piece, and correct to my

12 M Darrow, *Between Light and Shadow. The World Bank, The International Monetary Fund and International Human Rights Law* (Hart 2003).

13 M Darrow, 'World and International Monetary Fund', in D Forsythe (ed), *Encyclopedia of Human Rights* (OUP 2009), 373–381.

14 Ibid, 378.

mind, that '[m]ainstream international legal opinion would say that this translates into a minimum obligation that the Bank and the IMF respect (or at least not violate) human rights commitments in force in member countries and arguably also protect human rights within the scope of their influence and activities at the country level'.[15] In addition, according to him, '[m]any commentators go further still to argue that these institutions should promote or perhaps even fulfill human rights'.[16] Having said that, he also refers to the often cited 2006 'Legal Opinion on Human Rights and the Work of the World Bank' by the Bank's General Counsel at the time, Roberto Dañino.[17] The Legal Opinion, written upon a request by the Bank's senior management,[18] is labelled by Darrow and others as a 'watershed' which was a

> marked departure from the conservative doctrine of the 1980s and 1990s, this legal opinion posited a purposive and contextual interpretation of the Articles of Agreement, setting out an enabling framework for the bank to grapple explicitly with human rights issues arising within the increasingly broad and complex sphere of its operations and support its members in realizing their human rights obligations. Strikingly the opinion concluded that the Articles of Agreement permit, and in some cases require, the Bank to recognize the human rights dimension of its development policies and activities, since it is now evident that human rights are an intrinsic part of the Bank's mission.[19]

The legal opinion has not been brought before the Bank's executive board, but according to Darrow the 'persuasive effect of the opinion does not depend on the board's endorsement, although to formally bind the bank's operations the key provisions of the opinion would need to be reflected in the bank's operational policies, which do require such approval', and that is 'not a likely prospect'.[20] One can agree with the latter, although this also depends on the timeframe one has in mind. I would agree with Darrow's remark as far as it relates to the present and maybe the immediately foreseeable future, but things can and will change. It can anyhow be observed that whether the 2006 Legal Opinion has been a real 'watershed' or not, things are still gradually changing within the World Bank and are not carved in stone.

The Bank's next General Counsel, Ana Palacio, states that the 2006 Legal Opinion marks a clear evolution from the pre-existing restrictive legal

15 Ibid.

16 Ibid.

17 Also see R Daniño, 'The Legal Aspects of the World Bank's Work on Human Rights: Some Preliminary Thoughts', in P Alston and M Robinson (eds), *Human Rights and Development: Towards Mutual Reinforcement* (OUP 2005), *passim*.

18 A Palacio, *The Way Forward; Human Rights and the World Bank* (World Bank Institute 2006), Special Report Development Outreach, 36.

19 Darrow (n 13), 378.

20 Ibid, 379.

interpretation of the Bank's explicit consideration of human rights, but she reads it as 'permissive: allowing, but not mandating, action on the part of the Bank in relation to human rights'.[21] The word 'permissive' of course creates space for the IMF to act according to its own views on human rights issues and/or legal obligations. Later in this chapter this space will be further tested. Palacio herself adds that the 2006 Legal Opinion clarifies 'the state of the law' and that it 'gives the Bank the necessary leeway to explore its proper role in relation to human rights, updating the legal stance adopted internally to accord with the Bank's practice and the current international legal context'.[22] She also notes that it is clear that human rights 'can and sometimes should' be taken into consideration by the Bank as part of its decision-making process, amongst other things through the 'recognition of the role of human rights as *legal principles* [italics in the original text] which may inform a broad range of activities, and which may enrich the quality and rationale of development interventions'.[23] A few years later, Siobhán McInerney-Lankford and Hans-Otto Sano observed in a study done for the World Bank and the Nordic Trust Fund that despite such developments the official approach of the World Bank with regard to human rights 'remains non-explicit in terms of the direct or formal relevance of specific duties or international treaty obligations'.[24] As we saw, this still reflects the situation anno 2014 and shows how the WBG 'plays around' the legal obligations' part of the human rights field.

As to the IMF, one can refer to a range of publications by, amongst others, the former General Counsel, François Gianviti. He has explicitly reflected on the 'non-links' between the IMF and human rights law, more particularly the International Covenant on Economic, Social and Cultural Rights. Gianviti argued:

> There are three reasons for concluding that the Covenant does not apply to the Fund: the Fund is not a party to the Covenant; the obligations imposed by the Covenant apply only to States, not to international organizations; and the Covenant, in its Article 24, explicitly recognizes that '[n]othing in the present Covenant shall be interpreted as impairing the provisions ... of the constitutions of the specialized agencies which define the respective responsibilities ... of the specialized agencies in regard to the matters dealt with in the present Covenant.[25]

21 Palacio (n 18), 36.

22 Ibid.

23 Ibid.

24 S McInerney-Lankford and H-O Sano, *Human Rights Indicators in Development* (World Bank and the Nordic Trust Fund 2010), 6.

25 F Gianviti, General Council IMF (1987–2004), 'Economic, Social and Cultural Rights and the International Monetary Fund' (2002) available at *https://www.imf.org/external/np/leg/sem/2002/cdmfl/eng/gianv3.pdf* (accessed 27 January 2015), *passim*, esp paras 6, 16 and 60.

In addition, he discusses the often-heard argument that 'the obligations set forth in the Covenant are mandatory provisions of general public international law and, thus, binding on all subjects of international law, including international organizations' and that this would have to lead to the conclusion 'that the Fund's Articles of Agreement should be interpreted in a manner consistent with the objective of promoting the rights contained in the Covenant, or deemed to be amended if this was necessary to achieve these objectives'.[26] Gianviti concludes that once the principle would be admitted 'that the Covenant takes precedence over the Articles [of Agreement], the whole institutional and legal structure within which the Fund operates can be questioned'.[27] He clearly tries to escape the binding force of international human rights obligations.

But even a more modest view of the links between the IMF and human rights, one in which the IMF has to take human rights, more specially the International Covenant on Economic, Social and Cultural Rights, 'into consideration' and similar words, is not embraced by him. One of his key arguments is that the IMF is not a UN body and is not bound by general UN/international law: the IMF is 'an intergovernmental agency, not an agency of the United Nations'.[28] He observes that in accordance with Art 57 of the UN Charter, the Fund was brought into relationship with the UN by an agreement in which the UN recognizes that, 'by reason of the nature of its international responsibilities and the terms of its Articles of Agreement, the Fund is, and is required to function as, an independent organization'.[29] And most importantly: 'Article X of the Fund's Articles of Agreement, while requiring the Fund to cooperate with "any general international organization" [ie the United Nations], specifies that "Any arrangements for such cooperation which would involve a modification of any provision of [the Articles of Agreement] may be effected only after amendment to [the Articles]".'[30] It leads him to conclude that the relation between the IMF and the UN is not one of 'agency' but one of 'sovereign equals'.[31] This sovereignty issue will be discussed in a next section.

Darrow observes in relation to the IMF's Articles of Agreement that '[t]he ability, or obligation, of the IMF to consider human rights issues in connection with its work depends to a lesser degree than that of the bank upon the question of how its Articles of Agreement should be interpreted' and how its wishes to use and actually uses its 'implied powers'.[32] Thus, Darrow states, 'perhaps surprisingly, the IMF's articles [of Agreement] are relatively permissive in scope compared with those of the bank, and they contain no equivalent

26 Ibid, para 14.
27 Ibid.
28 Ibid, para 16.
29 Ibid.
30 Ibid.
31 Ibid.
32 Darrow (n 13), 379.

of the political prohibition ... that for so long dogged efforts to breathe life into the bank's constitution'.[33]

For now, the key question is to what extent the WBG and the IMF can be 'ordered', based on developments in the human rights field and in general international law, to accept direct human obligations and use their its position to address human rights issues as part of their mandates.

Incorporating the IFIs in the domain of international human rights law

Is the space the WBG and the IMF are creating for themselves still warranted? One can discern several aspects of international human rights law and general international law that are directly applicable to both IFIs. They are mentioned here in a schematic and non-exhaustive way, with a few references only.

First, both IFIs are necessarily bound by those human rights standards that qualify as peremptory standards of international law (*ius cogens*), such as the obligation to refrain from genocide, torture and racial discrimination, and the obligation to respect and actively protect the right to self-determination of peoples.

Secondly, the IFIs are bound by general principles of international (human rights) law, such as the obligation to make reparations in the case of an internationally wrongful act and the principle of due diligence as coined amongst other things in the context of human rights,[34] and by customary international law rules in the domain of human rights, such as the obligations following from certain of the 'human rights conventions' of the ILO, representing norms of an international customary law character: C29, on Forced Labour (1930); C87, on Freedom of Association and Protection of the Right to Organise (1948); C98, on the Right to Organise and Collective Bargaining (1949); C100, on Equal Remuneration (1951); C105, on Abolition of Forced Labour (1957); C111, on Discrimination ([in the context of] Employment and Occupation) (1958); C138, on Minimum Age (1973); and C182, on Worst Forms of Child Labour (1999).

Thirdly, as Specialized Agencies of the UN, which have entered into relationship agreements with the UN Economic and Social Council in accordance with Arts 57 and 63 of the UN Charter, the two institutions are bound to respect the principles and objectives of the UN, even though the IMF especially has occasionally retained the right to be seen independently from the UN.[35] One can agree with the observation by the International Law Commission, done in the context of its extensive studies on the fragmentation of international law, that the term 'self-contained regime', often also used

33 Ibid.

34 See, for instance, the wording of Human Rights Watch, used in 'Abuse-Free Development: How the World Bank Should Safeguard Against Human Rights Violations' (July 2013): 'Ongoing due diligence should include continually identifying and analyzing human rights risks throughout the course of a project and require the Bank to publicly acknowledge the human rights risks.'

35 See, most clearly and explicitly, Gianviti (n 25), paras 6, 16 and 60.

by and for the IFIs to justify their special position, is 'a misnomer' and that '[n]o legal regime is isolated from general international law'.[36]

Fourthly, there are many relevant pronouncements, both within certain treaties and emanating from particular supervisory bodies in the domain of human rights, which include the IFIs within the juridical domain of international human rights law. In particular, certain General Comments by the Committee on Economic, Social and Cultural Rights (CESCR) provide specific examples. In its 2002 General Comment on the right to water, for instance, the CESCR notes that '[t]he international financial institutions, notably the International Monetary Fund (IMF) and the World Bank, should take into account the right to water in their lending policies, credit agreements, structural adjustment programmes and other development projects ... so that the enjoyment of the right to water is promoted'.[37] Stating so, the CESCR addresses the IFIs themselves. In other General Comments, it addresses the member States of both IFIs. In its 2008 General Comment on social security, for instance, the CESCR observes that 'States parties should ensure that their actions as members of international organizations take due account of the right to social security' and that '[a]ccordingly, States parties that are members of international financial institutions, notably the International Monetary Fund, the World Bank, and regional development banks, should take steps to ensure that the right to social security is taken into account in their lending policies, credit agreements and other international measures'.[38] Such General Comments are not binding upon States, but, summarizing a long debate, one can agree with Conway Blake that General Comments are 'a testament to the dynamic nature of international law and its institutions', and that, while their authority 'cannot be viewed in traditional legal terms', they 'emerge as an authoritative interpretation, which gives rise to normative consensus on the meaning and scope of particular human rights'.[39]

A fifth aspect relates to the concept of 'the right to development', as laid down, *inter alia*, in the 1986 Declaration on the Right to Development.[40] Despite its perhaps limited *legal* value,[41] the Declaration as well as the concept of development as such can still serve as semi-legal (soft law) and practical tools for, in particular, human rights advocacy.[42] In addition, there is no misunderstanding possible on the relevance of the concept of development

36 Report of the Study Group of the International Law Commission, finalized by M Koskenniemi, 'Fragmentation of International Law: Difficulties Arising from the Diversification and Expansion of International Law', UN Doc A/CN.4/L.682, 13 April 2006, para 193.

37 UN Doc E/C.12/GC/15 (2002), 'The right to water', para 60.

38 UN Doc E/C.12/GC/19 (2008), para 58.

39 C Blake, 'Normative Instruments in International Human Rights Law: Locating the General Comment' (Center for Human Rights and Global Justice Working Paper No 17, 2008), 38.

40 UN Doc A/RES/31/128, 4 December 1986.

41 A Vandenbogaerde, 'The Right to Development in International Human Rights Law: A Call for its Dissolution' (2013) 31 *Netherlands Quarterly of Human Rights* 187–209.

42 In the same vain, see OO Oduwole, 'International Law and the Right to Development: A Pragmatic Approach For Africa', Inaugural Lecture as Professor to the Prince Claus Chair in

for the mandates of both the WBG and the IMF. Illustrating this point, one can refer to, for instance, the view of both IFIs themselves on the need to help realizing the 2000 Millennium Declaration, including the eight Millennium Development Goals, many of which directly relate to human rights.[43]

The 'political prohibition'

Discussing the manifold relations between the mandates of the IFIs and human rights, one also enters the domain of the so-called 'political prohibition', used by the WBG. Article IV, section 10, of the World Bank's Articles of Agreement provide that '[t]he Bank and its officers shall not interfere in the political affairs of any member; nor shall they be influenced in their decisions by the political character of the member or members concerned', and that '[o]nly economic considerations shall be relevant to their decisions'.[44] The inclusion of this 'political prohibition' relates to the vision of the founders of the Bank for an impartial and neutral institution. The original Articles of Agreement literally forbade the Bank to deal with any issues of a political character, and the Bank considered human rights to be part of that.

The original 'political prohibition' reflected the mainstream thinking on sovereignty and human rights after the end of WW II, while in the 1960s 'the Bank understood human rights issues in the context of whether or not it should deal with regimes which had a bad human rights record or were known to commit human rights, usually civil and political rights, violations'.[45] At that time, the Bank also used its Articles 'to fend off criticisms of involvement with such regimes by classifying human rights concerns as "political"'.[46] However, as we saw above, things are gradually changing, both IFIs being less reluctant, be it in different ways and to different degrees, to discuss 'non-economic concerns'. As to the latter wording, one can agree with Adam McBeth that 'the distinction between economic and non-economic matters is artificial and often unsustainable, particularly in placing human rights in the latter, prohibited category'.[47] 'Prohibited' links to 'the domestic affairs of sovereign States'.

Development and Equity 2013/2015 delivered on 20 May 2014 at the International Institute of Social Studies, The Hague, The Netherlands, 3.

43 See recently, 'The IMF and the Millennium Development Goals', IMF Fact sheet (2014), available at: *https://www.imf.org/external/np/exr/facts/pdf/mdg.pdf* (accessed 27 January 2015). Also see the successive annual World Bank and IMF Global Monitoring Reports (so far: 2004–2013), Washington, DC: World Bank, and World Bank and OECD. Also see OECD and World Bank, *Integrating Human Rights into Development: Donor Approaches, Experiences, and Challenges* (2nd edn 2013).

44 Articles of Agreement, International Bank For Reconstruction and Development (1944), drawn up at the United Nations Monetary and Financial Conference, Bretton Woods, New Hampshire.

45 S Fujita, 'The Challenges of Mainstreaming Human Rights in the World Bank' (2011) 15 *The International Journal of Human Rights* 374–396, at 376.

46 Ibid.

47 A McBeth, 'A Right by an Other Name: The Evasive Engagement of International Financial Institutions with Human Rights' (2009) 40 *The George Washington International Law Review* 1101–1156, 1110.

It is well-known, however, that as of now large parts of the human rights domain no longer belong to the domestic affairs of States. To mention just a few early markers of that development, one can refer to the 1970 judgment of the International Court of Justice in the Barcelona Traction case, with its famous dictum on *erga omnes* obligations (obligations that are 'the concern of all States'),[48] and to the 1993 Vienna Declaration and Program of Action ('the promotion and protection of all human rights is a legitimate concern of the international community').[49] Other outcomes of lengthy debates, such as the one on Art 48 of the Draft Articles on the Responsibility of States for Internationally Wrongful Acts – the Article that relates to the breach of obligations 'owed to the international community as a whole' (Art 48(1)(b)) - and the one on the Responsibility to Protect – a concept inspired by and based on the move from 'sovereignty as control' to 'sovereignty as responsibility'[50] – build on such notions as well. In line with and reflected within such judgments and documents, a global trend is developing asking for another view of sovereignty, being the basic concept behind the 'political prohibition'. The trend is clearly moving away from a rather exclusive focus on State sovereignty ('mind your own business') to a focus on elevating substantive human dignity over certain previously conceived sovereign rights and forms. One does not have to belong to those authors who state that human rights terminology and human rights goals should and actually already do permeate (nearly) *all* other domains of international law and policy, in order to see the relevance and actual occurrence of human rights terminology in other domains of the international legal order. In a recent article, overall extremely critical on the presumed actual dimensions of the 'humanization of the international legal order', Vassilis Tzevelekos comes to the conclusion – after having stripped all the inflated, *de lege ferenda* aspects of the humanization trend – that obligations *erga omnes (partes)* and the principle of due diligence are two 'systemic' tools, central to the humanization of international law, and that

> both these tools form part of modern positive law, but may also make a positive contribution towards the direction of deeper humanisation in international law, having the potential, inter alia, to limit state will, establish occasional material normative hierarchy consisting in conditional priority in the fulfillment of human rights, give a communitarian tone to international law and invite states to be pro-active in the collective protection of their common interests and values.[51]

48 See *http://www.icj-cij.org/docket/index.php?p1=3&p2=3&k=1a&case=50&code=bt2&p3=4* (accessed 28 January 2015), para 33 (and 34).

49 Adopted by the World Conference on Human Rights, Vienna, 1993, available at *http://www.ohchr.org/EN/ProfessionalInterest/Pages/Vienna.aspx* (accessed 28 January 2015), para I, 4.

50 International Commission on Intervention and State Sovereignty, *The Responsibility to Protect, Report of the International Commission* (IDRC 2001), para 2.14.

51 V Tzevelekos, 'Revisiting the Humanisation of International Law: Limits and Potential – Obligations Erga Omnes, Hierarchy of Rules and the Principle of Due Diligence as the Basis

It is a telling way of describing the state of the art as to the humanization trend. Further to that, Tzevelekos comes to the conclusion that the process of humanization of the international legal arena needs to be balanced with the decentralized and sovereignist origins of the pluralistic international legal system. I agree with that as well, the reference to sovereignty and the limits thereto being the key words in my mind.

Applying this to the IFIs, and once again reacting to Gianviti's interpretation of the IMF Articles of Agreement ending with his remark on 'sovereign equals', one can argue on very solid ground that the respective constitutive Articles of Agreement of both IFIs should be seen as dynamic and living instruments, to be interpreted in light of legal developments so far (*de lege lata*) and trends underway (a mix of *de lege lata* and *de lege ferenda*). The latter include the paradigm shift from sovereignty as an inward-looking way of protecting national interests towards sovereignty as co-responsibility for what is going on in the outside world, where problems are no longer 'intra-territorial'. In light of the foregoing and of current views on human rights extraterritorially, it is then clear that the original conceptualization of 'the political prohibition' is no longer tenable. In addition to the ILC statement, quoted above, that '[n]o legal regime is isolated from general international law', one can also refer to the Commission's observation that it

> is hard to see how regime-builders might have agreed not to incorporate (that is, opt out from) such general principles [of international law]. The debate about new states' competence to pick and choose the customary law they wish to apply ended after decolonization without there having been much 'rejection' of old custom. Few actors would care to establish relations with a special regime that claimed a blanket rejection of all general international law. Why, in such case, would anyone (including the regime's establishing members) take the regime's engagements seriously?[52]

The ILC thus calls upon States and, literally as well by implication, their international organizations, to step away from minimalistic approaches to international legal developments. Although this is a *de lege ferenda* call, the substantive arguments in the domain of existing international human rights law backing this call cannot be seen as negligible if both IFIs so desire.

for Further Humanisation' (2013) 6 *Erasmus Law Review*, *passim*. The quote is taken from the abstract of the article.

52 Report of the Study Group of the International Law Commission, finalized by Koskenniemi (n 36), para 185.

Human rights obligations of States, acting in the context of IFIs

The IFIs are by their very nature transnational, and IFI member States, while acting within the framework of the IFIs, do affect the enjoyment of human rights in borrowing States, positively and/or negatively, and thus act extraterritorially. In addition to what has been said above about the (General Comments of the) CESCR and the obligations of ICESCR States' parties when acting within the WBG and the IMF, the extraterritorial human rights obligations of member States of international organizations have been given ample attention in, for instance, the 2011 Maastricht Principles on Extraterritorial Obligations of States in the Area of Economic, Social and Cultural Rights (Maastricht ETO Principles).[53] According to the Principles, these obligations entail a prohibition of direct as well as indirect interference, ie conduct which 'impairs the ability of another State or international organization to comply with that State's or that international organization's obligations as regards economic, social and cultural rights' (Principle 21) or which 'aids, assists, directs, controls or coerces another State or international organization to breach that State's or that international organization's obligations as regards economic, social and cultural rights, where the former States do so with knowledge of the circumstances of the act'.[54] In light of general international law, it can be added to the words 'with knowledge ...' that ignorance is not always a legitimate defence (more on this aspect and related aspects below). In addition, the Maastricht ETO Principles affirm in a number of ways the States' obligation to fulfil human rights. Principle 29, for instance, requires States to take steps 'to create an international enabling environment conducive to the universal fulfilment of economic, social and cultural rights, including in matters relating to bilateral and multilateral trade, investment, taxation, finance, environmental protection, and development cooperation'.

Also relevant are the UN Guiding Principles on Business and Human Rights (UNGPs), in particular Principle 10:

States, when acting as members of multilateral institutions that deal with business related issues, should:

> (a) Seek to ensure that those institutions neither restrain the ability of their member States to meet their duty to protect nor hinder business enterprises from respecting human rights;
> (b) Encourage those institutions, within their respective mandates and capacities, to promote business respect for human rights and, where requested, to help States meet their duty to protect against human rights

53 'Maastricht Principles on Extraterritorial Obligations of States in the area of Economic, Social and Cultural Rights' (2011), available at *http://www.etoconsortium.org/en/library/maastricht-principles* (accessed 28 January 2015). For a detailed account, see Khalfan and Seiderman, chapter 2 in this volume, especially [16-23].

54 Ibid.

> abuse by business enterprises, including through technical assistance, capacity-building and awareness-raising;
> (c) Draw on these Guiding Principles to promote shared understanding and advance international cooperation in the management of business and human rights challenges.[55]

Although one can argue that the UNGPs may not apply equally to all WBG entities, they would in any event cover the International Finance Corporation that operates (and finances) together with the private sector. Similarly, there are also issues arising out of the IMF mandate in terms of its standby arrangements/conditionality policy and/or aid programmes that call for interaction with corporations and other business enterprises in the borrowing Member countries (for more on the relation between both IFIs and the private sector, see below).

In addition, it has to be observed that, when considering State participation within IFIs, the Executive Directors of the IFIs act as representatives of the IFI concerned, but also of the member State or States that appointed them. It would go too far, however, to detect in the present context all possible consequences of these dual capacity acts.[56] Some IFI member States have already adopted national human rights legislation imposing certain duties on the Executive Directors representing them. In the US, a Chapter of the US Code entitled 'Human Rights and United States Assistance Policies with International Financial Institutions' states that 'the United States' government, in connection with its voice and vote in the International Bank for Reconstruction and Development, the International Development Association, the International Finance Corporation … and the International Monetary Fund … *shall advance the cause of human rights* …'[57] (emphasis added). And: '… the Secretary of the Treasury shall instruct each Executive Director of the above institutions to consider in carrying out his duties: 1) specific actions by either the executive branch or the Congress as a whole on individual bilateral assistance programs because of human rights considerations; (2) the extent to which the economic assistance provided by the above institutions directly benefit the needy people in the recipient country'.[58] The law is explicitly reminding US Executive Directors to take human rights into consideration when taking decisions in the context of the IFIs, including the option *not* to take a decision if the programme at hand is not in the interest of addressing and solving the basic needs of people: 'is not in the interest of the

55 Guiding Principles on Business and Human Rights (OHCHR 2011).

56 See, in much detail, AS Barros and C Ryngaert, 'The Position of Member States in (Autonomous) Institutional Decision-Making: Implications for the Establishment of Responsibility' (2014) 11 *International Organizations Law Review* 53–82.

57 22 US Code § 262d – Human rights and United States assistance policies with international financial institutions, the section on Policy Goals.

58 Ibid, the section on Policy Considerations for Executive Directors of Institutions in Implementation of Duties.

realization of human rights such as the right to food, the right to adequate health care, and the right to housing of the people living in the borrowing States'. From a strictly legal point of view, such laws would not be needed, because States and their representatives would anyhow have the obligation to act in line with their human rights obligations when taking action with external human rights effects,[59] but on the other hand there is nothing wrong with making such obligations even more specific. The key question then is whether or not 'the cause of human rights' and 'serving the basic human needs' will be understood in line with existing international human rights law. If the latter would be the case, it would make sense for other IFI member States to follow the US example.

Obligations following from (legal) relationships between the IFIs and private subcontractors

Concluding this section on human rights obligations, a few remarks have to be made on the relationship between the IFIs and private subcontractors. Without discussing here the direct human rights obligations of businesses themselves, one can discern two different relationships between an IFI and its private subcontractors. The first concerns a *direct* link in, for instance, the case of security guards working for an IFI but legally employed by a private security company. An *indirect* relationship is created when an IFI supports collaboration between a State and a private subcontractor, for instance within the context of a public-private partnership.

When human rights standards are violated in the *direct* relationship, the IFI is obliged to act as carefully as possible when selecting the subcontractor, for example by doing an extensive check of past performance, and by including adequate provisions in the contracts to ensure the subcontractor does not violate norms in the field of human rights law. In such cases, the IFI would at least have a co-obligation to find adequate solutions, in whatever form (compensation, reparation, satisfaction), in case of human rights violations by the private contractor. Human rights obligations and the consequences of the violations thereof cannot be 'contracted away', and at the end the interests of the victims of violations of such obligations should not be neglected, if for instance the private subcontractor should go bankrupt or change its legal status after (or during) the contract period.[60]

59 F Coomans and MT Kamminga (eds), *Extraterritorial Application of Human Rights Treaties* (Intersentia 2004), and recently M Langford, W Vandenhole, M Scheinin and W van Genugten (eds), *Global Justice, State Duties. The Extraterritorial Scope of Economic, Social and Cultural Rights in International Law* (CUP 2013), *passim*.

60 More on such obligations and related (State) responsibility issues in W van Genugten, N Jägers and E Moyakine, 'Private Military and Security Companies, Transnational Private Regulation and Public International Law: From the Public to the Private and Back Again?', in J Letnar Černič and T Van Ho (eds), *Direct Corporate Accountability for Human Rights* (Wolf Legal Publishers 2015), 387–406, *passim*.

In April 2010, the heads of leading multilateral development banks (MDBs) signed an agreement to cross-debar firms and individuals found to have engaged in wrongdoings in MDB-financed development projects.[61] Under this agreement, entities debarred by one MDB may be sanctioned for the same misconduct in the context of other participating development banks. The goal is to use a list of debarred firms ('black list') to close a loophole that has previously allowed a firm that has been debarred by one MDB to continue obtaining contracts financed by other MDBs. Although this initiative is primarily situated in the battle against fraud and corruption, the system is such that its scope can be broadened to also include human rights violations.

When confronted with human rights violations in the *indirect* relationship, it will be more difficult, but not impossible, to establish the exact obligations of the IFI. Hereby it will be important to establish to what extent the IFI has control over the subcontractor hired by the borrowing State. As far as the IFI influences the decision on what private actor will be involved, it has obligations to act as described in the context of the direct relationship. In any event, and in whatever way the decision on hiring the subcontractor is taken, an examination of the factual control relationships between the IFI, the member State and the private corporation will time and again be called for. That, however, is a matter of attributing conduct rather than of (human rights) obligations per se.

Attributing unlawful conduct to IFIs and their member States

Being bound by human rights obligations is one thing, determining the exact responsibility for the violation of such obligations by the IFIs as co-duty-bearers in the domain of international human rights law is something else, as well as the logical next step to be discussed. This section discusses three items: the issue of attribution of unlawful conduct and establishment of the corresponding responsibility to the IFIs; what it means to be 'in control'; and primary, subsidiary and shared responsibility.

Attribution of unlawful conduct and establishing responsibility

The circumstances under which international organizations (IOs) may be held responsible for internationally wrongful acts have been laid down in the International Law Commission's (ILC) Draft Articles on the Responsibility of International Organizations (DARIO).[62] The DARIO rules are used here as one of the possible lenses through which one can look at the (co-) respon-

61 'Agreement for Mutual Enforcement of Debarment Decisions' (2010), available at *http://go.worldbank.org/B699B73Q00* (accessed 28 January 2015).

62 Adopted by the International Law Commission at its sixty-third session, in 2011, and submitted to the General Assembly as a part of the Commission's report covering the work of that session (A/66/10, para 87). See UN Doc A/RES/66/100, 27 February 2012, text and Annex.

sibility of IFIs for the violation of human rights obligations. In light of Art 4 of the DARIO, two conditions are required under international law for the responsibility of IFIs to be established: (1) the breach of one of their international obligations; (2) that the breach at issue is attributable to them. As to the latter requirement, the conduct to be attributed will most of the time be the official conduct of the organs and agents of the IFIs acting within the overall framework of their functions, irrespective of the excess of authority or contravention of instructions (cf Arts 2(c) and 8 of the DARIO).

The acts and omissions of the IFIs may give rise to human rights violations where they aid or assist (Art 14), or direct and control (Art 15) a State (or another IO) in the commission of a wrongful act. The ILC Commentary to the Draft Articles[63] further focuses especially on two conditions: the *competence* of the IO and the *intention* of the member State. Article 61 of the DARIO provides that the organization shall have *competence* in relation to the subject-matter of the State's international obligation at hand before it can be held responsible, and the Commentary to the Article makes clear that these situations are not limited to the transfer of States' functions to an organization only. It provides:

> What is relevant for international responsibility to arise under the present article, is that the international obligation covers the area in which the international organization is provided with competence. The obligation may specifically relate to that area or be more general, as in the case of obligations under treaties for the protection of human rights.[64]

The DARIO rules thus clearly address obligations linked to the IOs *themselves* and the responsibility that might be invoked if they fail to meet their obligations. As to the *intention* of member States, acting in the context of IOs, it is stated that

> [a] State member of an international organization incurs international responsibility if, by taking advantage of the fact that the organization has competence in relation to the subject matter of one of the State's international obligations, it circumvents that obligation by causing the organization to commit an act that, if committed by the State, would have constituted a breach of the obligation (Article 61 DARIO).

In the case of the member States, acting in the context of an IFI, the attribution of the misconduct relates to the obligations they have as sovereign States, either because they are a party to a convention, the substance of which is at stake in a concrete IFI decision, or because the relevant norm has a customary

63 See *http://legal.un.org/ilc/texts/instruments/english/commentaries/9_11_2011.pdf* (accessed 28 January 2015).

64 Commentary to Art 61 DARIO, para 6.

law character. Basically, it does not make a difference whether they act on their own, or in the context of one of the IFIs. As to the attribution of conduct violating such standards, the basic rule is that where they are 'in control' they have to accept the corresponding responsibility. The same goes, *mutatis mutandis*, for the IFIs themselves.

Although very relevant, it would go too far in the present context to discuss at length the specific responsibilities of both actors in relation to each of the elements of the tripartite human rights typology (respect, protect, fulfil).[65] Instead, it is decided to focus on two issues: first, what does it mean exactly that a State or an IFI is 'in control'; and secondly, how to divide responsibility between the IFIs themselves and the State members?

'In control'

In an earlier section of this chapter mention was made of two of the General Comments of the CESCR relevant for the present context, and 'reminding' States of what they have to do when acting in the context of IOs such as the WBG and the IMF. While specifying that conduct, the CESCR has also discussed at several occasions the reach of that 'desired behavior'. What can realistically be asked from the States parties to the ICESCR, when being active in the context of IOs, more specifically IFIs? In some of its Concluding Observations, for instance in 2001 in reaction to the periodic State report by Germany, the CESR encouraged 'the State party, as a member of international financial institutions, in particular the IMF and the World Bank, *to do all it can* to ensure that the policies and decisions of those organizations are in conformity with the obligations of States parties to the Covenant' (emphasis added).[66] I consider this to be an interesting formulation, which, however, at the same time is rather vague and far from being outcome-oriented or linked to hard duty language. Nevertheless, I do agree with Sepúlveda that the words can also be read as a call upon States to perform 'an active role aimed at the implementation of the Covenant'.[67] But what is 'active'? Khalfan observes that '[r]equiring that a State "do all it can" to ensure that international organizations conform to the ICESCR implicitly requires that States have obligations to respect, protect and fulfill ESC rights in the context of their participation within such organizations'.[68] Although literally speaking Khalfan reads something into the findings of the CESCR, I think he draws

65 See, extensively, Khalfan and Seiderman, chapter 2 in this volume.

66 Example taken from M Langford, F Coomans and F Gómez Isa, 'Extraterritorial Duties in International Law', in M Langford, W Vandenhole, M Scheinin and W van Genugten (eds), *Global Justice, State Duties. The Extraterritorial Scope of Economic, Social and Cultural Rights in International Law* (CUP 2013), 51–113, at 104.

67 Ibid.

68 A Khalfan, 'Division of Responsibility amongst States', in M Langford, W Vandenhole, M Scheinin and W van Genugten (eds), *Global Justice, State Duties. The Extraterritorial Scope of Economic, Social and Cultural Rights in International Law* (CUP 2013), 299–331, at 311.

the right conclusion from the intention of the Committee, while making that intention more specific than the wording chosen by the Committee itself. But unless we think that the obligations to respect, protect and fulfil human rights are totally clear in each and every situation – which is not the case despite numerous legal and semi-legal instruments and extensive case-law – one still needs to go a few steps further. In an attempt to create more clarity on such issues, the Maastricht ETO Principles refer to the obligation to avoid causing harm:

> States must desist from acts and omissions that create *a real risk* of nullifying or impairing the enjoyment of economic, social and cultural rights extraterritorially. The responsibility of States is engaged where such nullification or impairment is a *foreseeable result* of their conduct. *Uncertainty* about potential impacts *does not constitute justification for such conduct* (Principle 13, emphasis added).

I consider this to be a good overall guideline, although applying it in full in the context of IFIs seems to be a nearly impossibly high threshold. More on that below.

Before returning to the responsibility of the IFIs specifically, it makes sense to have a look at related standard-setting efforts and outcomes in the domain of 'in control'. Apart from the CESCR, several other human rights supervisory bodies as well as, for instance, the International Court of Justice and a number of International Criminal Tribunals and researchers reflecting upon such case-law, have developed standards such as 'effective control', 'overall control', 'decisive influence', 'due diligence', 'positive obligations' and 'proximity', and looking at the outcome rather than the input side, for instance, the 'equivalent protection', 'conduct doctrine' and the 'effects doctrine'.[69] The search is time and again for an adequate coining of the scope of human rights obligations of whatever actor and the establishment of the corresponding responsibility for human rights violations if the actor is indeed 'in control'. However, in many

69 See, out of many sources, S Narula, 'International Financial Institutions, Transnational Corporations and Duties of States', in M Langford, W Vandenhole, M Scheinin and W van Genugten (eds), *Global Justice, State Duties. The Extraterritorial Scope of Economic, Social and Cultural Rights in International Law* (CUP 2013), 114–149, at 120–125, 140–147; M den Heijer and R Lawson, 'Extraterritorial Human Rights and the Concept of "Jurisdiction"', in M Langford, W Vandenhole, M Scheinin and W van Genugten (eds), *Global Justice, State Duties. The Extraterritorial Scope of Economic, Social and Cultural Rights in International Law* (CUP 2013), 153–191, at 172–182; C Ryngaert, 'Jurisdiction: Towards a Reasonableness Test', in M Langford, W Vandenhole, M Scheinin and W van Genugten (eds), *Global Justice, State Duties. The Extraterritorial Scope of Economic, Social and Cultural Rights in International Law* (CUP 2013), 192–211, *passim*; A Reinisch, 'Aid or Assistance and Direction and Control between States and International Organizations in the Commission of Internationally Wrongful Acts' (2010) 7 *International Organizations Law Review*, *passim*; P De Hert and F Korenica, 'The Doctrine of Equivalent Protection: Its Life and Legitimacy Before and After the European Union's Accession to the European Convention on Human Rights' (2012) 13 *German Law Journal* 874–895.

cases, although not exclusively, these efforts have been undertaken in the context of violations of civil and political rights, of international humanitarian law, of international criminal law and of 'hard parts' of general international law, such as the duty to respect the territorial integrity of States. It will not be easy to apply them in - cumulatively! - the context of (a) violations of economic, social and cultural rights, (b) taking place extraterritorially, by and through (c) the channels of the IFIs and/or their member States. In some situations and cases it would not be too difficult to do that – one can think of the construction of the typical World Bank funded dam leading to the forced eviction of a local indigenous community (the phenomenon also known as 'villagization'[70]), which would include a number of violations of human rights, amongst them economic, social and cultural rights, depending on the concrete situation at hand – but such examples are often *too* easy and not very well suited to be copied in less clear situations.

This becomes even more apparent if the nuances of the issue of 'causation of human rights violations' is added to the spectrum. Under what circumstance can one speak of a sufficient causal link between an activity of an IFI or an IFI member State and a specific human rights violation, in order to keep that actor responsible for the violation? Or even more difficult: the relation between an omission to act and the non-prevention of serious violations. Again, in some cases one might be able to establish such links, and the above-mentioned forced evictions can again serve as a possible example, although even there it depends on the exact facts of the case as to whether or not the actor might claim the presence of circumstances precluding wrongfulness (cf Chapter V of the Draft Articles on the Responsibility of States for Internationally Wrongful Acts). Skogly has observed how difficult it is to determine causality in the context of extraterritorial human rights obligations. Doing that, she identifies two types of 'hurdles': 'First, the determination of which acts and omissions actually led to outcomes that may be categorised as human rights violations; and, second, the identification of international legal requirements that may make those acts and omissions unlawful.'[71] Taking such key legal issues into account in the context of the work of IFIs, and including the (interplay of) obligations discussed in an earlier section, it is clear that it will not be easy to establish a standard of control which will be workable in each and every situation which the IFIs and their member States have to face in the context of drafting and executing their policies, programmes and projects. But having such an overall, all-embracing standard or not, case-by-case analyses would be needed in order to establish the exact level of control and the corresponding responsibilities. I agree with Scheinin, who has observed on several occasions that 'facticity creates normativity', meaning that a 'contex-

70 See, for instance, Human Rights Watch (n 34), *passim*.

71 S Skogly, 'Causality and Extraterritorial Human Rights Obligations', in M Langford, W Vandenhole, M Scheinin and W van Genugten (eds), *Global Justice, State Duties. The Extraterritorial Scope of Economic, Social and Cultural Rights in International Law* (CUP 2013), 233–258, at 235.

tual assessment of the factual circumstances'[72] of a case or a situation should be leading in the discussion on establishing jurisdiction and the consequences thereof. Such a case-by-case approach does not have to be undertaken without any guidance. In the end, it is all about establishing sufficient factual links between the decision and the (negative) outcomes, to be done by independent third parties (courts, committees, fact-finding commissions) leading to justifiable and reasonable outcomes. One can refer here to Ryngaert's 'reasonableness test', inspired by US tort law.[73] Combining the perspectives taken by Skogly, Scheinin and Ryngaert, we are in the domain of analysing and judging concrete situations, done, inspired and steered by the human rights obligations of the actors concerned and by the system of attribution of unlawful conduct as developed in the context of the Draft Articles on the Responsibility of States for Internationally Wrongful Acts and the DARIO rules, and further specified by key legal and semi-legal organs, endowed with legal and semi-legal authority. If this judging and analysing work will be done by independent experts in human rights law, acting in whatever frame (again: courts, committees, fact-finding commissions) and, if relevant, in interaction with other disciplines (economics, finance, anthropology), one can trust that also in the context of the IFIs progress can be made along the lines discussed in this chapter.

Primary, subsidiary and shared responsibility

As observed, there is a direct link between 'being in control', including the establishment of causal links between decision and outcome, the attribution of conduct violating international human rights law to the actor concerned and the establishment of the corresponding responsibility. The same reasoning can be applied when the IFI and the member State are not taking action separately but jointly. They will then (have to) face the consequences of their shared responsibility, established through procedures as sketched above, and leading to apportioning the responsibility according to the relative weight of the (non-)acts conducted and the violations caused.

The DARIO rules and the Commentary to it make a division between the invocation of primary and subsidiary responsibility and of joint and several responsibility. The first is to my mind rather a matter of dividing responsibility and providing for a back-up in case the invocation of the primary responsibility fails; the second one relates to what is called here and elsewhere in this book 'shared responsibility'. As to the first, the DARIO rules state that '[w]here an international organization and one or more States or

72 M Scheinin, 'Just Another Word? Jurisdiction in the Roadmaps of State Responsibility and Human Rights', in M Langford, W Vandenhole, M Scheinin and W van Genugten (eds), *Global Justice, State Duties. The Extraterritorial Scope of Economic, Social and Cultural Rights in International Law* (CUP 2013), 212–229.

73 Ryngaert (n 69), 198.

other international organizations are responsible for the same internationally wrongful act, the responsibility of each State or organization may be invoked in relation to that act' (Art 48, para 1), and that that responsibility 'may be invoked insofar as the invocation of the primary responsibility has not led to reparation' (Art 48, para 2). The primary responsibility might either relate to the IFI *or* the member States, depending on the policy, programme or project at hand. The ILC Commentary adds as to the corresponding obligation to provide reparation, that there will be cases 'in which a State or an international organization bears only subsidiary responsibility, to the effect that it would have an obligation to provide reparation only if, and to the extent that, the primarily responsible State or international organization fails to do so'.[74] Conceptually speaking, this is clear language.

As to the shared responsibility, the Commentary to the DARIO states, without being very specific, that '[a]cceptance of responsibility by a State could entail either subsidiary responsibility or joint and several responsibility', while adding that 'the same applies to responsibility based on reliance', and that '[as] a general rule, only a rebuttable presumption may be stated'.[75] I do agree with Khalfan and Seiderman, as argued in chapter 2, that the principle of joint responsibility does not apply to a State that can show it has taken all reasonable steps to secure human rights in its conduct that has effect beyond borders.[76] Although this remark relates to the joint responsibility of States acting extraterritorially, the same reasoning can be applied to the responsibilities shared by a State and an IFI. The 'persistent objector', a concept developed in the context of customary international law but by analogy useful in the present context as well, cannot be blamed for the conduct if it has indeed taken all reasonable steps to avoid that conduct.

The question then arises whether or not the concepts discussed in relation to 'in control' are adequate and sufficient to address all attribution aspects of 'shared responsibility' as well. Measuring the level of control of each actor individually might lead to either an overlap in attributing conduct to each actor or, alternatively, a gap in such attribution. Both actors might also hide behind one another, thus creating the risk that the victims of such conduct might end up without the recognition of the responsibility, either primary, subsidiary or shared, and adequate measures of reparation, in whatever way. I agree with Vandenhole that we might then need concepts such as 'complicity'.[77] He observes that in the international domain the term is used in the context of direct human rights obligations of companies ('corporate complicity'), while one can also refer to the domain of international criminal law and concepts such as a 'joint criminal enterprise'. In both contexts these

74 Commentary (n 64), 77.

75 Ibid, 99.

76 Khalfan and Seiderman, chapter 2 in this volume.

77 Vandenhole, chapter 6 in this volume. Also see the complexities he discusses when introducing the term in another context than usual.

words do have a specific meaning, while the application of the layered composition of the concept – for instance: 'direct, indirect and silent complicity', also discussed by Vandenhole – will lead to specific outcomes in whatever new context the concept will be applied. The key, however, is clear: in case of joint actions violating whatever parts of international human rights law, there is a need of concepts addressing the issue of overlapping and shared responsibilities. And while authorizing the previously mentioned 'independent third bodies' to do the analyses and judging of concrete situations and cases, weighing all this and apportioning responsibility accordingly, again the criteria unfolded in the section 'in control' will be relevant.

In all cases the bottom line is that, according to present international human rights law, the responsibility for not causing human rights harm, for actively implementing human rights norms according to the leading tripartite typology and for taking effective remedial measures in case of violations, concerns all actors whose activities in fact affect people's lives. A realistic approach to the establishment of the level of control and the corresponding responsibilities, taking all the difficulties the IFIs are facing into account, will unavoidably have to lead and, I am convinced, also actually lead to the acceptance of these responsibilities as well.

Concluding remarks

Over the last two decades, many commentaries have been released on the way both IFIs have taken human rights obligations on board or have refrained from doing so. The chapter could have set the strict legal obligations and the corresponding responsibilities for both IFIs higher, for instance by presenting more extensive interpretations of existing case-law, or by extrapolating trends in the human rights field more progressively than I have done. That, however, could to my mind have overstretched the legal validity and applicability of developments in the field of international human rights law to both IFIs. Instead, the chapter took a threefold route, by establishing first what is already going on within both IFIs in terms of human rights (law), followed by a treatment of existing human rights law and a 'localization' of existing human rights law into the mandates of the IFIs, and by discussing a number of issues relevant to a realistic understanding of the primary, subsidiary or shared responsibility the IFIs will have to face in case their conduct causes in one way or another human rights violations.

Overall, there is a lot of pressure on both organizations and, *mutatis mutandis*, on other MDBs not discussed in this chapter to accept more accountability under international human rights standards. This chapter has made clear by what standards they are already bound, given the state of the art of international human rights law anno 2014, while as to the extent to which both IFIs, be it in different degrees, still argue that they are *not* bound by such standards, it has been shown that the space for such an argumentation is becoming more and more limited. Discussing that, it also helps to my mind to underscore that both IFIs are moving themselves in a direction in which the relevance of human rights for the fulfilment of their mandates is recognized (small) step after (small) step, even if one accepts that their pronouncements are only partly legally relevant and, more importantly, that the present chapter is not about the application of their claims in daily practice. Human rights law is best seen as living law and actors such as the IFIs can best be considered as non-static entities, even given their sometimes static approaches to their own mandates. Both IFIs have entered the human rights doorway, be it to different degrees. Should they want to move backwards or to reconsider their respective ways forward, the state of the art of international human rights law anno 2014 can serve as an invitation, but also as a stop sign.

4 Corporate responsibility for human rights: towards a pluralist approach

Jernej Letnar Černič[1]

Introduction

Chiquita Brands Inc, is an American food corporation, based in Charlotte, North Carolina.[2] Chiquita has been in past two decades subjected to countless allegations that it has been complicit in serious systematic and continuous violations in Colombia.[3] In this way, it has been subjected to several lawsuits, particularly before the courts in the United States.[4] The Business and Human Rights Resource Centre has reported that 'in March 2007, Chiquita admitted that it made payments from 1997 to 2004 to the United Self-Defense Forces of Colombia …' and that 'Chiquita settled a criminal complaint by the US Government at that time and agreed to pay a $25 million fine'.[5] The most recent complaint has alleged that the corporation 'throughout the late 1980s to the mid 1990s' aided 'terrorist organizations in Colombia in their campaign of terror against the civilian population of the Urabá region, in order to maintain its profitable control of Colombia's banana growing region. Plaintiffs are family members'.[6] The complaint has further alleged that 'Chiquita funded, armed, and otherwise supported the FARC. The deaths of Plaintiffs' relatives were a direct, foreseeable, and intended result of Chiquita's illegal and tortuous support of this terrorist organization. Chiquita's actions violated not only Colombian law and U.S. law, but also international law prohibiting crimes against humanity, war crimes, terrorism, and other abuses'.[7] The complaint is at the moment still pending before the United States District Court for the

1 I would like to thank Wouter Vandenhole, Tara van Ho, Cedric Ryngaert and Margot E Salomon for their comments on earlier versions of this chapter. Usual disclaimers apply.

2 See *http://www.chiquita.com/Home.aspx* (accessed 28 January 2015).

3 Business and Human Rights Resource Centre, Chiquita Lawsuits (re Colombia), *http://www.business-humanrights.org/Categories/Lawlawsuits/Lawsuitsregulatoryaction/LawsuitsSelectedcases/ChiquitalawsuitsreColombia* (accessed 28 January 2015).

4 Ibid.

5 Ibid.

6 *Does 1 through 254 v Chiquita Brands International Inc*, 17 March 2011, para 1, *http://www.business-humanrights.org/media/documents/chiquite-complaint-1-9-jun-2011.pdf* (accessed 28 January 2015).

7 Ibid.

District of Columbia, which on 3 June 2011 dismissed Chiquita's motion to dismiss. No legal proceedings have been so far started against Chiquita in Colombia.

The above example illustrates a clear connection between corporate human rights violations and the lack of responsibility for such acts and omissions. It poses a number of pertinent questions relating to corporate human rights obligations. Who are duty-bearers of human rights[8] obligations in the context of violations committed by or involving corporations? Do corporations have direct human rights obligations under international law? Do home states have extra-territorial human rights obligations? How, if necessary, can one distribute responsibility between corporations, states and individuals?

The enjoyment of human rights is crucial for the survival and well-being of an individual. Corporations often have 'enormous economic power' and an 'often considerable size of ... social footprint'.[9] Whereas the impact of corporations on daily lives of individuals has extended in past decades, development of their human rights obligations has taken a much slower pace. Nonetheless, globalisation 'has generated a set of new duty bearers in the area of human rights'.[10] In the same way, it has shed a new perspective on already present actors such as corporations, which have so far not been seen as duty-bearers. On the other hand, corporations can commit direct human rights violations, they act in complicity with a state or another state actor or they are not directly involved in violations but fail to speak or act against human rights violations in the country where they do business.[11] Corporations therefore play an important role in the realisation of the civil, political, economic, social and cultural rights. The primary responsibility for realising human rights remains with states, however this should not undermine emerging corporate human rights obligations in international settings.[12]

Against this background, this chapter subscribes to a pluralist approach to corporate human rights responsibilities and their enforcement. In doing so,

8 This chapter follows a broad definition of human rights, which also includes environmental rights and anti-corruption norms.

9 D Kinley and R Chambers, 'The UN Human Rights Norms for Corporations: The Private Implications of Public International Law' (2006) 6 Human Rights Law Review 447–497, at 493. See, for example, Opinion of Advocate General Trstenjak, *Maribel Dominguez v Centre informatique du Centre Ouest Atlantique and Préfet de la région Centre*, Case C-282/10, 8 September 2011, para 117.

10 ME Salomon, A Torstensen and W Vandenhole, 'Human Rights, Development and New Duty-Bearers', in ME Salomon, A Torstensen and W Vandenhole (eds), *Casting the Net Wider: Human Rights, Development and New Duty-Bearers* (Intersentia 2007), 3.

11 See, for example, A Clapham and S Jerbi, 'Categories of Corporate Complicity in Human Rights Abuses' (2001) 24 Hastings International and Comparative Law Review 339–349.

12 Special Representative of the Secretary-General on the Issue of Human Rights and Transnational Corporations and Other Business Enterprises, Guiding Principles on Business and Human Rights: Implementing the United Nations 'Protect, Respect and Remedy' Framework, UN Doc A/HRC/17/31 (21 March 2011) (by John Ruggie); 2011 Update of the OECD Guidelines for Multinational Enterprises, *http://www.oecd.org/document/33/0,3746,en_2649_34889_44086753_1_1_1_1,00.html* (accessed 30 July 2013).

it advances three main arguments. First, it is submitted that that there is no fundamental legal problem with conceptualising such direct obligations *de lege ferenda*, and that at this moment of time corporations have already direct human rights obligations, even though in a limited field, deriving from international and national legal orders as sources of international law. Secondly, as corporations must be held accountable for the failure to meet their human rights obligations, one of the main questions therefore concerns whether and where victims can claim any kind of responsibility for corporate human rights violations. The third main argument advances a holistic approach towards responsibility for corporate human rights violations.

The remainder of this chapter argues that no legal conceptual arguments exist to argue against human rights obligations of corporations in domestic systems and international law and pleads for a holistic approach to corporate human rights violations. The task will be divided into five steps. Section 2 discusses and examines the state of the art on human rights and business. Section 3 analyses sources of corporate human rights obligations. It does so in two steps: first, by discussing and analysing corporate human rights obligations in international law; secondly, by examining corporate human rights obligations in national legal orders. Section 4 attempts to answer the question on the division of responsibility between corporations, states and individuals and proposes a holistic approach based on the concurrence of responsibilities. The conclusion in section 5 summarises the findings and identifies foundational principles for responsibility for violations in a pluralist duty-bearer setting.

Background of human rights and business

This section sets the scene for the arguments in the following sections. The association of human rights with business has gained a strong foothold in international, as well as domestic, law. A great number of United Nations (UN) initiatives include a reference to corporate responsibility for human rights. A number of attempts to regulate corporate activities notoriously failed at the UN level in the 1970s and 1980s when no consensus was reached to adopt a code of conduct for transnational corporations (TNC); however, the United Nations Centre for Transnational Corporations was inaugurated in 1977. Some decades later, on 13 August 2003, the UN Sub-Commission on the Promotion and Protection of Human Rights approved the 'Norms on the Responsibilities of Transnational Corporations and Other Business Enterprises with regard to Human Rights' together with an accompanying Commentary as a document specifying the human rights obligations of corporations.[13] The Norms were eventually not adopted by the then UN Commission on Human Rights.

13 ECOSOC, Sub-Commission on the Promotion and Protection of Human Rights, Norms on the Responsibility of Transnational Corporations and Other Business Enterprises with Regard

Instead, the Commission asked the UN Secretary-General to appoint a Special Representative on the issue of corporations and human rights. In July 2005, John Ruggie, a professor at Harvard University, was appointed Special Representative of the UN Secretary-General on the Issue of Human Rights and Transnational Corporations and Other Business Enterprises. Ruggie criticised the 2003 Norms and has submitted that the 'norms exercise became engulfed by its own doctrinal excesses'.[14] The 2008 Ruggie Report proposed a three-pillar framework for corporate accountability for human rights, which he describes as 'Protect, Respect and Remedy'.[15] The UN Human Rights Council thereafter adopted the Guiding Principles on Business and Human Rights in June 2011.[16] Ruggie recognises that corporations already have responsibility to respect ('obligation to do no harm'), but he refrains from addressing the question as to whether corporations also have obligations and responsibility to protect and fulfil human rights of individuals.[17] This is somehow surprising, particularly as some corporations have already recognised that they also have obligations to protect and fulfil human rights.[18] Bilchitz and Deva argue in their 2013 edited volume that 'the book does not claim that the Framework and the GPs are devoid of any merit. Nevertheless, we believe that critical insights will be vital to further the cause of putting in place a robust framework regarding the human rights obligations of companies'.[19] In this light, it may well be argued that not

to Human Rights, UN Doc E/CN.4/Sub.2/2003/12/Rev.2, 26 August 2003. ECOSOC, Commission on Human Rights, Responsibilities of Transnational Corporations and Related Business Enterprises with Regard to Human Rights, UN Doc E/CN.4/DEC/2004/116, 20 April 2004. The Commission, in Resolution 2004/116 of 20 April 2004, expressed the view that, while the Norms contained 'useful elements and ideas' for its consideration, as a draft the proposal had no legal standing.

14 J Ruggie's 2008 report, UN Human Rights Council, Promotion and Protection of All Human Rights, Civil, Political, Economic, Social and Cultural Rights, Including the Right to Development: Protect, Respect and Remedy: A Framework for Business and Human Rights, UN Doc A/HRC/8/5, 7 April 2008, *http://www.reports-and-materials.org/Ruggie-report-7-Apr-2008.pdf* (accessed 28 January 2015), para 59. He further suggests that 'even leaving aside the highly contentious though largely symbolic proposal to monitor firms and provide for reparation payments to victims, its exaggerated legal claims and conceptual ambiguities created confusion and doubt even among many mainstream international lawyers and other impartial observers'.

15 Ibid, para 69.

16 Ruggie (n 12).

17 Ruggie's 2008 report suggests that corporate 'responsibilities cannot and should not simply mirror the duties of States', Ruggie (n 14), 53.

18 BP, Promoting security and human rights: 'We recognize that we also have a responsibility to contribute to protecting the security of the communities where we operate. We have therefore continued our work to implement the Voluntary Principles on Security and Human Rights, which aim to help extractive industry companies maintain the safety and security of their operations in a framework that upholds respect for human rights', *http://www.bp.com/sectiongenericarticle.do?categoryId=9022092&contentId=7044181* (accessed 28 January 2015).

19 S Deva and D Bilchitz, 'The Human Rights Obligations of Business: A Critical Framework for the Future', in S Deva and D Bilchitz (eds), *Human Rights Obligations of Business: Beyond the Corporate Responsibility to Respect* (CUP 2013), 1–26, at 4.

only states have obligations to respect, protect and fulfil human rights, but also that corporations have obligations to respect, protect and fulfil human rights.

After Ruggie's mandate expired in 2011, the UN Human Rights Council appointed a five-member Working Group primarily to 'promote the effective and comprehensive dissemination and implementation of the Guiding Principles on Business and Human Rights: Implementing the United Nations "Protect, Respect and Remedy" Framework'.[20] The Working Group has so far produced two reports, which mainly followed Ruggie's mandate. Both reports have been so far heavily criticised by non-governmental organisations and academics.[21] Against this backdrop, the Republic of Ecuador at the Human Rights Council in September 2014 proposed the adoption of 'an international legally binding instrument, concluded within the UN system, which would clarify the obligations of transnational corporations in the field of human rights, as well as of corporations in relation to States'.[22] Such initiative is reported to be supported by 85 states and various civil society organisations.[23] On 26 June 2014, the UN Human Rights Council voted on two resolutions on the topic.[24] One resolution was drafted by Ecuador and South Africa and supported also by Bolivia, Cuba and Venezuela[25] and the other was proposed by Norway.[26] The Resolution proposed by Ecuador and South Africa creates 'an open-ended intergovernmental working group on a legally binding instrument on transnational corporations and other business enterprises with respect to human rights; whose mandate shall be to elaborate an international legally binding instrument to regulate, in international human

20 The UN Human Rights Council, Resolution, para 6(a), 15 June 2011, *http://www.business-human-rights.org/media/documents/un-human-rights-council-resolution-re-human-rights-transnational-corps-15-jun-2011.pdf* (accessed 28 January 2015).

21 Dejusticia, Conectas, Justica Global, A Review of the first two and a half years of work, November 2013, *http://conectas.org/arquivos/editor/files/6_Dej_Con_JG_WG2years_Nov2013.pdf* (accessed 28 January 2015). See also Declaration of the African Coalition for Corproate Accountability, 22 January 2014, *http://www.globalrights.org/sites/default/files/news-items/ACCA_Press_Release.pdf* (accessed 28 January 2015).

22 Statement of the Republic of Ecuador on behalf of a Group of Countries the 24rd Session of the Human Rights Council, September 2013, *http://business-humanrights.org/media/documents/statement-unhrc-legally-binding.pdf* (accessed 28 January 2015).

23 See also S Deva, 'The Human Rights Obligations of Business: Reimagining the Treaty Business', *http://business-humanrights.org/media/documents/reimagine_int_law_for_bhr.pdf* (accessed 24 March 2014), 1; *http://www.escr-net.org/node/365340* (accessed 28 January 2015).

24 For a detailed account see, I Pietropaoli, High tide in Lake Geneva. Business and human rights events at the 26th session of the UN Human Rights Council, 27 June 2014, *http://business-humanrights.org/sites/default/files/media/high_tide_in_lake_geneva.pdf* (accessed 28 January 2015).

25 Elaboration of an international legally binding instrument on Transnational Corporations and Other Business Enterprises with respect to human rights, Ecuador and South Africa resolution adopted by the UN Human Rights Council on 26 June 2014, signed by Bolivia, Cuba, Ecuador, South Africa and Venezuela.

26 Business and Human Rights Resource Centre, *http://business-humanrights.org/en/binding-treaty-pros-and-cons* (accessed 28 January 2015) (accessed 10 July 2014).

rights law, the activities of Transnational Corporations and Other Business Enterprises'.[27] The Resolution further notes 'that the Chairperson-Rapporteur of the working group should prepare elements for draft legally binding instrument [*sic*]'.[28] An international treaty would 'provide appropriate protection, justice and remedy to the victims of human rights abuses directly resulting from or related to the activities of some transnational corporations and other businesses enterprises'.[29] Even though the resolution moves away from the ongoing work of the United Nations on business and human rights, 20 states supported it, 14 voted against it and 13 abstained.[30] Nonetheless, as correctly noted by Arvin Ganesan of Human Rights Watch, 'A fundamental flaw lies in Ecuador's insistence that the treaty focus on multinational companies, even though any company can cause problems and most standards, including the UN [guiding] principles, don't draw this artificial distinction.'[31] A day later, a resolution proposed by Norway was adopted consensually.[32] This resolution expressed support for 'the work of the Working Group on the issue of human rights and transnational corporations and other business enterprises in the fulfilment of its mandate'.[33] Ruggie noted recently that 'the resolution introduced by Argentina, Ghana, Norway, and Russia – currently overshadowed by Ecuador's resolution – will play an important role going forward'.[34] It it submitted that both conflicting approaches are often one-dimensional and that the most appropriate way forward would be to allow for pluralist approaches to the questions of (non-)binding initative in the field of human rights and business.

27 Ecuador and South Africa resolution, Elaboration of an international legally binding instrument on Transnational Corporations and Other Business Enterprises with respect to human rights, para 1.

28 Ibid.

29 Statement on behalf of a Group of Countries at the 24rd Session of the Human Rights Council, September 2013, *http://business-humanrights.org/sites/default/files/media/documents/statement-unhrc-legally-binding.pdf* (accessed 28 January 2015).

30 For an exact distribution of votes, see Business and Human Resources, *http://business-humanrights.org/en/binding-treaty-pros-and-cons* (accessed 28 January 2015).

31 A Ganesan of Human Rights Watch: 'Dispatches: A Treaty to End Corporate Abuses', available at *http://www.hrw.org/news/2014/07/01/dispatches-treaty-end-corporate-abuses* (accessed 28 January 2015).

32 Human rights and transnational corporations and other business enterprises, Norway resolution adopted by the UN Human Rights Council on 27 June 2014, signed by Andorra, Argentina, Australia, Austria, Bulgaria, Colombia, France, Georgia, Ghana, Greece, Guatemala, Iceland, India, Lebanon, Liechtenstein, Mexico, New Zealand, Norway, Russia, Serbia, the former Yugoslavia, Turkey, *http://business-humanrights.org/en/binding-treaty-pros-and-cons* (accessed 28 January 2015.

33 Ibid, para 1.

34 J Ruggie, 'The Past as Prologue? A Moment of Truth for UN Business and Human Rights Treaty', 8 July 2014, *http://www.ihrb.org/commentary/board/past-as-prologue.html* (accessed 28 January 2015).

Pluralist approach to corporate human rights obligations

It is uncontentious that international law should regulate corporations given their powerful position in the global economy and countless allegations that they violate human rights. A far more important question, however, is: do corporations already have human rights obligations in international law? This section will illustrate in two steps that there exists evidence, perhaps scattered in different subfields of international law but evidence nevertheless, of direct corporate human rights obligations in international law. First, it will argue that certain international law obligations already apply to corporations, either on the basis of international treaty provisions or rules of customary international law; secondly it will show that international law obligations derive from a plethora of national legal orders.

Towards corporate human rights obligations at the international level

International level provides an important layer of support for corporate human rights obligations. However, legal academia still seems reluctant in imposing direct obligations on corporations.[35] International human rights treaties can nowadays still be signed and ratified only by states, however, does this mean that they do not bind, for instance, corporations? Several commentators have argued that, despite the primary focus on states, corporations can have additional obligations under international human rights law.[36] Additionally, the UN Working Group on Business and Human Rights in its 2013 report recognised that businesses have 'duties and responsibilities'.[37] What is more, the UN Working Group further notes that 'Today, policymakers and busi-

35 See discussions by Radu Mares and Cedric Ryngaert at the Glothro Project Final Confernce, 26–28 March 2014, Turku, Finland.

36 SR Ratner, 'Corporations and Human Rights: A Theory of Legal Responsibility' (2001) 111 Yale Law Journal 443–545; A Clapham, *Human Rights Obligations of Non-State Actors* (OUP 2006), 266–270; N Jägers, *Corporate Human Rights Obligation: In Search of Accountability* (Intersentia 2002), 75–95; PT Muchlinski, *Multinational Enterprises and the Law* (2nd edn OUP 2007), 519–524; D Kinley and J Tadaki, 'From Talk to Walk: The Emergence of Human Rights Responsibilities for Corporations at International Law' (2004) 44 Virginia Journal of International Law 931–1023, at 961–993; N Stinnet, 'Regulating the Privatization of War: How to Stop Private Military Firms from Committing Human Rights Abuses' (2005) 28 BC Int'l & Comp L Rev. 211–224, at 217–218; D Weissbrodt and M Kruger, 'Current Development: Norms on the Responsibilities of Transnational Corporations and Other Business Enterprises with Regard to Human Rights' (2003) 97 Am J Int'l L 901–922, at 919–20; L Van den Herik and JL Černič, 'Regulating Corporations under International Law: from Human Rights to International Criminal Law and Back Again' (2010) 8 Journal of International Criminal Justice 725–743; J Letnar Černič, *Human Rights Law and Business* (Europa Law Publishing 2010). For a contrary view, see JE Alvarez, 'Are Corporations »Subjects« of International Law?' (2011) 9 Santa Clara Journal of International Law 1–36.

37 The UN Working Group 2013 Report, Report of the Working Group on the issue of human rights and transnational corporations and other business enterprises, A/HRC/23/32, 14 March 2013, para 69.

ness enterprises broadly acknowledge that States have a duty to protect and that companies have a responsibility to respect human rights'.[38] In contrast, Ruggie has concluded that the main international human rights instruments do not seem to impose direct legal responsibilities on corporations.[39] As Ratner has observed, such an approach 'confuses the existence of responsibility with the mode of implementing it'.[40] Clapham argues that it 'makes sense to talk about the parties to a human rights treaty rather than use the expression States parties, which indicates that states are exclusive members of every human rights regime'.[41] That only states can sign and ratify international treaties does not, therefore, mean that those treaties can bind only states. Rather, one should use a teleological method of interpretation that every actor which is capable of violating a human rights norm is also bound by it. Such method of interpretation takes into consideration purpose and values of a particular human rights provision. Moreover, international human rights bind corporations even if there does not exist so far an international mechanism for enforcing them.[42] The recognition of the international human rights obligations of corporations cannot be subject to the existence of potential international jurisdiction. Ratner has suggested a method for translating obligations under current international human rights law to the corporate context by employing four criteria: '[a corporation's] relationship with the government, its nexus to affected populations, the particular human right at issue, and the place of individuals violating human rights within the corporate structure'.[43] He submits that such a theory 'offers a starting point for global actors to develop a corpus of law that would recognise obligations on businesses to protect human rights'.[44] However, his proposal does not provide a definitive answer as to the legal strength of corporate human rights obligations.

What is more, individuals are already nowadays obliged to comply with prohibitions of genocide, crimes against humanity, war crimes, torture and slavery in customary international law.[45] If individuals are bound by such obligations, it is implied that corporations that are made out of individuals are also bound by such obligations.[46]

38 Ibid, para 14.

39 J Ruggie, *Just Business; Multinational Corporations and Human Rights* (Norton & Co 2013), 47. See also Representative of the Special Representative of the Secretary General, *Business and Human Rights: Mapping International Standards of Responsibility and Accountability for Corporate Acts*, 44, UN Doc A/HRC/4/035 (9 February 2007).

40 Ratner (n 36), 481.

41 Clapham (n 36), 91.

42 Ibid.

43 Ratner (n 36), 496–497.

44 Ibid, 530.

45 E van Sliedregt, *Individual Criminal Responsibility in International Law* (OUP 2013); C Ochoa, 'The Individual and Customary International Law Formation' (2007–08) 48 Virginia Journal of International Law 119–186.

46 S Deva, *Regulating Corporate Human Rights Violations: Humanizing Business* (Routledge 2012).

Several international environmental treaties place obligations on corporations. For instance, the Council of Europe Convention on Civil Liability for Damage Resulting from Activities Dangerous to the Environment provides that 'the operator ... shall be liable for the damage caused by the activity as a result of incidents at the time or during the period when he was exercising the control of that activity'.[47] The International Convention on Civil Liability for Oil Pollution Damage provides similiarly that '... the owner of a ship at the time of an incident, or, where the incident consists of a series of occurrences, at the time of the first such occurrence, shall be liable for any pollution damage caused by the ship as a result of the incident'.[48] Both treaties potentially extend their applicability to corporations. What is more, the Paris Convention on Third Party Liability in the Field of Nuclear energy[49] hold operators of nuclear facilities liable for damages or loss of life to persons and property from private nuclear accidents.[50] Further, Article 2 of the OECD Convention on Combating Bribery of Foreign Public Officials in International Business Transactions states that 'each Party shall take such measures as may be necessary, in accordance with its legal principles, to establish the liability of legal persons for bribery of a foreign public official'.[51] Such treaties indirectly impose responsibilities also on corporations.

What is more, international investment law provides further evidence that corporations are obliged to comply with human rights norms. For instance, the Canada 2014 Draft Model BIT, albeit non-binding, provides that '... it is inappropriate to encourage investment by relaxing domestic health, safety or environmental measures'.[52] The Norway 2007 Draft Model BIT in Article 32 includes a provision on Corporate Social Responsibility, which provides 'the Parties agree to encourage investors to conduct their investment activities in compliance with the OECD Guidelines for Multinational Enterprises and to participate in the United Nations Global Compact'.[53] This approach would suggest that the rights of investors are also curtailed by their obligation to respect human rights. Further, a number of international legal instruments,

47 The COE Convention on Civil Liability for Damage Resulting from Activities Dangerous to the Environment, 21 June 1993, *http://conventions.coe.int/treaty/en/treaties/html/150.htm* (accessed 28 January 2015), Art 6(1).

48 The International Convention on Civil Liability for Oil Pollution Damage, 29 November 1969, Art 3(1).

49 Paris Convention on the Third Party Liability in the Field of Nuclear Energy, done 29 July 1960, 956 UNTS 251.

50 The Brussels Convention Relating to Civil Liability in the field of Maritime Carriage of Nuclear Material, 17 December 1971, 974 UNTS.

51 OECD Convention on Combating Bribery of Foreign Public Officials in International Business Transactions, 18 December 1997, S Treaty Doc 105-43 (1998), 37 ILM, entered into force 15 February 1999.

52 Canada 2014 Model BIT, Art 11, *http://italaw.com/documents/Canadian2004-FIPA-model-en.pdf* (accessed 28 January 2015).

53 The Norway 2007 Draft Model BIT, Investment Treaty Arbitration, Draft version 1912207, Art 32, *http://ita.law.uvic.ca/documents/NorwayModel2007.doc* (accessed 28 January 2015).

such as the OECD Guidelines for Multinational Enterprises,[54] the UN Global Compact[55] and the ILO Tripartite Declaration[56] provide a growing support for corporate human rights obligations. The 2003 UN Norms on the Responsibilities of Transnational Corporations and Other Business Corporations and Other Business Enterprises with Regard to Human Rights state that corporations are required to promote, respect and protect 'human rights recognised in international as well as national law'.[57] The OECD 1976 Guidelines for Multinational Enterprises (revised in 2011) require multinational enterprises to 'respect the human rights of those affected by their activities consistent with the host government's international obligations and commitments'.[58] Further, the National Contact Points (NCPs) under the OECD Guidelines for Multinational Enterprises may provide an avenue for the enforcement of some rights against corporations. A number of cases against corporations have so far been brought before respective NCPs.[59] The ILO Tripartite Declaration states that 'all parties (including corporations) should contribute to the realization of the ILO Declaration on Fundamental Principles and Rights at Work and follow-up adopted in 1998'.[60] Such emerging obligations represent strong evidence of the commitments corporations must obey.[61] Transnational private regulation in human rights provides further support of direct human rights obligations of corporations.[62]

From this analysis of distinctive fields of international law, it is clear that a mixture of scattered corporate human rights obligations already exists in

54 2011 Update of the OECD Guidelines for Multinational Enterprises, *http://www.oecd.org/document/33/0,3746,en_2649_34889_44086753_1_1_1_1,00.htmlhttp://www.oecd.org/document/33/0,3746,en_2649_34889_44086753_1_1_1_1,00.html* (accessed 30 March 2013).

55 UN Global Compact, *http://www.unglobalcompact.org/* (accessed 30 March 2013).

56 ILO, Tripartite Declaration of Principles concerning Multinational Enterprises and Social Policy, 204th Sess, 83 ILO Official Bulletin (2000), para 8. For a critical discussion, see J Letnar Černič, 'Corporate Responsibility for Human Rights: Analyzing the ILO Tripartite Declaration of Principles Concerning Multinational Enterprises and Social Policy' (2009) 6 *Miskolc Journal of International Law* 24–34.

57 HR Commission, *Norms on the Responsibilities of Transnational Corporations and Other Business Enterprises with Regard to Human Rights*, UN Doc E/CN.4/Sub.2/2003/12/Rev.2, at 1 (26 August 2003).

58 OECD, OECD Guidelines for Multinational Enterprises: Text, Commentary and Clarifications 14 (2001).

59 European Center for Constitutional and Human Rights, A Comparison of National Contact Points – Best Practices in OECD Complaints Procedures, Berlin, November 2011, *http://www.ecchr.de/index.php/ecchr-publications/articles/a-comparison-of-national-contact-points-best-practices-in-oecd-complaints-procedures-1333.html* (accessed 2 February 2015).

60 ILO, Tripartite Declaration of Principles concerning Multinational Enterprises and Social Policy (3rd edn, 2000); see also Letnar Černič (n 56).

61 See, for example, Glothro exporatory workshop on Direct human rights obligations of corporations in international law, Bled, 17–19 January 2013, Bled, http://www.glothro.org/main.aspx?c=.GLOTHRO&n=105963 (accessed 28 January 2015).

62 C Ryngaert, 'Transnational Private Regulation and Human Rights: The Limitations of Stateless Law and the Re-Entry of the State', in J Letnar Černič and T Van Ho (eds), *Direct Corporate Accountability for Human Rights* (Wolf Legal Publishers 2014), 99–130.

international law. This is further corroborated by the recent proposal for a treaty on human rights and business. However, the glass remains only half-full and therefore such a comprehensive framework of corporate human rights obligations should be expanded in international law in order to achieve the objective to effectively enforce corporate human rights obligations.[63] Such international legal sources are reinforced by the obligations stemming from national legal orders.

Corporate human rights obligations in national legal orders as a evidence of international legal obligations

National legal orders could provide a primary layer of corporate obligations to observe human rights.[64] The majority of national constitutions provides protection for human rights. Such protection applies also to legal persons such as corporations. What is more, a number of domestic courts have protected enjoyment of human rights against the activities of corporations. Hence, the normative thrust of corporate human rights obligations derives not only from the international but also from the national level which acts as the source of international law. This was somehow surprisingly confirmed also in the 2013 Report of the UN Working Group on Business and Human Rights, which notes that 'while business enterprises generally do not have legal obligations directly relating to human rights emanating from international instruments, they will often have legal obligations resulting from State laws that incorporate international standards, or contractual obligations with regard to respecting international standards'.[65] Article 38(1)(d) of the Statute International Court of Justice provides that judicial decisions can be regarded as sources of international law, whereas constitutional, statutory provisions, and domestic decisions offer evidence of state practice and *opinio juris* necessary for the creation of a rule of international customary law.

National constitutional courts have in the past reaffirmed the importance of human rights, including against corporations.[66] Several national jurisdictions have upheld human rights claims against corporations.[67] Corporate human rights obligations in domestic orders mostly derive from statutory provisions in criminal law, civil law and administrative law legislations.

63 Statement of the Republic of Ecuador on behalf of a Group of Countries the 24rd Session of the Human Rights Council, September 2013, *http://business-humanrights.org/media/documents/statement-unhrc-legally-binding.pdf* (accessed 28 January 2015).

64 J Letnar Černič, 'An Elephant in a Room of Porcelain: Establishing Corporate Responsibility for Human Rights' in J Letnar Černič and Tara Van Ho (eds), *Direct Corporate Accountability for Human Rights* (Wolf Legal Publishers 2014), 134–144.

65 Report of the Working Group on the issue of human rights and transnational corporations and other business Enterprises, A68/279, 6 August 2013, para 19.

66 *Mazibuko and Others v City of Johannesburg and Others* (CCT 39/09) [2009] ZACC 28; 2010 (3) BCLR 239 (CC); 2010 (4) SA 1 (CC) (8 October 2009). See Letnar Černič (n 36).

67 See, for example, Comision Estatal de Derechos Humanos, Nuevo Leon, Mexico, CEDH/242/2011, 31 December 2012.

A number of jurisdictions have introduced corporate criminal liability for all or some international crimes. Australia,[68] Belgium,[69] Canada,[70] France,[71] India,[72] Japan,[73] the Netherlands,[74] Slovenia,[75] South Korea, South Africa,[76] the United Kingdom[77] and the United States[78] have introduced legislation that extends domestic legislation on international crimes to legal persons. The extraterritorial application of these pieces of domestic criminal legislation varies from country to country. A number of national criminal jurisdictions allow, however, for active and passive extraterritorial jurisdiction over their nationals.[79] In France, for example, 'legal persons may incur criminal liability for crimes against humanity pursuant to the conditions set out under Article 121-2'.[80] Under Dutch law, the conditions of corporate criminal liability for international crimes are identical to those of natural persons.[81] The Dutch Criminal Code does not distinguish between the 'criminal liability of natural and legal persons'.[82] Likewise, corporations can be prosecuted under Australian law for international crimes.[83] What is more, a number of

68 J Kyriakakis, 'Freeport in West Papua: Bringing Corporations to Account for International Human Rights Abuses Under Australian Criminal and Tort Law' (2005) 31 Monash University Law Review 95–119, at 104–114, and J Kyriakakis, 'Australian Prosecution of Corporations for International Crimes: The Potential of the Commonwealth Criminal Code' (2007) 5 Journal of International Criminal Justice 809–826.

69 B Demeyere, Survey Response, Laws of Belgium, 'Commerce, Crime and Conflict: A Survey of Sixteen Jurisdictions', Fafo AIS, 2006.

70 A Ramasastry and RC Thompson, Survey Response, Laws of Canada, 'Business and International Crimes', Fafo AIS, 2004.

71 French Criminal Code, Art 213(3).

72 S Muralidhar, Survey Response, Laws of India, 'Commerce, Crime and Conflict: A Survey of Sixteen Jurisdictions', Fafo AIS, September 2006.

73 Human Rights Now, Survey Response, Laws of Japan (Human Rights Now), 'Commerce, Crime and Conflict: A Survey of Sixteen Jurisdictions', Fafo AIS, 2006.

74 N Jägers, Survey Response, Laws of the Netherlands, 'Commerce, Crime and Conflict: A Survey of Sixteen Jurisdictions', Fafo AIS, 2006.

75 Criminal Liability of Legal Entities Act (Slovenia), Official Gazette, no 59/1999.

76 A Katz, 'An Act of Transformation, The Incorporation of the Rome Statute of the ICC into National Law in South Africa' (2003) 12 African Security Review 25–30.

77 S Powles et al., Survey Response, Laws of the United Kingdom, 'Business and International Crimes', Fafo study, Commerce, Crime, and Conflict: A Comparative Survey of Legal Remedies for Private Sector Liability for Grave Breaches of International Law And Related Illicit Economic Activities, United Kingdom, Fafo AIS, 2004.

78 RC Thompson, Survey Response, Laws of the United States of America, Fafo AIS, September 2006 .

79 Ramasastry and Thompson (n 70), 16.

80 French Criminal Code, Art 213(3).

81 Jägers (n 74), 16.

82 Ibid, 9.

83 The Australian Commonwealth Criminal Code Act of 1995, Sections 12(1) and 268. Fafo study, R Meeran, 'Survey on Australia' conducted as part of 'Commerce, Crime, and Conflict: A Comparative Survey of Legal Remedies for Private Sector Liability for Grave Breaches of International Law and Related Illicit Economic Activities', September 2006.

recent prosecutions in domestic jurisdictions show that corporations can be held criminally liable for human rights violations.

The majority of national legal orders provide for civil claims to be brought against corporations.[84] Most national legal orders provide for civil recovery for victims of negligent torts or delicts, among them all national legal orders discussed in this chapter. Mass claims have been also processed before governmental commissions and courts in the context of Holocaust litigation, including against corporations in Austria,[85] Belgium,[86] France,[87] Germany,[88] the Netherlands[89] and the United States.[90] Several claims have been successful, particularly in Australia,[91] the Netherlands,[92] Canada[93] and England.[94] Fifteen of the 16 countries surveyed in the Fafo Report[95] allow for civil claims

84 See, for example, *Association France-Palestine Solidarité v Société Alstom Transport SA*, Judgment, Court d'appel de Versailles de 22 mars 2013, *http://www.volokh.com/wp-content/uploads/2013/04/French-Ct-decision.pdf* (accessed 28 January 2015).

85 See cases under the Austrian General Settlement Fond, http://de.nationalfonds.org/ (accessed 3 September 2013).

86 Belgian Jewish Community Indemnification Commission, http://www.combuysse.fgov.be/en/index.html (accessed 3 September 2013).

87 French Commission for the Compensation of Victims of Spoliation Resulting from the Anti-Semitic Legislation in force during the Occupation, http://www.civs.gouv.fr/ (accessed 3 September 2013).

88 German Foundation, 'Remembrance, Responsibility and Future', http://www.stiftung-evz.de/start.html (accessed 3 September 2013).

89 The Netherlands' Foundation for Individual Bank Claims Shoah, *http://www.ushmm.org/information/exhibitions/online-features/special-focus/holocaust-era-assets/the-netherlands* (accessed 3 September 2013).

90 *Bodner v Banque Paribas*, 114 F Supp 2d 117 (EDNY 2000) (settled); *In re Holocaust Victim Assets Litigation*, 105 F Supp 2d 155–157 (settled). See also the official website of the Swiss Banks Settlement: *In re Holocaust Victim Assets Litigation*, http://www.swissbankclaims.com/ (accessed 30 July 2013). See also MT Allen, 'The Limits of Lex Americana: The Holocaust Restitution Litigation as a Cul-de-Sac of International Human-Rights Law' (2011) 17 Widener L Rev 1–68; and MJ Bazayler, *Holocaust. Justice: The Battle for Restitution in America's Courts* (New York University Press 2003). See further, SA Bilenker, 'In Re Holocaust Victims' Assets Litigation: Do the U.S. Courts Have Jurisdiction Over the Lawsuits Filed by Holocaust Survivors Against the Swiss Banks?' (1997) 21 Maryland Journal of International Law & Trade 251–278; and L Bilsky, 'Transnational Holocaust Litigation' (2012) 23 Eur J Int Law 349–375; MJ White, 'Asbestos and the Future of Mass Torts' (2004) 18 Journal of Economic Perspective 183–204. See also Permanent Court of Arbitration (ed), *Redressing Injustices through Mass Claims Processes* (OUP 2006).

91 *Dagi v BHP (No 2)* [1997] 1 VR 428 (Austl).

92 *Akpan v Royal Dutch Shell PLC*, District Court of the Hague, 30 January 2014, Case no C/09/337005/HA ZA 09-1580 (ECLI:NL:RBDHA:2013:BY9854). See *https://www.milieudefensie.nl/english/shell/oil-leaks/courtcase/* (accessed 28 January 2015).

93 *Recherches Internationales Québec v Cambior Inc* [1998] QJ No 2554 (SCJ) (Canada); *Anvil Mining Ltd v Association Canadienne contre l'Impunité* [2012] CA 117 (Canada).

94 *Connelly v RTZ Corporation* (1997) 3 WLR 373 (HL); *Lubbe and 4 Others v Cape plc* [2000] 1 WLR 1545 (HL).

95 Fafo Institute, Report on Assessing the Liability of Business Entities for Grave Violations of International Law Business and International Crimes Project, Fafo, Norway, 2006.

on the basis of common law torts or civil delict against corporations for human rights violations.

Two other jurisdictions that have recognised corporate human rights obligations deriving from civil law sources are Japan and the United States. In Japan, several cases have been brought in relation to human rights violations committed by or involving corporations, particularly in relation to forced labour during the Second World War. To date, several civil compensation lawsuits against corporations have succeeded on the basis of international humanitarian law or international criminal law.[96] Most decisions, however, were delivered against corporations for violations of human rights not on the basis of international criminal law, but under Japanese tort law.[97]

The US Alien Tort Statute (ATS) has provided one of the few channels for an individual to bring an action for damages against corporations for alleged human rights violations by having knowledge of or directly assisting in such violations. The US Congress enacted the ATS as part of section 9 of the Judiciary Act of 1789. The relevant section provides as follows: 'the district courts shall have original jurisdiction of any civil action by an alien for a tort only, committed in violation of the law of nations or a treaty of the United States'.[98] International non-governmental organisations in the field of human rights have therefore put their hopes in domestic legal systems, particularly in the legal system of the United States which has so far been a relatively favourable forum for claims against transnational corporations for human rights violations. More specifically, the ATS has been one of the few forums to also allow non-US victims of human rights violations to enforce the accountability of transnational corporations for violations committed outside US territory. All that has been necessary is that a corporation is established in US territory or does business there. US courts have so far dealt with more than 100 ATS cases brought against corporations. Several claims are currently pending against several corporations for, *inter alia*, alleged involvement in crimes against humanity, war crimes, torture and forced labour and, to date, 13 claims against corporations have been settled.[99] In two cases the victims were successful.[100] US courts have dealt with a number of cases against corporations. However, most of them have not resulted in a positive outcome for the

96 See 'Commerce, Crime, and Conflict: A Comparative Survey of Legal Remedies for Private Sector Liability for Grave Breaches of International Law and Related Illicit Economic Activities Report on Japan'. Niigata District Court, Judgment of 26 March 2004, 50-12 SHOMU GEPPO 3444, Fukuoka High Court, Judgment of 24 May 2004, 50-12 SHOMU GEPPO 3646. See Hiroshima High Court, Judgment of 19 January 19 2005, 51-12 SHOMU GEPPO.

97 Ibid.

98 Alien Torts Claims Act of 1789, 28 USC § 1350. Judiciary Act of 1789, ch 20, § 11, 1 Stat 73, 78. Human rights claims against corporations can also be brought in the US under the Torture Victims Protection Act, 28 USC, Section 1350.

99 MD Goldhaber, 'Corporate Human Rights Litigation in Non-U.S. Courts: A Comparative Scorecard' (2013) 3 UC Irvine Law Review 127–150, at 128–129.

100 *Licea v Curacao Drydock Co*, 584 F Supp 2d 1355 (SD Fla 2008), *Aguilar v Imperial Nurseries*, No 3-07-cv-193 (JCH), 2008 WL 2572250. Cited in Michael D Goldhaber, 'Corporate Human

victims.[101] The ATS was hit with a powerful punch when on 17 April 2013 the US Supreme Court delivered its long-awaited decision in the case of *Kiobel et al v Royal Dutch Petroleum Co.* The US Supreme Court confirmed the presumption against the extraterritorial validity of the ATS. Moreover, it noted that 'there is no indication that the ATS was passed to make the United States a uniquely hospitable forum for the enforcement of international norms'.[102] American courts will now only in exceptional cases consider actions against a company, 'and even where the claims touch and concern the territory of the United States, they must do so with sufficient force to displace the presumption against extraterritorial application … Corporations are often present in many countries, and it would reach too far to say that mere corporate presence suffices'.[103] The *Kiobel* decision will have the greatest impact on individuals from countries with inoperative and inefficient legal systems as they are left empty-handed with regard to a potential forum for their claims.

All in all, it has been illustrated that corporate human rights obligations under criminal and civil national legislation provide an authoritative legal source for development of direct international legal obligations. Therefore, one cannot claim that the direct human rights obligations do not derive from national level.

Division and concurrence of responsibility between corporations, states and individuals

The existing international documents do not provide any guidance on the relationship between state and corporate responsibility.[104] As we have argued before, the corporate responsibility represents an additional and independent type of responsibility for human rights violations.[105] The current framework is, as Deva argues, 'inadequate and has been unable to ensure effective accountability of companies for human rights violations'.[106] In this context, Vandenhole argues that 'business enterprises themselves have a complementary obligation, albeit simultaneously with States'.[107] Ruggie's framework 'rests on differentiated but complementary responsibilities', in which the

Rights Litigation in Non-U.S. Courts: A Comparative Scorecard' (2013) 3 UC Irvine Law Review 127, at 128.

101 See, for instance, *Khulumani v Barclay Nat Bank Ltd*, United States Court of Appeals, Second Circuit, 12 October 2007, 2007 WL 2985101.

102 *Kiobel et al v Royal Dutch Petroleum Co* (US Supreme Court, 17 April 2013), 12.

103 Ibid, 14.

104 Ruggie (n 12); Maastricht Principles on Extraterritorial Obligations of States in the area of Economic, Social and Cultural Rights, 28 September 2011.

105 J Letnar Černič, 'Human Rights and Business: In Search of Effective Remedial Measure' (2012) 55/56 Dignitas – Slovene Journal of Human Rights 152–165.

106 S Deva, *Regulating Corporate Human Rights Violations* (Routledge 2012), 188.

107 W Vandenhole, *Emerging Normative Frameworks on Transnational Human Rights Obligations*, EUI Working Paper RSCAS 2012/17 (2011), 15.

state duty to protect occupies the primary position.[108] The Guiding Principles remain salient on the exact relationship between state and corporate responsibility. However, both notions of state and corporate responsibility are included in the concept of complicity. The UN Global Compact stipulates in Principle Two: 'businesses should make sure they are not complicit in human rights abuses'.[109] For instance, the South African Truth and Reconciliation Commission distinguished between first, second and third order of involvement.[110] With regard to first order of involvement, it noted that:

> To the extent that business played a central role in helping to design and implement apartheid policies, it must be held accountable. This applies particularly to the mining industry which, for this reason, is dealt with in some detail below. Direct involvement with the state in the formulation of oppressive policies or practices that resulted in low labour costs (or otherwise boosted profits) can be described as first-order involvement. This is clearly of a different moral order to simply benefiting from such policies. Businesses that were involved in this way must be held responsible and accountable for the suffering that resulted.[111]

It continued that 'those who made their money through second-order involvement clearly have more to answer for than did those who made their money in other business activities. The argument is that, as entrepreneurs, they could have chosen not to engage in such business allocating their capital and energies elsewhere'.[112] It follows that at least two forms of complicity can be distinguished: direct and indirect. However, it is not clear and must be further elaborated how the concept of complicity as a notion taken from domestic criminal law can provide any guidance on the relationship between state and corporate responsibility for human rights violations in the context of international law.

While individual responsibility and corporate responsibility function mainly in the national legal order, state responsibility functions best in the international legal order. Emphasising corporate or individual responsibility does not absolve states of their human rights obligations.[113] This chapter advances a holistic approach, however, which includes a plurality of types of responsibility. When corporate responsibility offers no remedy, claimants may often be forced to seek redress through individual or state responsibility.

108 Ruggie (n 17), para 9.

109 UN Global Compact, http://www.unglobalcompact.org/ (accessed 28 January 2015), Principle 2.

110 South African Truth and Reconciliation Commission, Final Report 1998, vol 4, ch 2, paras 23–36.

111 Ibid, para 23.

112 Ibid, para 27.

113 V Engström, *Who Is Responsible for Corporate Human Rights Violations?* (Åbo Akademi University Institute for Human Rights, January 2002), 49–50.

When state responsibility proves ineffective, claimants may have some success utilising avenues of corporate and/or individual responsibility. A convincing and compelling argument can be made that the holistic approach should be employed when pursuing responsibility for corporate human rights violations.

A pluralist and holistic approach for corporate human rights violations suggests that responsibility can be established against a corporation, a state and an individual at the same time. For example, the concurrence between individual and corporate criminal responsibility in national legal orders is theoretically feasible. One example is the parallel attribution of complicity in crimes against humanity in Iraq to Mr Van Anraat and his corporation.[114] During the Rome Conference debates, the Greek delegate Daskalopoulou-Livada argued that there is no 'need for establishing the principle of criminal responsibility of legal persons under the Statute of the Court, not because Greek law did not provide for the criminal responsibility of such persons, but because there was no criminal responsibility which could not be traced back to individuals'.[115] However, it appears that sole reliance on either corporate or individual criminal liability cannot adequately address corporate human rights violations. In other words, individual and corporate criminal responsibility can coexist side by side. What is more, a number of national legal orders offers the possibility of the concurrence of corporate and individual criminal law responsibility. Article 51(2) of the Criminal Code of the Netherlands provides, for example, that corporate and individual criminal responsibility can arise concurrently.[116] Likewise, the French Criminal Code states that 'the criminal liability of legal persons does not exclude that of natural persons'.[117] Similarly, Australian law also allows for the concurrence of corporate and individual responsibility.[118]

The concurrence of responsibilities is also recognised at the international level. Paragraph 3 of Article 10 of the UN Convention against Transnational Organised Crime states, for instance, that the liability of legal entities 'shall be without prejudice to the criminal liability of the natural persons who have committed the offences'.[119] All in all, the moral rationale behind corporate responsibility is that arguments for concurrent responsibility leave the door

114 *Public Prosecutor v Van Anraat*, LJN: BA4676, Court of Appeal The Hague, 2200050906-2, 9 May 2007. For a detailed discussion, see H van der Wilt, *Public Prosecutor v Van Anraat*, Judgment of The Hague Court of Appeal, LJN BA4676, 2200050906-2, Oxford Reports on International Law in Domestic Courts; ILDC 753 (NL 2007), 9 May 2007, http://www.oxfordlawreports.com/ (accessed 28 January 2015).

115 Summary Records of the Meetings of the Committee as a Whole, United Nations Diplomatic Conference of Plenipotentiaries on the Establishment of an International Criminal Court, 1st meeting, UN Doc A/CONF.183/C.1/L.3, 16 June 1998, Vol 2, para 57, p 136.

116 Criminal Code of the Netherlands, Art 51(2).

117 Criminal Code of the French Republic, 121-2, Act no 2000-647, 10 July, Art 8, Official Journal of 11 July 2000.

118 The Australian Commonwealth Criminal Code Act, No 12, 1995, Section 12.1.

119 The United Nations Convention against Transnational Organized Crime, adopted by General Assembly resolution 55/25, 15 November 2000, Art 10.

open for victims to pursue different avenues for establishing responsibility for corporate human rights violations. Corporate, state and individual responsibility, taken together, are more likely to satisfy those concerned with enforcing responsibility for corporate violations. Similarly, Kamminga notes that 'individual responsibility under international law has not replaced … state responsibility for the same offences'.[120] Different levels of responsibility coexist concurrently in international law. In international human rights law, states, corporations and individuals share responsibility to respect, protect and fulfil human rights. If state responsibility has been already well developed in international law, much work remains to develop corporate responsibility under international human rights law. Nonetheless, in an ideal case, states, corporations and individuals carry responsibility to observe human rights.

International human rights law currently does not provide a mechanism whereby individuals can protect their rights *vis-à-vis* corporate conduct.[121] A holistic approach underlines the pivotal function of human rights law in maintaining a 'victims-oriented perspective' to human rights problems. Such an approach may allow for concurrence of different levels of responsibility. Different possibilities of concurrence can be distinguished, for example: concurrence between individual and state responsibility; concurrence between corporate and state responsibility; concurrence between corporate and individual responsibility; and concurrence between individual, corporate and state responsibility. In most cases, the victims remain without the right to effective judicial protection at the international level, leaving victims to seek recourse in the domestic courts. A victim of a human rights violation should have multiple claims available: not only against corporations, but also against the state that failed in its obligation to protect the human rights in question and also against the individual behind corporate legal fictions: directors, managers and employees. These claims cannot be conflicting or mutually exclusive, but are instead complementary and concurrent.

Towards a pluralist understanding of corporate human rights responsibilities

A plausible argument can be made that not only home and host state, but also the Chiquita corporation mentioned in the introduction, failed in their obligations to protect individuals against the corporate conduct. This chapter has shown that international law at this point of time is gearing towards corporate human rights obligations in international law. Those obligations may

120 MT Kamminga, 'Corporate Obligations under International Law', paper presented at the 71st Conference of the International Law Association, plenary session on Corporate Social Responsibility and International Law, Berlin, 17 August 2004, *http://www2.ohchr.org/english/issues/globalization/business/docs/kamminga.doc* (accessed 28 January 2015), 6. See PA Nollkaemper, 'Concurrence between Individual Responsibility and State Responsibility in International Law' (2003) 52 International and Comparative Law Quarterly 615–640.

121 Van den Herik and Letnar Černič (n 36).

be scattered over different fields of international law and have a minor scope, but they, nevertheless, do exist. What is more, international human rights norms reach corporations indirectly through already existing human rights treaties, domestic norms and extra-territorial obligations of home states. In this way, corporate human rights obligations fall within transnational human rights obligations.

Which foundational principles for distribution of obligations and responsibility across the different fields of human rights obligations of foreign states, transnational corporations and international organisations can be discerned from the preceding discussion? We can identify at least three over-reaching principles and one novel pluralist approach that could be employed in a plural duty-bearer setting in the context of responsibility for human rights violations.

First, the preambular paragraph of the Universal Declaration of Human Rights (UDHR) already recognised the plurality of actors in globalised societies and stipulated: 'that the General Assembly proclaimed the Declaration as a common standard of achievement for all peoples and all nations, to the end that every individual and every organ of society ... shall strive by teaching and education to promote respect for these rights and freedoms and by progressive measures, national and international, to secure their universal and effective recognition and observance ...'.[122] Reading the preamble, Henkin notes that: 'every individual includes juridical persons. Every individual and every organ of society excludes no one, no company, no market, and no cyberspace. The Universal Declaration applies to them all'.[123] Human rights obligations to respect, protect and fulfil do not rest at this point of time only with states, but also with corporations, and to the some extent with individuals. Those obligations are independent, inter-dependent, equal, interrelated and are not placed in any particular hierchical order. All in all, there exists a plurarity of human rights obligations of corporations in domestic, international and internal corporate settings.

Secondly, establishing responsibility for violation of corporate obligations should be based on concurrent responsibility, which offers a victims-friendly approach. Corporate, state and individual responsibility can work together to establish responsibility for corporate human rights violations. Ratner recognised this when he noted that the 'challenge is to construct a theory both down from state responsibility and up from individual responsibility ... Some principles of state and individual responsibility (both primary and secondary rules) are quite similar, permitting us to rely upon them in the corporate context. Such a methodology acknowledges that ... a corporation is, as it

122 Universal Declaration of Human Rights, adopted and proclaimed by UN General Assembly Res 217 A (III) of 10 December 1948.

123 L Henkin, 'The Universal Declaration at 50 and the Challenge of Global Markets' (1999) 25 Brooklyn Journal of International Law 17–26, at 25.

were, more than an individual and less than a state'.[124] It appears to be more effective to take a pluralist and holistic approach and to make a range of approaches and sanctions (civil and criminal, individual, state and corporate) available to regulators to allow for a dynamic and integrated approach to enforcement.

Thirdly, all actors should focus on bottom-up law-making in order to take account of the human rights of ordinary people living ordinary lives, particularly at the time of a stalemate in the field of human rights and business. For instance, Backer argues that 'Within its own logic, and in the context of emerging complex non-state governance orders, a recognition of anarchy in governance might liberate norm production from state control and permit more active engagement directly by civil society elements....'[125] There are several examples, for instance the Maastricht Principles on Extraterritorial Obligations of States in the area of Economic, Social and Cultural Rights,[126] the UNCTAD principles on promoting responsible sovereign lending and borrowing[127] and the Guiding Principles on Business and Human Rights,[128] that have been developed from the bottom up or at least with some involvement of civil society. For example, a good example of a bottom-up approach would be an obligation to secure the prior consent of an indigenous community in order for a corporation to invest in areas where a community lives.[129] Such methods would also enforce the bottom-up obligations and responsibility in plurality of duty-bearers. What is more, Deva notes that 'if norms of international law can be developed "bottom-up" by the participation of non-state actors, the same could be said about the enforcement of such norms by informal means and by using social sanctions'.[130] The latter informal methods could thus later turn into formal pressure on domestic and international institutions.

This chapter has argued that the corporate human rights obligations even at this point of time may derive from a plurality of sources. However, they

124 Ratner (n 36), 496.

125 LC Backer, At the 2nd UN Forum on Business and Human Rights – Reflections on Bilchitz and Deva (eds), 'Human Rights Obligations of Business: Beyond the Corporate Responsibility to Respect?', 1 December 2013, *http://lcbackerblog.blogspot.com/2013/12/at-2nd-un-forum-on-business-and-human.html* (accessed 28 January 2015).

126 Maastricht Principles on Extraterritorial Obligations of States in the area of Economic, Social and Cultural Rights, 28 September 2011.

127 UNCTAD principles on promoting responsible sovereign lending and borrowing, April 2012, *http://www.unctad.info/en/Debt-Portal/Project-Promoting-Responsible-Sovereign-Lending-and-Borrowing/About-the-Project/Principles-on-Responsible-Sovereign-Lending-and-Borrowing/* (accessed 28 January 2015).

128 Ruggie (n 12).

129 Piplinks, 'Making Free Prior and Informed Consent a Reality: Indigenous Peoples and the Extractive Sector', 2013, *http://www.piplinks.org/report%3A-making-free-prior-%2526amp%3B-informed-consent-reality-indigenous-peoples-and-extractive-sector* (accessed 28 January 2015).

130 S Deva, 'Multinational, Human Rights and International Law: Time to Move beyond the "State-Centric" Conception' in J Letnar Černič and T Van Ho (eds), *Direct Corporate Accountability for Human Rights* (Wolf Legal Publishers 2014), 14.

require further development in order for the glass to become full. Further, this chapter has argued that states too have obligations to respect, protect and fulfil the human rights within and outside their territorial borders. Corporations must primarily ensure that they will not violate the human rights of individuals when doing business at home and abroad. Finally, it has advanced a holistic approach to responsibility for corporate human rights obligations. In sum, these inherently interconnected sections taken together offer an understanding on how corporate human rights and transnational human rights obligations could be further developed and conceptualised.

5 Litigating transnational human rights obligations

Mark Gibney

This chapter looks into experiences with litigating extraterritorial human rights obligations. Although States now operate outside their territorial boundaries almost as a matter of course and in doing so will often exert a profound influence on the human rights protections of individuals living in other lands, the story that is about to be told is not an encouraging one. Rather, adjudicatory bodies – assuming, of course, that an appropriate institution can even be found – have displayed a dismaying tendency to avoid dealing with transnational harms. Ironically enough, as will be explained here, there is something about the act of crossing national borders that seems to disrupt the workings of international law.

I present three reasons for this failure. *Establishing responsibility* focuses on the law of State responsibility, particularly in light of the recent ascension of the Articles on State Responsibility (ASR) and the serious negative effect this most likely will have on the protection of human rights in the context of extraterritorial harms. *Assigning responsibility* involves the difficulty of allocating blame where there are a myriad of actors (State and non-State alike) but also human rights adjudicatory bodies that are restricted by jurisdictional limitations. Finally, the section *Resisting responsibility* analyses how various regional and domestic institutions have taken a narrow view of State responsibility and we will consider several of the most noteworthy examples of this. One involves the European Court of Human Rights' interpretation of the scope of the European Convention. A second has been the manner in which regional and domestic courts have repeatedly given the principle of sovereign immunity primacy over international human rights standards. A third example involves the unwillingness of Western governments to rein in private actors, especially their own multinational corporations, which are violating human rights standards in other lands. The final example involves the Alien Tort Statute (ATS) litigation in the United States, which for years has been used as a major vehicle for pursuing extraterritorial claims of human rights abuse, including those in which multinational corporations (MNCs) were involved. However, with the Supreme Court's recent ruling in *Kiobel v Royal Dutch Petroleum*,[1] the viability of the ATS is now in serious doubt.

1 (2013) 133 S Ct 1659.

Establishing responsibility

Like other international lawyers, throughout this chapter I will speak about what is commonly referred to as the 'law on State responsibility', which, as I will explain, now generally refers to the International Law Commission's ASR.[2] However, unlike many others, I have serious reservations about this 'law', and in the past have even gone so far as to call it the 'law on State (non) responsibility'.[3]

Notwithstanding its high-sounding name, the 'law on State responsibility' is not only of quite recent origin but it rests on an uncertain legal foundation as well. It was only in 2001 that the ILC completed nearly four decades of work and forwarded the ASR to the United Nations General Assembly. In response, the GA adopted a resolution that did nothing more than to commend the ASR 'to the attention of Governments without prejudice to the question of their future adoption or other appropriate action'.[4] Yet, since that time the ASR have achieved a certain stature under international law. However, this is in large part due to the International Court of Justice's heavy reliance on the ASR in its ruling in *Bosnia v Serbia* (*Genocide Case*)[5] – a decision that, ironically enough, has been severely criticised by international lawyers and scholars. Thus, it is important to see how the ICJ used the ASR in this case.

The backdrop for *Bosnia v Serbia* was the attempt by Bosnia and Herzegovina to break away from the former Yugoslavia (Serbia) in order to establish its own independent State. The fighting that ensued pitted Bosnia forces against a range of Bosnian Serb paramilitary groups that were very closely allied with the Serbian government. The horrible conflict that engulfed this region in the early 1990s resulted in the deaths of an estimated 200,000 civilians and the displacement of upwards of 2 million people.

In 1993, Bosnia and Herzegovina brought a claim before the ICJ against Serbia and Montenegro alleging responsibility for gross and systematic violations of human rights, including genocide. Based on jurisdictional grounds, genocide was the only claim addressed by the ICJ.[6] Article I of the Genocide

2 J Crawford, *The International Law Commission's Articles on State Responsibility: Introduction, Text and Commentaries* (CUP 2002).

3 M Gibney, *International Human Rights Law: Returning to Universal Principles* (Rowman & Littlefield 2008), Chapter 2.

4 GA Res 56/83, para 3 (12 December 2001).

5 (2007) ICJ Reports.

6 The case was brought under Article IX, which provides:

> Disputes between the Contracting Parties relating to the interpretation, application or fulfillment of the present Convention, including those relating to the responsibility of a State for genocide or any of the other acts enumerated in Article III (conspiracy to commit genocide, incitement to commit genocide, attempt to commit genocide, and complicity in genocide), shall be submitted to the International Court of Justice at the request of any of the parties to the dispute.

Convention provides: 'The Contracting Parties confirm that genocide, whether committed in time of peace or in time of war, is a crime under international law which they undertake to prevent and to punish.'[7]

Based on a literal reading of Article I, an argument could be made that the only duty (or duties) that State parties have is 'to prevent and to punish' those who have carried out genocide. Although the Court ultimately did address these issues, it is noteworthy that it devoted most of its ruling to whether Serbia had committed genocide itself (through its Bosnian Serb allies), and then whether Serbia was responsible for 'aiding and assisting' genocide. More than this, the ICJ held that such an analysis was antecedent to whether a State had met its obligations 'to prevent' and 'to punish' genocide.

As an initial matter, the Court had to address whether genocide had occurred. Here, the Court relied heavily on the rulings of the International Criminal Tribunal for the Former Yugoslavia (ICTY) and it concluded that genocide had taken place – but only during a short period of time immediately following the fall of Srebrenica.[8] The next question was whether Serbia was 'responsible' for this genocide.

Rather than making any attempt to discern 'State responsibility' from the treaty itself, the Court instead turned immediately to the ASR. It began by examining whether the Bosnian Serb forces could be considered as 'State organs' of the Serbian government so that the actions of the former could be attributed to the latter, but concluded they were not, on the basis that there was no evidence that these forces had 'complete dependence' on the Serbian State.[9] The Court then examined whether the Bosnian Serb forces were acting under the 'direction and control' of Serbian officials.[10] In addressing this matter, the ICJ invoked the standard it first enunciated in *Nicaragua v United States*,[11] ruling that in order to hold Serbia responsible for the acts of genocide carried out by the Bosnian Serb military forces there must be conclusive proof that Serbia had exercised 'effective control' with respect to each operation in which the alleged violations occurred, and not generally in respect of the overall operations taken by the persons or groups of persons having committed the violations. Making reference to what it perceived as 'differences'

7 Convention on the Prevention and Punishment of the Crime of Genocide, 78 UNTS 277.

8 Although I will not address the Court's conclusion on this matter as such, or even its approach at reaching these findings, this should not be interpreted to mean that I agree with this. For a critique of how the ICJ proceeded with this case see, generally, M Gibney, 'Genocide and State Responsibility' (2007) 7 Human Rights Law Review 760–773.

9 Article 4 provides: 'The conduct of any State organ shall be considered an act of that State under international law, whether the organ exercises legislative, executive, judicial or any other functions....'

10 Article 8 provides: 'The conduct of a person or group of persons shall be considered an act of a State under international law if the person or group of persons is in fact acting on the instruction of, or under the direction or control of, that State in carrying out the conduct.'

11 (1986) *Military and Paramilitary Activities In and Against Nicaragua* (*Nicaragua v USA*), Merits Judgment, ICJ Reports.

between the Bosnian Serbs and the Serbian government, the Court ruled that this requisite level of 'effective control' had not been achieved.

The final issue was whether Serbia had 'aided and assisted' or was 'complicit' in this genocide. Article 16 of the ASR, which is entitled 'Aid or assistance in the commission of an internationally wrongful act', provides:

> A State which aids or assists another State in the commission of an internationally wrongful act by the latter is internationally responsible for doing so if:
> a) That State does so with knowledge of the circumstances of the internationally wrongful act; and
> b) The act would be internationally wrongful if committed by that State.

In addressing this issue, the ICJ first referred back to the Genocide Convention and noted that under Article III not only is genocide itself a punishable crime, but so is *conspiracy* to commit genocide, *directing and inciting* genocide, *attempts* to commit genocide, and finally, *complicity* in genocide. The Court then proceeded to equate 'complicity' in Article III of the Genocide Convention with 'aiding and assisting' under Article 16 of the ASR. Following this, it ruled that in order to be responsible for aiding and assisting in genocide, the sending State had to have full knowledge of the genocidal intent of the receiving entity and, presumably, take measures in furtherance of this genocidal goal. According to the Court's interpretation of events, this had not been established 'beyond any doubt'.

In sum, although the Genocide Convention only makes mention of State parties having the duty to prevent and to punish genocide, the Court seemingly sought to establish the principle that there are varying degrees of State responsibility for genocide, with the commission of genocide at its apex. Although the ICJ should be applauded because such an analysis provides a much more nuanced and accurate portrayal of possible wrongdoing, the Court's analysis can be faulted on at least two grounds.

The first involves the standards themselves, not only the way in which they were summarily announced by the ICJ, but the near-impossibility of ever meeting these various tests. In determining whether the Bosnian Serb paramilitary forces were acting as Serbian 'State organs', the Court demanded that these groups must be completely dependent on the Serbian government. In that way, notwithstanding the massive amounts of military, economic and political assistance that Serbia had provided to its Bosnian Serb allies, the ICJ (somehow) concluded that this standard had not been achieved. With respect to whether these forces were operating under the 'direction and control' of the Serbian State, the ICJ employed an 'effective control' standard – which in reality is much closer to an 'absolute control' test.[12] And finally, in terms of

12 For a further critique of *Nicaragua v United States* in general and the 'effective control' test in particular, see M Gibney, K Tomasevski and J Vedsted-Hansen, 'Transnational State Responsibility for Violations of Human Rights' (1999) 12 Harvard Human Rights Journal 267–296.

the issue of 'aiding and assisting', the Court read an 'intent' requirement into Article 16 that simply does not exist in the article itself.[13]

The point is that under these standards there will be few (if any) situations where a State will be 'responsible' for committing genocide or aiding and assisting in genocide that occurs in another country. Moreover, although the Court made some reference to the seriousness of the crime (genocide) involved in the case as a way of justifying these heightened standards, there is no indication that these would not be applied to all areas of human rights. In that vein, what is important to note is that the *Nicaragua* case did not involve claims involving genocide, yet the standards in that case were nearly identical to those applied in the *Genocide Case*.

The second problem with the ICJ's approach, at least in this part of its decision, is that it made no attempt to discern different levels or degrees of State responsibility. Instead, responsibility was treated as an either-or concept. Thus, for the ICJ the question was whether Serbia was responsible in full – or not responsible at all. In that way, one of the most striking (and even shocking) aspects of the Court's ruling is that, ultimately, Serbia was treated as being no more 'responsible' for the genocide that had occurred in Bosnia than, say, Canada or Tanzania or any other country that had no involvement in the political and military situation in this region of the globe. In short, the Court's commission/complicity analysis is both surprising and disappointing, but because of this, establishing State responsibility for extraterritorial harms will be no easy task.

Unfortunately, but perhaps understandably, what has received considerably less scholarly attention has been the 'other' part of the ICJ opinion in which the Court ruled that Serbia had failed to meet its obligation under the Convention to 'prevent' genocide.[14] First, the ICJ specified that the obligation to 'prevent' genocide was an obligation of conduct and not of result, and that State parties had to take 'all measures' to prevent genocide that were within their power that might contribute toward this end – whether these efforts ultimately were ever successful or not and notwithstanding whether other States were undertaking their own obligations under the Convention. Secondly, the ICJ interpreted the Convention as demanding that State parties exercise 'due diligence' that is based on State capacity. For the ICJ, what was paramount was the ability of a State 'to influence effectively the actions of persons likely to commit, or already committing, genocide'.[15] The Court continues:

13 Note that 'intent' is absent in Article 16. However, the issue is raised in the accompanying Commentary. See Crawford (n 2), 149. For a critical analysis of this discrepancy between the Articles and the Commentary on this point, see K Nahapetian, 'Confronting State Complicity in International Law' (2002) 7 UCLA Journal of International Law and Foreign Affairs 99–127.

14 The ICJ also found that Serbia had not met its obligation 'to punish', based on the government's lack of cooperation with the ICTY.

15 *Bosnia v Serbia*, para 430.

> This capacity itself depends, among other things, on the geographical distance of the State concerned from the scene of the events, and on the strength of the political links, as well as links of all other kinds, between the authorities of that State and the main actors in the events.[16]

What this means is that different States will have different duties based upon differences in circumstances. All, however, have a legal duty to contribute as much as they can towards the elimination of the substantive evil (genocide). Finally, in contrast to its approach to the issue of 'aiding and assisting' where the ICJ had ruled that in order to be 'responsible' sending States had to be fully aware of the genocidal intent of the recipient, in the context of the duty to 'prevent' the Court did not demand anything close to such certainty. Instead, the ICJ ruled that State responsibility arose whenever there was a 'serious risk' of genocide occurring. Because of the strong ties between Serbia and its Bosnian Serb allies, the Court concluded that this standard had been met in the present case.

In short, the *Genocide Case* sets forth two different – in my view competing – standards for establishing State responsibility. The test for aiding/complicity is a very high one and if this standard gains general acceptance, as appears to be the case, establishing State responsibility for extraterritorial human rights harms will be extraordinarily rare. In sharp contrast to this is the much lower 'due diligence' standard the ICJ employed in its analysis of whether Serbia had failed to prevent acts of genocide from occurring. The obvious point is that the systematic application of the Court's own 'due diligence' standard would immediately have an enormous impact on the protection of human rights for transnational harms.

Assigning responsibility

Even when State responsibility can be established, a further difficulty is assigning responsibility, especially when there are a myriad of actors involved, as there often will be in claims involving extraterritorial human rights violations. Global warming provides perhaps the perfect example of this. Not only do all States contribute to this problem, but emissions of carbon dioxide and other greenhouse gases have been occurring for centuries. How, then, do we assign State responsibility?[17] In addition, even if only present-day emissions are taken into consideration, should responsibility be based on a per capita basis – in which case the United States would be the single most responsible actor – or should only the overall levels of greenhouse gas emissions from a

16 Ibid.

17 See, generally, MG Faure and A Nollkaemper, 'Climate Change Liability and the Allocation of Risk: International Liability as an Instrument to Prevent and Compensate for Climate Change' (2007) 43A Stanford Journal of International Law 123–179; J Knox, 'Linking Human Rights and Climate Change at the United Nations' (2009) 33 Harvard Environmental Law Review 477–498.

country be considered – in which case China, as the world's leading polluter, would be assigned the greatest degree of responsibility.

But matters get even more complicated in the sense that a large percentage of greenhouse gases are produced by non-State actors. As its name suggests, State responsibility involves itself with actions by the State. No doubt, it would make little sense to only hold States accountable for the contributions to global warming that the State itself produces. But, on the other hand, is it fair to hold States responsible for the actions of private individuals – actions that States might oftentimes be powerless to prevent or even regulate?

Yet, even in situations when only State actors are involved there will be many instances where assigning State responsibility will not be easy. Consider a case where an international financial institution (IFI) provides the sole funding for an enormous dam project that turns out to be an environmental disaster. Is only the IFI responsible, or are the constituent member States responsible as well?[18] And if one assumes the latter, should responsibility be pegged to the voting power that a State has within this institution – so that if Sweden has 8 per cent of the total votes in this particular IFI it would then be 8 per cent responsible for the environmental and/or human rights harms that ensue? But what if Sweden actively opposed the loan, perhaps on the basis of human rights considerations, but wound up on the losing side and funding for the project still went through. Should Sweden be responsible as a member of the IFI but exempt in its individual capacity?[19]

But going beyond the multiplicity of actors, what compounds the problem of assigning responsibility are the jurisdictional limits of various human rights adjudicatory bodies. In that way, for example, the European Court of Human Rights can only entertain claims against those States that are party to the European Convention. How, then, should the ECHR deal with something like an extraordinary rendition case where only one part of the legal wrong has occurred within the territorial boundaries of a European country? Perhaps a suspected terrorist is arrested in Ghana, flown to Poland where he is held in a secret detention facility for three weeks, and then taken to Afghanistan where he is subjected to months of harsh interrogation and torture. And, of course, all of this is being carried out at the behest – and perhaps even under the direction – of the United States. If this individual were to pursue a claim against Poland for his unlawful detention and for violating the prohibition against *non-refoulement*, to what extent should the ECHR consider the actions (and inactions) of the other actors involved in this case (including the other European States whose air space was crossed for this individual's flights to and from Poland), but which are not before the Court?

Perhaps this is an argument for holding States joint and severally liable,

18 I do not see any answers to these questions in the International Law Commission's document: 'Responsibility of International Organizations', UN General Assembly, 63rd Sess, Geneva, A/CN.4/L.778 (2011).

19 See also van Genugten, chapter 4 in this volume.

with the idea that, in a case like this, Poland could be held to account and a judgment rendered against it for the total harm done to the detainee. In that way, it would be Poland – and not the claimant – that would have to seek indemnification from the other States involved. This certainly would be a better outcome than denying any recovery at all, which, with rare exceptions, has become the norm.[20] However, what is discomforting about this result is that Poland's contribution is miniscule to that of Ghana and Afghanistan, not to mention the United States.

Yet, while jurisdictional limitations can certainly impose severe obstacles, what is an even bigger problem is the manner in which existing avenues for adjudication and redress have been almost systematically ignored, with the desuetude of the UN inter-State complaint system serving as perhaps the prime example of this. Thus, one of the goals of the book project *Litigating Transnational Human Rights Obligations: Alternative Judgments*[21] was to spotlight human rights adjudicatory bodies that already exist, while at the same showing how a progressive interpretation of present-day international law human rights standards could much better protect against extraterritorial harms.

Given all these complexities and factors, what is much needed is a theory of shared responsibility.[22] The problem, however, is that State responsibility has long been premised on the notion of individual international responsibility.[23] Under this principle, a State is only responsible for international wrongs that it has committed itself. Yet, this does not square well with a reality that is considerably messier than this, invariably involving a wide array of actors, some of which interact with one another but many others that do not. Unfortunately, this situation has often led to a form of judicial paralysis: with so much responsibility, ultimately no State is held responsible.

Yet, I would suggest that much of the problem is self-inflicted and this goes back to the issue of how State responsibility has come to be established

20 Compare the handling of the case of Khaled El-Masri, a German national who was suspected of terrorist activities leading to his being kidnapped in Macedonia. Macedonian officials turned El-Masri over to CIA officials, who flew him to Afghanistan where he was held for four months during which time he was subjected to repeated torture. Although the US government acknowledged making a mistake in this matter, his suit in federal district court was dismissed on the basis of the State's secret doctrine. *El-Masri v Tenet et al* (2006) 437 F Supp 530 (ED Va) *aff'd* (2007) 479 F 3d 296 (4th Cir), *cert denied* (2007) 128 S Ct 373. In sharp contrast to this, El-Masri was successful in his suit against Macedonia in his case before the European Court of Human Rights (*El-Masri v Macedonia*, App no 29630/09 (ECtHR, 13 December 2012). See, generally, F Fabbrini, 'The European Court of Human Rights, Extraordinary Rendition and the Right to the Truth: Ensuring Accountability for Gross Human Rights Violations Committed in the Fight Against Terrorism' (2014) 14 Human Rights Law Review 85–103.

21 M Gibney and W Vandenhole (eds), *Litigating Transnational Human Rights Obligations: Alternative Judgments* (Routlege 2014).

22 S Skogly, 'Global Responsibility for Human Rights' (2009) 29 Oxford Journal of Legal Studies 827–847.

23 A Nollkaemper and D Jacobs, 'Shared Responsibility in International Law: A Conceptual Framework' (2013) 34 Michigan Journal of International Law 359–438.

in the first place, particularly the 'legalistic' approach reflected in the ASR. As shown in the earlier discussion of the 'other' part of the *Bosnia v Serbia* ruling, a due diligence approach would be much less concerned with determining exact levels of 'responsibility' – the ICJ certainly made no reference to the degree to which Serbia was responsible for its failure to prevent genocide in Bosnia[24] – and much more intent on evaluating State behaviour more broadly.

Resisting responsibility

International human rights law not only promises all individuals certain rights but this same law also provides for some form of 'effective remedy' when those rights have been violated. The immediate goal is to offer some restitution to victims, but there is a prophylactic purpose behind such provisions as well. Although there have been substantial advances in this realm, due in large part to the work of the regional human rights adjudicatory bodies, double victimization remains common: a person whose human rights have been violated is quite often also denied any form of effective remedy.

This section analyses different ways in which various institutions, but mainly adjudicatory bodies, have resisted invoking responsibility. These examples are not meant to be exhaustive but they do provide some indication of how State responsibility has been avoided. What is particularly noteworthy about these examples is that all involve Western States and institutions. The first example involves the European Court of Human Rights and the manner in which the world's premier human rights adjudicatory body continues to follow a narrow (and self-serving) interpretation of the geographic scope of its work. The second involves (foreign) State sovereignty immunity and the manner in which this principle of international law has repeatedly been given primacy over international human rights standards – including *jus cogens* norms such as the prohibition against torture. The third example involves the unwillingness of States to ensure that private actors under their jurisdiction and control do not violate human rights standards. The final example involves what appears to be the demise of ATS litigation in the United States.

European Court of Human Rights

Article 1 of the European Convention provides: 'The High Contracting Parties shall secure to everyone within their jurisdiction the rights and freedoms defined in … this Convention.' A vital issue the European Court of Human Rights (ECtHR) continues to wrestle with is the meaning of the term 'jurisdiction'. The leading case in this realm is the ECtHR's decision in

24 As Andrea Gattini has pointed out, Bosnia also seriously considered bringing a case against other States, including the United Kingdom, for their own breach of duty to prevent the commission of genocide. A Gattini, 'Breach of the Obligation to Prevent and Reparation Thereof in the ICJ's Genocide Judgment' (2007) 18 European Journal of International Law 695–713.

Bankovic et al v Belgium et al,[25] which was based on a 1999 NATO bombing mission over Serbia that resulted in the death or injury of 32 civilians. Since Serbia was not a State party to the ECHR, the question before the Court was whether these Serb civilians were within the 'jurisdiction' of the other European countries at the time of the bombing. The ECtHR ruled that they were not, and on this basis it dismissed the case as being inadmissible.[26] In arriving at this conclusion, the Court held that the Convention was 'primarily' or 'essentially' territorial in nature, but that individuals who were outside of Europe could be brought within the jurisdiction of the contracting States under 'exceptional circumstances', namely, when these States exercised 'effective control' over them. The ECtHR never provided a definitive accounting of when this 'effective control' test will be met, although we know from the Court's ruling that dropping bombs and killing and injuring people on the ground does not meet this standard.

In proceedings since then, the ECtHR has tempered its *Bankovic* ruling, at least to some degree. In *Öcalan v Turkey*,[27] the Court ruled that an individual who was arrested and detained by Turkish officials at the airport in Nairobi, Kenya was thereby within the 'jurisdiction' of this one contracting State. In *Ilaşcu v Russia and Moldova*,[28] the Court reaffirmed a territorial reading of the European Convention by holding Moldova responsible for human rights violations in parts of the country that were outside of its authority and control and which were governed by the self-proclaimed Moldovian Republic of Transdniestria (MRT). However, the ruling also recognized an extraterritorial dimension to the Convention by holding Russia responsible due to its 'decisive influence' over the MRT. And in what seems to be the Court's strongest move away from *Bankovic*, in *Issa v Turkey*[29] the Court ruled that if Turkish soldiers had gone on to Iraqi soil and had mutilated and killed a group of Iraqi civilians as alleged, the protections of the Convention would thereby apply on the basis that Turkey had exercised what it termed as 'temporary effective control'. The Court reasoned that: 'accountability in such situations stems from the fact that Article 1 of the Convention cannot be interpreted so as to allow a State party to perpetrate violations of the Convention on the territory of another State, which it could not perpetrate on its own territory'.[30] However, after enunciating what appears to be a new standard, the Court then went on to dismiss the case on the basis that the applicants had not provided sufficient evidence that Turkish troops had actually carried out these human rights violations.

25 *Bankovic et al v Belgium et al*, App no 52207/99 (ECtHR, 12 December 2001).

26 For a highly critical analysis of this case, see E Roxstrom, M Gibney and T Einarsen, 'The NATO Bombing Case (*Bankovic et al. v. Belgium et al.*) and the Limits of Western Human Rights Protection' (2005) 23 Boston University International Law Journal 55–136.

27 *Öcalan v Turkey*, App no 46221/99 (ECtHR, 12 May 2000).

28 *Ilaşcu v Russia and Moldova*, App no 47887/99 (ECtHR, 8 July 2004).

29 *Issa v Turkey*, App no 31821/96 (ECtHR, 16 November 2005).

30 Ibid, para 71.

Relying on these Court precedents, in *Al-Skeini v United Kingdom*[31] the British High Court ruled that only one of six civilian deaths in a British controlled area of Iraq were protected under the ECHR. According to the High Court, what differentiated this one case from the other five was that at the time of the killing the deceased had been in custody in a British-run prison, while all the other deaths had occurred on 'the street'. However, in what has been heralded by some as a historic ruling, the ECHR overturned this decision,[32] holding that at the time of their deaths at the hands of British security forces all six individuals were within the 'jurisdiction' of the United Kingdom, although it is important to note that the Court placed a strong emphasis on the occupation itself, suggesting, perhaps, that a different result would have been reached otherwise.[33]

This jurisprudence notwithstanding, the larger point is that there appears to be only a severely limited class of cases involving the actions of the European States acting outside their borders that the ECHR will be willing to address: the occupation of another country;[34] an extraterritorial arrest; interdiction and coercive law enforcement on the high seas;[35] and (possibly) a military incursion in another country, but only when there are boots on the ground and perhaps only in situations involving a formal military occupation. Yet, what this completely ignores is that there are many ways in which European States will have a profound effect on human rights protections in other lands.[36]

The primacy of sovereign immunity

Many (arguably most) victims of human rights violations have no realistic way of pursuing an effective remedy. A person who has been tortured by agents of his home country is certainly not going to press a claim in the domestic courts of that State. Because of the dearth of human rights adjudicatory bodies quite generally, some victims have sought redress in other countries. However, in nearly all instances what has thwarted such suits has been the principle of sovereign immunity.

31 Session 2006–07, (2007) UKHL 26.

32 *Al-Skeini v United Kingdom*, App No 55721/07 (ECtHR, 7 July 2010).

33 This issue was confronted directly by Nico Moons in his 'alternative judgment' of the *Al-Skeini* decision. N Moons, 'Military Interventions in Non-European States', in M Gibney and W Vandenhole (eds), *Litigating Transnational Human Rights Obligations* (Routledge 2014), 325–338.

34 Prior to *Bankovic*, in a series of cases involving Turkey's occupation of part of Cyprus, both the European Commission of Human Rights and the European Court of Human Rights had given the European Convention an extraterritorial reading to cover Turkey's actions. In a way, then, *Bankovic* represented a reversal of these cases.

35 *Medvedyev v France*, App no 3394/03 (ECtHR, 29 March 2010); *Hirsi Jamaa and Others v Italy*, App no 27765/09 (ECtHR, 23 February 2012).

36 In one of the chapters in his book *Complicity and the Law of State Responsibility* (CUP 2011), HP Aust devotes an entire chapter to ways in which extraterritorial human rights violations can be carried out. I would suggest that this is only the tip of the iceberg, especially if one were to consider – as one should – violations of economic, social and cultural rights.

The leading case in this area is the ECtHR's ruling in *Al-Adsani v United Kingdom*.[37] The case involved a Kuwaiti-UK dual national who was tortured in Kuwait during the first Persian Gulf War. After being released from the hospital and returning to his home in the United Kingdom, Al-Adsani brought suit against the Kuwaiti government. The case eventually went up to the House of Lords, the highest judicial body in the country, but Al-Adsani's claim was dismissed on the basis of the sovereign immunity provisions under British law.

Following this, however, Al-Adsani then brought another suit, but rather than going against Kuwait, he sued the United Kingdom and he did so on the grounds that by providing sovereign immunity to a State (Kuwait) that tortured him, the United Kingdom has violated his rights under the European Convention. This case was eventually heard by the Grand Chamber of the ECtHR, but by the narrowest of margins (9–8) the Court ruled that the United Kingdom had not violated Al-Adsani's rights under the European Convention.

But it is not only regional courts that have placed a premium on the principle of sovereign immunity over the protection of human rights. Consider two domestic court cases, one from Canada and the other from the United States, but both arriving at the same result.

The first involves Houshang Bouzari, an Iranian businessman who alleges he had been tortured by Iranian officials.[38] Bouzari was eventually able to flee his country and he settled in Canada. A few years later, he brought suit against the Iranian government in the Canadian court.[39] The basis of Bouzari's suit is that as a State party to the Convention Against Torture (CAT), Canada has an obligation to ensure all victims some form of redress and compensation. While Article 13 of the CAT provides for a remedial system for 'any individual who alleges he has been subjected to torture in any territory under its jurisdiction …' Article 14 makes no mention of either 'territory' or 'jurisdiction'. Instead, it merely refers to 'the victim'.[40]

The drafting history of the Convention is instructive. The drafters considered briefly, adopted without discussion, and then abandoned one year later, a proposal by the Netherlands to restrict the unconditional obligation in Article 14 to torture committed in territory under the jurisdiction of the State

37 *Al-Adsani v United Kingdom*, App no 35763/97 (ECtHR, 21 November 2001).

38 See, generally, NB Novogrodsky, 'Immunity for Torture: Lessons from *Bouzari v. Iran*' (2007) 18 European Journal of International Law 939–953.

39 (2002) *Bouzari v Islamic Republic of Iran*, 2002 ACWSJ LEXIS 2293; 2002 ACWSJ 3390; 114 ACWS (3d).

40 Article 14(1) reads in full:

> Each State Party shall ensure in its legal system that the victim of an act of torture obtains redress and has an enforceable right to fair and adequate compensation, including the means for as full rehabilitation as possible. In the event of the death of the victim as a result of an act of torture, his dependants shall be entitled to compensation.

party.[41] Furthermore, there was no indication by the Working Group that was responsible for drafting the Convention that this lack of any geographic scope posed any special problem. Rather, the only country that has consistently given Article 14 an exclusively territorial reading has been the United States, which ratified the Torture Convention with this 'understanding'.

Notwithstanding this, Canadian courts dismissed Bouzari's claim on the grounds of sovereign immunity protection. However, the UN Committee Against Torture (CAT Committee) responded by expressing concern at Canada's failure to provide a civil remedy for all victims of torture. In its 2005 Concluding Observations to Canada's report, CAT recommended that Canada 'review its position under Article 14 of the Convention to ensure the provision of compensation through its civil jurisdiction to all victims of torture'.[42] Thus, there is a disjuncture between the views of the CAT Committee, the UN body that has been assigned to implement and monitor CAT, and various judicial bodies, in Canada but also elsewhere, that have granted sovereign immunity protection for States accused of carrying out torture.[43]

While this result might possibly be explained on the basis that Mr Bouzari was not a Canadian national at the time he filed suit, the same is not true for Scott Nelson, a US citizen, who claimed he had been tortured in Saudi Arabia. After his eventual return to the United States, Nelson brought suit against the Saudi government in a case that was ultimately decided by the US Supreme Court, which upheld the dismissal of Nelson's case.[44]

Since 1976, the governing law in the United States is the Foreign Sovereign Immunity Act (FSIA)[45] which specifies that foreign States enjoy sovereign immunity protection in US courts – subject to a list of specified exceptions. However, an important additional exception was added in 1996 through the passage of the Antiterrorism and Effective Death Penalty Act (AEDPA)[46] for actions against States that are caused by 'personal injury or death that was caused by an act of torture, extrajudicial killing, aircraft sabotage, hostage taking, or the provision of material support or resources . . . for such an act'. Although this might look like a general 'human rights' exception, it is not. For one thing, it is limited to US nationals. Beyond this, the exception only applies against those States that have been designated by the US Department of State as 'State sponsors of terrorism'. The original list consisted of: North

41 CK Hall, 'The Duty of States Parties to the Convention Against Torture to Provide Procedures Permitting Victims to Recover Reparations for Torture Committed Abroad' (2007) 18 European Journal of International Law 921–937.

42 CAT Committee, Conclusions and recommendations, 34th Sess, 2–20 May 2005, UN Doc CAT/C/CR/34/CAN, 7 July 2005, paras 4(g), 5(f).

43 A Orakhelashvili, 'State Immunity and Hierarchy of Norms: Why the House of Lords Got It Wrong' (2007) 18 European Journal of International Law 955–970.

44 *Saudi Arabia v Nelson*, 507 US 349 (1993).

45 Foreign Sovereign Immunity Act, 28 USC 1602–1611 (2004).

46 Antiterrorism and Effective Death Penalty Act, 22 USC Sec 2377–2378 (2004).

Korea, Syria, Cuba, Sudan, Libya, Iran and Iraq (the present list has been whittled down to four countries: Cuba, Iran, Sudan and Syria).

Although the Saudi government has had a long history of carrying out torture, Saudi Arabia is not included on this list. Because of this, Scott Nelson could not proceed with his claim under the AEDPA. Instead, Nelson had to try to fit into the FSIA exemption for 'commercial activities' within the United States on the basis that the Saudi government had recruited him in Virginia. However, the Supreme Court rejected this argument (as perhaps it should have). But consider what US law has done. It eliminates sovereign immunity protection for *some* States that carry out torture and the like, but it continues to protect *other* States that do exactly the same thing.

While the discussion thus far has revolved around the issue of (foreign) State sovereign immunity, there is also the matter of (domestic) sovereign immunity. As shown in *Saleh v Titan*,[47] under such laws, not only does the 'sovereign' protect its own self, but this immunity has been extended to entities performing services for the government. In the *Saleh* case, former Abu Ghraib detainees brought suit in the federal (US) court against the private corporations whose employees subjected them to torture and other inhuman treatment that a worldwide audience is now familiar with. In ordering the petitioners' complaint be dismissed, the DC Circuit Court extended governmental immunity to the Titan Corporation on the basis that because of the close ties between the corporation and the US government such suit would in effect serve as an indirect challenge to the actions of the US military. In a powerful dissent, Judge Garland pointed out that the Federal Tort Claims Act,[48] the governing law in this area, specifically excludes private contractors from its coverage. Moreover, as Garland also noted, rather than carrying out government policy, federal officials – including President Bush himself – unequivocally condemned the actions of these military contractors involved in carrying out the abuses.

Finally, an interesting twist to the issue of sovereign immunity arose in *Belhag and Anor v Straw and Others*,[49] a decision handed down by the British High Court of Justice. The case involved an extraordinary rendition carried out against a couple living in China. The husband is a Libyan national and a staunch opponent of the Gaddafi regime. His wife is a Moroccan national. The two sought to travel to the United Kingdom in order to claim political asylum. Working with the CIA, British intelligence officials informed the Libyan government of the couple's travel plans and they were then kidnapped and tortured. The second claimant suffered a miscarriage during the course of these proceedings. The first claimant was imprisoned and tortured throughout the period of 2004–08. After the overthrow of the Gaddafi government,

47 580 F 3d 1 (DC Cir, 2009).
48 28 USC Sec 1346(b), 2671–2680 (2010).
49 (2013) EWHC 4111 (QB).

the claimants gained access to intelligence information which clearly established the British government's involvement in their rendition.

Using the principle of joint and several liability, the petitioners sought to hold the British defendants liable for the entirety of their claim. The defendants, British officials, sought to counter this by arguing that if they had committed a tort they were only 'secondary wrongdoers' and not 'primary wrongdoers', and according to their reading of the law, the doctrine of joint and several liability is not appropriate where there is such a differentiation in legal responsibility. Reserving judgment on this matter, the court proceeded to address the issue of sovereign immunity. The issue for the court was whether the petitioners' claim would necessarily and unlawfully 'implead' the other States involved in this rendition: China, Thailand, Malaysia, the United States and Libya. The court concluded that it would not and it refused to dismiss the suit on the basis of this doctrine.

However, Judge Simon, the presiding officer, then applied the Act of State doctrine and it upheld dismissal of the case on this basis:

> I have concluded, with hesitation, that the Defendants are correct in their submission that the case pleaded against them depends on the Court having to decide that the conduct of US officials acting outside the United States was unlawful, in circumstances where there are no clear and incontrovertible standards for doing so and where there is incontestable evidence that such an enquiry would be damaging to the national interest (par. 150).

Proceeding further, but once again expressing his reservations:

> My hesitation arises from a residual concern that … what appears to be a potentially well-founded claim that the UK authorities were directly implicated in the extra-ordinary rendition of the Claimants, will not be determined in any domestic court; and that Parliamentary oversight and criminal investigations are not adequate substitutes for access to, and a decision by, the Court. Although the act of State doctrine is well-established, its potential effect is to preclude the right to a remedy against the potential misuse of executive power and in respect of breaches of fundamental rights, and on a basis which defies precise definition. It is a doctrine with a long shadow but whose structure is uncertain (par. 151).

Thus, even in a case where there is substantial evidence implicating British security officials and where the reviewing judicial body provides a restrictive reading of the principle of sovereign immunity, there always seems to be another legal doctrine silently waiting in the wings in order to shield offending States.

Multinational corporations rule

Another example where State institutions have resisted against any finding of State responsibility involves the unwillingness of 'home' States to regulate the behaviour of their own MNCs, even in the face of strong evidence of massive levels of human rights violations by these MNCs. The well-documented case involving TVI Pacific will serve as a case study for these purposes.[50]

TVI Pacific is a Canadian-based MNC that has a mining operation in the Siocon Zamboanga del Norte municipality in the Philippines. Local residents claim that TVI Pacific's operations have caused widespread levels of environmental degradation and other violations of international human rights standards. In November 2004, a delegation from this community travelled to Canada and met with government officials there. A few months later, two community members returned to Canada to testify before the Parliamentary Subcommittee on Human Rights and International Development (Subcommittee) of the Standing Committee on Foreign Affairs and International Trade (SCFAIT). In June 2005, SCFAIT adopted a report of the Subcommittee and presented it to the Canadian Parliament. The SCFAIT Report States as fact that:

> Mining activities in some developing countries have had adverse effects on local communities, especially where regulations governing the mining sector and its impact on the economic and social wellbeing of employees and local residents, as well as on the environment, are weak or non-existent, or where they are not enforced.

Noting that Canada does not have any legislation to help ensure that Canadian mining companies in developing countries conform to human rights standards, the Subcommittee recommended that the government put in place stronger incentives to encourage compliance with international human rights standards as well as stronger monitoring and complaint mechanisms. The SCFAIT Report also called for the establishment of 'clear legal norms' to ensure that Canadian corporations and residents were held accountable for environmental and human rights violations. However, in October 2005, the government tabled a response that rejected many of the recommendations in the SCFAIT Report. According to this government Report, the international community is still in the early stages of defining and measuring corporate social responsibility, especially in terms of human rights standards. Moreover, the recommendation to establish clear legal norms to hold Canadian corporations accountable was rejected, with a commitment only to examining the 'best practices' of States. The government Report noted that Canadian law does not generally provide for extraterritorial application, and to do so would

50 S Seck, 'Home State Responsibility and Local Communities: The Case of Global Mining' (2008) 11 Yale Human Rights and Development Law Journal 177–206.

raise several problems including 'conflict with the sovereignty of foreign States; conflicts where States have legislation that differs from that of Canada; and difficulties with Canadian officials taking enforcement action in foreign States'.

In sum, the Canadian government refuses to regulate the extraterritorial activities of Canadian mining corporations, even in the face of the lack of regulation and protection by the 'host' State and even after being presented with first-hand accounts of the violations carried out by TVI Pacific and other Canadian mining companies.[51] In that way, Canada – like other industrial countries – has adopted a narrow interpretation of State responsibility under international human rights law.

To be clear, the Philippines as the 'host' State has the strongest obligation to regulate all corporate behaviour operating within its territorial borders. This principle needs to be underscored and it is certainly not being questioned. However, what is being questioned is the conclusion that Canada bears no responsibility for the manner in which its own multinational corporations operate in the world. Yet, the position taken by the Canadian government is consistent with the *Ruggie Principles*.[52] The operative provision is Principle 2, which is entitled: *States should encourage business enterprises domiciled in their territory and/or jurisdiction to respect human rights throughout their global operations, including those conducted by their subsidiaries and other related legal entities.*

The accompanying Commentary provides:

> The role that States should play to ensure that business enterprises domiciled in their territory and/or jurisdiction do not commit to human rights abuses abroad is a complex and sensitive issue. States are not at present generally required under international human rights law to regulate the extraterritorial activities of businesses domiciled in their territory and/or jurisdiction, nor are they generally prohibited from doing so provided there is a recognised jurisdictional basis, and that the exercise of jurisdiction is reasonable. Various factors may contribute to perceived and actual reasonableness of States' actions, including whether they are grounded in a multilateral agreement.

The Commentary continues:

> Furthermore, the exercise of extraterritorial jurisdiction is not a binary matter but comprises a range of measures, not all equally controversial

51 In a follow up article, Seck has described how the Canadian government has continued to wrestle with this problem, all the while Canadian-based MNCs remain unregulated – at least under Canadian law. SL Seck, 'Canadian Mining Internationally and the UN Guiding Principles for Business and Human Rights' (2011) The Canadian Yearbook of International Law 51–116.

52 *Guiding Principles for the Implementation of the United Nations 'Protect, Respect and Remedy' Framework* *http://www.ohchr.org/Documents/Issues/Business/A-HRC-17-31_AEV.pdf* (accessed 3 February 2015).

> under all circumstances. The permissible options which may be available range from domestic measures with extraterritorial implications, such as requirements on 'parent' companies to report on their operations at home and abroad, to direct extraterritorial jurisdiction such as criminal regimes which rely on the nationality of the perpetrator no matter where the offense occurs. Indeed, strong policy reasons exist for home States to encourage businesses domiciled in their territory and/or jurisdiction to respect human rights abroad, especially if the State is involved in the business venture.

In contrast to this is the approach of the *Maastricht Principles on Extraterritorial Obligations of States in the Area of Economic, Social and Cultural Rights*.[53] Rather than being permissive, the *Maastricht ETO Principles* specify that States 'must' take actions to ensure that private actors under their jurisdiction and control do not cause harm. The operative provision is Principle 24: *Obligation to Regulate*:

> All States must take necessary measures to ensure that non-State actors which they are in a position to regulate, as set out in Principle 25, such as private individuals and organisations, and transnational corporations and other business enterprises, do not nullify or impair the enjoyment of economic, social and cultural rights. These include administrative, legislative, investigative, adjudicatory and other measures. All other States have a duty to refrain from nullifying or impairing the discharge of this obligation to protect.

To conclude this section by returning to the TVI Pacific example, under the *Ruggie Principles* Canada's refusal to regulate would not constitute an internationally wrongful act. According to this reading of international law, while it would be permissible for Canada to regulate these practices it is not required to do so. The *Maastricht ETO Principles* would provide a different result. Based on what the Canadian government already knows about the overseas operations of TVI Pacific, its refusal to prevent environmental and human rights harms brought on by the operations of one of its own corporations would constitute an internationally wrongful act. How or whether Canadian courts would respond to this charge still remains unknown.

Responsibility lost

For more than four decades, the ATS,[54] adopted as part of the Judiciary Act of 1789 enacted by the initial US Congress, has served as a powerful tool

53 O de Schutter et al, 'Commentary to the Maastricht Principles on Extraterritorial Obligations of States in the Area of Economic, Social and Cultural Rights' (2012) 34 Human Rights Quarterly 1084–1169.

54 28 USC Sec 1350. The ATS reads in its entirety: 'This district courts shall have original

by which foreign victims of human rights abuses have been able to pursue civil claims in US courts. On the basis of this once moribund law, foreign nationals can bring suit in federal (US) court for violations of the 'law of nations'. In 1992, Congress passed the Torture Victim Protection Act,[55] thereby providing US citizens who are victims of torture or extrajudicial killings these same rights. The first modern case (1980) to make use of the ATS was *Filartiga v Pena-Irala*[56] where suit was brought by a Paraguayan citizen whose brother had been tortured and killed in Paraguay against the police chief responsible for his abuse and ultimate demise. The Second Circuit Court of Appeals overturned the lower court's dismissal ruling that the case involved a foreign national bringing suit for a violation of the law of nations (torture). What soon followed were a flurry of civil cases against both high and low-ranking officials from a geographic spread of States that included the Philippines, Argentina, Guatemala and even an (unsuccessful) attempt to hold the Palestinian Liberation Organization civilly liable.[57] All of these cases truly are extraterritorial in the sense that the atrocities in question occurred in a foreign land and both the plaintiff and the defendant are foreign nationals. The only connection to the US is that the defendant happened to be found within the territorial boundaries of the United States.

Although suits against foreign State officials dominated the earliest ATS proceedings, within a period of time cases also began to be brought against corporate actors. In addition to the change in legal personality, one of the important differences is that in situations involving individual State officials, the defendant's assets were seldom, if ever, within the United States. Thus, in virtually every case, plaintiffs would win a default judgment against the foreign defendants who, because of the civil nature of the case, would quickly return to his homeland, none the poorer. In that way, ATS suits were more symbolic than anything else simply because the defendants' assets remained out of the reach of the US judgment.

Cases directed against corporate actors are qualitatively different because many of the multinationals being targeted are either incorporated in the US and/or have their primary place of business in the United States. What this meant, essentially, was that real money was at stake and, seemingly, because of this, the American judiciary began to give a much more restrictive reading to the ATS than it had previously.[58] Given the fact that massive tort litigation

jurisdiction of any civil action by an alien for a tort only, committed in violation of the law of nations or treaty of the United States.'

55 Pub L No 102-256, 106 Stat 73 (1992) (codified at 28 USC Sec 1350 note).

56 (1980) 630 F 2d 876 (2nd Cir).

57 (1981) *Tel-Oren v Libyan Arab Republic*, 517 F Supp 542 (DCC) *aff'd* (1984) 726 F 2d 774 (DC Cir).

58 A 2011 article computed that plaintiffs had filed 155 ATS cases against corporations with nearly 80% arising in the preceding 15 years. These cases have arisen from approximately 60 countries. Success was elusive and federal courts routinely dismissed ATS cases. However, since 2007 there had been some movement in the other direction. Not only have there been a few out-of-court

was simply unknown in these States and that damage awards were oftentimes statutorily limited to amounts that were miniscule compared to American legal practice, this resulted in the quick demise of such cases.

While this case-law was developing, the US Supreme Court was further limiting the reach of the ATS. First, in *Sosa v Alvarez-Machain*[59] the Court narrowed the statute's expanse by limiting claims to those torts that are widely recognized under international law, concluding that the plaintiff's claim of arbitrary arrest did not reach this standard. However, in *Kiobel* the Court appeared to go much further than this. This case involved a suit brought by Nigerian nationals living in the United States who brought suit against a group of Dutch, British and Nigerian multinationals on the grounds that these corporate actors had aided and abetted the Nigerian government in committing human rights violations against those who protested against environmental degradation in the Ogoni region. In particular, the plaintiffs, political refugees, claimed that these foreign companies, including Royal Dutch Shell, had violated the law of nations by providing material support to the Nigerian government, which had carried out: (1) extrajudicial killings, (2) crimes against humanity, (3) torture and cruel treatment, (4) arbitrary arrest and detention, (5) violations of the right to life, liberty, security and association, (6) forced exile, and (7) property destruction.

Essentially bypassing decades of ATS litigation by lower federal courts, the Supreme Court ruled that the presumption against the extraterritorial application of federal statutes applied to the ATS and that there was nothing in the statute to rebut this presumption. Thus, while the ATS apparently would still apply to violations of international law committed on the high seas and within the territorial borders of the United States, its application to human rights violations occurring within the territory of another State is now questionable. As should be obvious, the implications of this for protecting human rights are enormous.[60]

Future directions

This chapter has analysed how various adjudicatory bodies – international, regional and domestic courts, alike – have struggled when faced with claims involving extraterritorial human rights harms. One enormous problem is

settlements, but four ATS actually went to trial an in two cases judgment was rendered against corporate defendants. JC Drimmer and SR Lamoree, 'Think Globally, Sue Locally: Trends and Out-of-Court Tactics in Transnational Tort Actions' (2011) 29 Berkeley Journal of International Law 456–527.

59 (2004) 542 US 692.

60 Perhaps the torch is being passed to the European States, which recently have shown much more willingness to address transnational human rights claims. See, generally, JA Kirshner, 'Why is the US Abdicating the Policing of Multinational Corporations to Europe? Extraterritoriality, Sovereignty, and the Alien Tort Statute' (2012) 30 Berkeley Journal of International Law 259–302.

the 'law' itself, particularly the (nearly) impossible standards set forth in the ASR for States that are charged with 'aiding and assisting' in the carrying out of human rights violations in other countries. Under the ICJ's rulings in both *Nicaragua* and in *Bosnia*, States have been given tremendous leeway to pursue policies that have a negative effect on human rights protections in other lands, but what remains unclear is whether it is the ASR – as opposed to the ICJ's interpretation of these articles – that has led to these results. While the ASR are certainly important to the development of the law on State responsibility they should not be seen as *the* law on State responsibility. Rather, there are other sources for this law, most notably international treaties themselves.

Another problem has been assigning responsibility when there are multiple actors and judicial institutions involved. All too often this has resulted in no State responsibility at all. Yet, there is no reason for this result. Instead, it is important for international law to reflect the fact that in many instances State responsibility will be shared responsibility. In this regard, however, the rigid nature of the ASR has been more hindrance than help. A better approach is something like the 'due diligence' standard the ICJ itself used in the 'forgotten' part of its *Genocide* ruling.

Finally, we explored several ways in which Western bodies have avoided responsibility altogether. There are at least two reasons for this result. The first is the overload problem or, more accurately, the perception of an overload problem. Thus, what is implicit (although at times explicit) in many extraterritorial human rights claims is the fear that if the door to justice is opened just a crack this will result in massive numbers of victims the world over racing to Western courtrooms. Given the dearth of available judicial institutions in which to pursue the 'effective remedy' promised by international human rights law, this is a very real concern. But what is never considered is how sharply human rights violations would decline if and when States no longer enjoy the impunity that they presently do.

The second reason for the avoidance of responsibility relates to the continued judicial deference to political institutions. Perhaps this can be seen most clearly when *jus cogens* norms such as the prohibition against torture are repeatedly trumped by a battery of defences, some judicially created and some not. This would include: Act of State, sovereign immunity, State secrets, *forum non conveniens*, and so on. The point is no matter what 'doctrine' is relied upon the result is nearly always the same, namely, double victimization. This, of course, is directly contrary to why international human rights law exists in the first place. Above all else, then, what must happen is that the rights of victims must be given priority over the political interests of States – not only in theory, but in actual practice.

Notwithstanding this otherwise dreary report, there remains hope, or at least promise. Consider how differently the world would look if the ECtHR's 9–8 ruling in *Al-Adsani* had gone in the opposite direction and the United Kingdom had been found to be in violation of the ECHR for providing

Kuwait sovereign immunity protection in a case involving its own torture. Such a decision would have gone far in puncturing the shield of sovereign immunity, thereby providing victims something they truly have never had before: a forum in which to protect their human rights.

Part 2

Towards foundational principles for a globalised duty-bearer human rights regime

6 Obligations and responsibility in a plural and diverse duty-bearer human rights regime

Wouter Vandenhole

Introduction

Economic globalisation has changed the State's role and power.[1] As a result of the increasing prevalence of transnational processes the State has lost power and many of its traditional functions are now transferred to the global and regional realm.[2] Non-State actors have become much more prominent. The ability of State and other actors to impact human rights far from home – both positively and negatively – has never been clearer. This means that ensuring human rights enjoyment is less exclusively in the hands of the State of which one is a citizen or on the territory of which one finds oneself.

Economic globalisation has so far not been paralleled by a 'globalisation of human rights law'.[3] The 'institutions of the global economy'[4] – the International Financial Institutions (IFIs)[5] such as the World Bank and the International Monetary Fund (IMF), the World Trade Organisation (WTO) and transnational corporations (TNCs) all have grown in importance and impact,[6] but human rights law has not followed suit. Whereas 'problems have

1 A Mcbeth, 'Human Rights in Economic Globalisation', in S Joseph and A McBeth (eds), *Research Handbook on International Human Rights Law* (Edward Elgar 2010), 139–166.

2 P Evans, *The Politics of Human Rights: A Global Perspective* (Pluto Press 2005).

3 The expression is borrowed from Morais, though it seems he used it in a different sense: HV Morais, 'The Globalization of Human Rights Law and the Role of International Financial Institutions in Promoting Human Rights' (2000) 33 The George Washington International Law Review 71–96.

4 D Kinley, *Civilising Globalisation. Human Rights and the Global Economy* (CUP 2009), 3.

5 Whereas the notion of International Financial Institutions (IFIs) is broader than the World Bank and IMF, and includes also the regional development banks, for ease of reference we will use IFIs here to mean World Bank and IMF.

6 See, eg, with regard to transnational corporations, DD Bradlow and C Grossman, 'Limited Mandates and Intertwined Problems: A New Challenge for the World Bank and the IMF' (1995) 17 Human Rights Quarterly 411–442, at 423 and Kinley and Chambers, who have stressed the 'enormous economic power that TNCs wield and the often considerable size of their social footprint' (D Kinley and R Chambers, 'The UN Human Rights Norms for Corporations: The Private Implications of Public International Law' (2006) 6 Human Rights Law Review 447–497, at 493). Bradlow and Hunter have pointed out 'the profound, and sometimes irreversible, impact that IFI operations can have in many of those Member States that actually use their

become transnationalized',[7] human rights law has continued to focus on the (domestic) State as the primary or exclusive duty-bearer.

There is meanwhile a growing body of scholarship that takes issue with the expansion of the duty-bearer side of human rights law.[8] The Research Networking Programme GLOTHRO (Beyond Territoriality: Globalisation and Transnational Human Rights Obligations) has been part of this development. Much of the debate centres on whether transnational human rights obligations do exist as legal obligations, and how they can be further grounded. Important work has also been done on some of the specific 'newer' duty-bearers like IFIs, companies, peace operations or the UN. More recent standard-setting exercises on foreign States, IFIs and business enterprises include the following:[9]

- the 2011 *Maastricht Principles on Extraterritorial Obligations in the Area of Economic, Social and Cultural Rights*, which focus almost exclusively on the human rights obligations of foreign States;
- the 2003 *Norms on the Responsibilities of Transnational Corporations and Other Business Enterprises with regard to Human Rights* (UN Norms) and the 2011 *UN Guiding Principles on Business and Human Rights* (UNGPs), which address the obligations of home States and of transnational companies as direct duty-bearers. The latter have also had a considerable impact on the 2011 revised OECD Guidelines for Multinational Enterprises;
- the 2002 *Tilburg Guiding Principles on the World Bank, IMF and Human Rights* (Tilburg Principles), which address the obligations of member States of international organisations (the international financial institutions in particular) and of these organisations themselves as direct duty-bearers. The Tilburg Guiding Principles have undergone revision and were updated in early 2015.[10]

financial services' and the 'growing discretion, power, and reach of the IFIs in carrying out their expanding mission' (DD Bradlow and DB Hunter, 'Conclusion: The Future of International Law and International Financial Institutions' in DD Bradlow and DB Hunter (eds), *International Financial Institutions and International Law* (Kluwer Law International 2010), 387–397, at 387 and 389.

7 Bradlow and Grossman (n 6), 415.

8 For references and further discussion, see other chapters in this book and D Garcia-Sayan, 'Human Rights and Peace-Keeping Operations' (1994) 29 University of Richmond Law Review 41–65.

9 For an elaborate account, see W Vandenhole, 'Shared Responsibility of Non-State Actors: A Human Rights Perspective', in N Gal-Or, C Ryngaert and M Noortmann (eds), *Responsibilities of the Non-State Actor in Armed Conflict and the Market Place: Theoretical Considerations and Empirical Findings* (Brill 2015), forthcoming.

10 The legal, moral and political status of each of these documents varies enormously. None of them is the final word on the topic, and none of them has binding legal effect. However, they often reflect an emerging consensus, politically and/or academically. They have at least a declaratory importance to the extent that they codify existing international law, and they may be or become indirectly binding (see also Kinley and Chambers (n 6), 483–488).

This chapter does not deal with questions of legal grounding or actor-specific regimes as such. Rather, it seeks to take a meta-view and tries to articulate some emerging or possible foundational principles on the attribution of human rights obligations and the apportioning of responsibility for violations, regardless of the type of actor. Assigning particular obligations to a particular actor (that we therefore call duty-bearer) logically precedes the question as to whether that actor can subsequently be held responsible for a violation or infringement of a human right (ie constituting an internationally wrongful act).[11]

There is a fairly sophisticated and workable toolbox of legal concepts in human rights law to deal with the domestic State, including a mainly territorial notion of jurisdiction to identify which State in particular has obligations in a specific setting, and standards and principles to assess whether a violation has occurred. This toolbox is somewhat more advanced and applied in the field of civil and political rights thanks to litigation, but increasingly there is also a better understanding of these issues in the area of economic, social and cultural rights (ESC rights). But do these concepts and principles still work when expanding the duty-bearer side of human rights law to foreign States, international organisations like the IFIs and non-State actors like corporations?

In this chapter, we look into these two questions in particular, ie which concepts and notions to use for attributing human rights *obligations* to a particular actor, and how to assign *responsibility* for human rights violations. A double challenge stands out, as we have to deal not only with a *plurality* but also a *diversity* of duty-holders (State and non-State).

In what follows, we will for both puzzles (1) introduce key issues/options; (2) map existing and emerging principles; (3) examine whether and how these principles can underpin a plural and diverse human rights duty-holders regime. The implications for *actor-specific* regimes of *common* principles governing human rights obligations and responsibility of a plurality and diversity of actors may be flagged here and there, but is not fully fleshed out.

A fundamental tension and key question is whether foundational principles for the allocation of obligations and apportioning of responsibility in a plural and diverse duty-bearer regime can be built incrementally from the current sole duty-bearer (the domestic State) paradigm, or whether a radical overhaul is needed, whereby the regime is re-built from scratch. As long as we only deal with foreign *States* as human rights duty-holders, reasoning by analogy may still be possible and justified. However, once we also include non-State actors, the point made by Bradlow and Hunter on the responsibility of IFIs, but of much broader relevance, is worth recalling:

11 The European Court of Human Rights has acknowledged that distinction in *Jaloud v The Netherlands*, App no 47708/08 (ECtHR, 20 November 2014), para 154.

> [T]he ILC process has stumbled by relying too heavily on State responsibility as an analogue for the responsibility of international organizations. [footnote omitted] Although the analogy has value, over-reliance on it tends to underplay the differences between States, which are geographically defined and have general powers and responsibilities, and international organizations, which can operate across regions and national borders, but have particular structures and limited powers and mandates defined by their founding treaties.[12]

This observation applies to TNCs and, for example, international non-governmental organisations (INGOs) as well: unlike States, these non-State actors are typically not geographically defined, have particular structures and limited mandates. The different nature of non-State actors raises fundamental questions on the appropriateness of reasoning by analogy with the current State-based regime.[13]

The factually different nature of non-State actors also demonstrates how this exercise necessitates us to revisit other basic questions, such as the rationale for applying human rights law to a diversity of actors beyond the domestic State,[14] and how we understand law. These two questions are explored in the introductory chapter, and that exercise is not reiterated here. Suffice it to say that we focus on those that hold or exercise *considerable* or decisive and *asymmetrical* power which has, or has the potential to have, a considerable impact on a number of persons or situations. Obvious actors to be included are, therefore, IFIs, companies operating globally, international territorial administrations and armed groups when they assume control over territory and persons. As to the second question how we understand law, the notion of transnational human rights obligations does not necessarily imply international law standards in the sense of State-made binding norms agreed upon in a treaty, and may compel us to revisit the process of international law-making.

Obligations

In this section, we (1) introduce key issues/options for assigning human rights obligations; (2) map existing and emerging principles; (3) examine whether and how these principles can underpin a plural and diverse human rights duty-holders regime.

12 Bradlow and Hunter (n 6), 392.

13 Contra Ratner, who argues 'that, in general terms, a corporation is, as it were, more than an individual and less than a State': SR Ratner, 'Corporations and Human Rights: A Theory of Legal Responsibility' (2001) 111 The Yale Law Journal 443–545, at 496.

14 This question has been explored in more depth in M Düwell et al, *The Cambridge Handbook of Human Dignity: Interdisciplinary Perspectives* (CUP 2014).

Issues at stake

There are two basic strands of thinking on allocating human rights obligations to a range of duty-bearers beyond the domestic State, in order to include foreign States and non-State actors (NSAs). One favours an incremental approach whereby the 'newer' duty-bearers are gradually and possibly only partially included. The incremental approach prevails in the recent standard-setting exercises on transnational human rights obligations referenced in the introductory session of this chapter. Human rights obligations incumbent on other actors than the domestic State mirror those incumbent on the domestic State, and are in part or fully extended by analogy. The other strand is more radical, in that it proposes a complete overhaul of the current thinking, and takes global obligations of all States as its starting point. It is grounded in arguments that human rights are universal ('all people have human rights and ... all States have the responsibility to protect those rights – for all people'[15]) or that there are global obligations. The latter strand of thinking found strong support in GLOTHRO's inquiry into inspirational sources outside the human rights framework, ie in legal philosophy and global ethics (see chapter 7) and in common interest regimes in international law (see chapter 8). In human rights law, one of the most prominent proponents of this line of thinking is Salomon.[16] Most of these primarily focus on other States or the international community, but do not explicitly include NSAs. At first sight, the Maastricht Principles on extraterritorial obligations of foreign States belong to the incremental strand, but since they include also 'obligations of a global character' (§ 8), they seem to rather bridge both.

Regardless of the strand of thinking, key issues include how to assign human rights obligations to an actor in a particular instance; whether and how to define the scope of obligations of each actor; and how to distributively allocate obligations to a plurality of actors.

Mapping: existing and emerging principles

Assigning obligations

In order to identify which State has human rights obligations and in which setting or situation, human rights law tends to resort to the notion of jurisdiction (arguably with the exception of the ICESCR).[17] The Maastricht Principles

15 M Gibney, 'On Terminology: Extraterritorial Obligations', in M Langford, W Vandenhole, M Scheinin and W van Genugten (eds), *Global Justice, State Duties. The Extraterritorial Scope of Economic, Social and Cultural Rights in International Law* (CUP 2013), 32–47, at 47. Compare M Gibney and S Skogly (eds), *Universal Human Rights and Extraterritorial Obligations* (University of Pennsylvania Press 2010).

16 ME Salomon, *Global Responsibility for Human Rights* (OUP 2007).

17 For an unequivocal statement of the ECtHR that jurisdiction is not to be equated with establishing responsibility for an internationally wrongful act, and the different tests that apply, see *Catan v Moldavia and Russia*, App no 43370/04 (ECtHR, 19 October 2012), para 115.

too use the concept of jurisdiction to assign obligations to extraterritorial States. Principle 9 on the scope of jurisdiction reads: 'A State has obligations to respect, protect and fulfil economic, social and cultural rights in any of the following….' This is also confirmed in the Commentary to the Principles, which explains under Principle 8 on which basis a 'State's extraterritorial obligations in the area of human rights may arise'.[18]

The Maastricht Principles imbue the notion of jurisdiction with a very broad meaning, including situations over which a State exercises authority or effective control; situations over which State actions or omissions bring about foreseeable effects; and situations in which a State is in a position to exercise decisive influence or to take measures to realise ESC rights extraterritorially (Principle 9). The Maastricht Principles stretch the meaning of jurisdiction so far, that they in fact re-define and revolutionise its meaning. In particular, the inclusion of situations where a State is simply in a position to take measures to further ESC rights as bringing about obligations for that State is rather new. The inclusion of the latter ground for jurisdiction had become inevitable because of the recognition of obligations of a global character.[19] Once obligations of a global character to realise human rights are universally accepted, regardless of any notion of causation or effect through acts or omissions, the only way the concept of jurisdiction can still be used to assign obligations is by giving it a very broad meaning.

Whereas the notion of jurisdiction may still work with regard to regional organisations with a clear territorial delineation like the EU,[20] it may be too strongly connected with sovereignty and State notions to apply it to NSAs across the board. In the UN Norms, the notion of sphere of activity and influence[21] was used as the 'functional equivalent to a State's jurisdiction'.[22] In the words of Kinley and Chambers, corporations have 'only those human rights obligations proximate to a corporation's business'.[23] The UN Guiding Principles use the concept of impact, in the meaning of causing human rights harm. Ruggie has explicitly rejected the broader concept of influence, which

18 O De Schutter et al, 'Commentary to the Maastricht Principles on Extraterritorial Obligations of States in the Area of Economic, Social and Cultural Rights' (2012) 34 Human Rights Quarterly 1084–1169, at 1101.

19 This is explicitly acknowledged in De Schutter et al (n 18), 1109.

20 See the language of jurisdiction used in Art 1(6) of the draft EU accession agreement to the European Convention on Human Rights (Draft revised agreement on the accession of the European Union to the Convention for the Protection of Human Rights and Fundamental Freedoms as Appendix I to the final report to the CDDH of the Fifth Negotiation Meeting between the CDDH Ad Hoc Negotiation Group and the European Commission on the Accession of the European Union to the European Convention on Human Rights, Doc 47+1(2013)008rev2 (2013)).

21 UN Norms, para 1.

22 J Ruggie, 'Report of the Special Representative of the Secretary-General on the Issue of Human Rights and Transnational Corporations and Other Business Enterprises, John Ruggie, Clarifying the Concepts of "Sphere of Influence" and "Complicity"' (2008), 5.

23 Kinley and Chambers (n 6), 462.

may in his understanding also include leverage over actors that are causing harm or could prevent harm.[24] The Tilburg Guiding Principles limit human rights obligations of IFIs to 'situations where the institutions' own projects, policies or programmes negatively impact or undermine the enjoyment of human rights'.[25]

Undeniably, there is the need for a test to assign human rights obligations to duty-bearers. However, the notion of jurisdiction is too much associated with States, but other notions like sphere of influence may be equally objected to. In the end, rather than the notion, what matters is the type of touchstone to apply. At one end is the approach that tends towards an abstract test, independent of the particular act or omission in question, like the overall or effective control tests with regard to States,[26] or sphere of influence or proximity tests with regard to companies. At the other end is a contextual and inductive approach that leans towards fact-based tests.[27] Here, the focus is on the actual or potential use of power or activity, and its *effects* or *impact* on rights-holders. Rather than to look for the most suitable notion, it may be more fruitful to decide which type of test (or combination of tests) is most amenable to operationalisation. Assigning obligations often happens in a more abstract way, prior to and outside the realm of alleged violations. In principle, an abstract touchstone (degree of control; influence; leverage[28]) is therefore to be preferred.

Scope of obligations

In the Maastricht Principles, a general, negative obligation to 'avoid causing harm' has been identified: 'States must desist from acts and omissions that create a real risk of nullifying or impairing the enjoyment of economic,

24 Ruggie (n 22), 5.

25 Tilburg Guiding Principles, para 5.

26 To which Besson adds an appeal for compliance as a third cumulative element in what she calls a 'political notion of jurisdiction'. Besson has put forward that jurisdiction is about de facto legal and political authority, and consists of three constitutive elements: not only effective power and overall control, but also an appeal for compliance. The latter is also referred to as the normative-guidance element. Key to her argument is that jurisdiction cannot be reduced to effective and overall control only, but needs this normative-guidance element of reason-giving or an appeal for compliance. In building her argument, she strongly draws on democratic theory, in which affectedness is not enough, but where normative subjectedness is required. Besson submits that the European Court of Human Rights' case-law endorses these three constitutive elements. S Besson, 'The Extraterritorialiy of the European Convention on Human Rights: Why Human Rights Depend on Jurisdiction and What Jurisdiction Amounts To' (2012) 25 Leiden Journal of International Law 857–884, at 872–873.

27 M Scheinin, 'Extraterritorial Effect of the International Covenant on Civil and Political Rights', in F Coomans and M Kamminga (eds), *Extraterritorial Application of Human Rights Treaties* (Intersentia 2004), 73–82.

28 Wood has suggested the notion of leverage, see S Wood, 'The Case for Leverage-Based Corporate Human Rights Responsibility' (2011) 22 Business Ethics Quarterly 63–98.

social and cultural rights extraterritorially'.[29] Inherent to the obligation to avoid causing harm is the procedural obligation to conduct prior impact assessments.[30] The scope of extraterritorial obligations is unpacked along the well-established tripartite typology of obligations to respect, to protect and to fulfil. The general, negative obligation to avoid causing harm is reflected in the obligation to respect: ie 'to refrain from conduct which nullifies or impairs the enjoyment and exercise of economic, social and cultural rights of persons outside their territories', which is coined direct interference.[31] In addition, States need to refrain from conduct that impairs the ability of another State or international organisation with its obligations, or that 'aids, assists, directs, controls or coerces' another State or international organisation to breach its obligations (indirect interference).[32]

The obligation to protect against violations by NSAs, ie private individuals and organisations, TNCs and other business enterprises, has been disentangled as an obligation to regulate, to influence and to cooperate. The obligation to influence is a minimal obligation, which applies 'even if [States] are not in a position to regulate [the conduct of NSAs]'.[33] The obligation to regulate is limited to circumscribed positions to regulate, defined by leads such as territory; nationality; or simply a reasonable link between the State and the conduct. Specifically for business enterprises, the centre of activity, place of registration or domicile, or main place of business or substantial business activities are mentioned. Finally, a category of conduct is added that qualifies as violations of a peremptory norm of international law.[34] An obligation to cooperate is incumbent on all States in order to 'prevent human rights abuses by NSAs, to hold them to account for any such abuses, and to ensure an effective remedy for those affected'.[35] Only under the obligation to fulfil is the scope of the obligation of foreign States defined more narrowly than the domestic State's obligation, and only with regard to the obligation to provide international assistance. The latter is defined as a *contribution to* the fulfilment of ESC rights.[36]

29 Principle 13.

30 Principle 14.

31 Principle 20.

32 Principle 21. The latter categories are borrowed from the ILC Articles on State Responsibility for Internationally Wrongful Acts, see further.

33 Principle 26.

34 Principle 25. For this category, the meaning of the obligation to protect if these violations also constitute a crime under international law is spelt out: 'States must exercise universal jurisdiction over those bearing responsibility or lawfully transfer them to an appropriate jurisdiction.'

35 Principle 27.

36 For a scholarly suggestion on this, see R Künnemann, 'Extraterritorial Application of the International Covenant on Economic, Social and Cultural Rights', in F Coomans and M Kamminga (eds), *Extraterritorial Application of Human Rights Treaties* (Intersentia 2004), 201–231; for a critique, see W Vandenhole and W Benedek, 'Extraterritorial Human Rights Obligations and the North-South Divide', in M Langford, W Vandenhole, M Scheinin and W van Genugten (eds), *Global Justice, State Duties. The Extraterritorial Scope of Economic, Social and Cultural Rights in International Law* (CUP 2013), 332–363, at 337–338.

The Norms define the substantive obligation of all business enterprises, including transnational corporations, in the same way as that incumbent on States, ie they have the 'obligation to promote, secure the fulfilment of, respect, ensure respect of and protect human rights recognized in international as well as national law'.[37] However, in para 12, with regard to ESC rights, reference is made to *contribution* to their realisation.[38]

The UN Guiding Principles evoke a weak corporate responsibility (in its plain sense, so not referring to a legal obligation) to respect human rights, ie to 'avoid infringing on the human rights of others and … [to] address adverse human rights impacts with which they are involved'.[39] It mainly entails a negative obligation of abstention, besides a positive one to 'address adverse human rights impacts with which they are involved'.[40] The latter is further clarified, and arguably partly watered down, in Principle 13, which holds that business enterprises need to address adverse human rights impacts of their own activities, as well as '*[s]eek* to prevent or mitigate adverse human rights impacts that are directly linked to their operations, products or services by their business relationships …' (emphasis added).[41] The corporate responsibility to respect is said to apply up to parent companies and down to the supply chain.[42]

In the Tilburg Guiding Principles, the scope of IFIs' direct human rights obligations is limited to respect obligations, ie negative obligations. In the Guiding Principles part proper, it is said that the macro-economic policy of the IFIs 'should take into account its impact on human development objectives, including human rights', and that they 'should integrate human rights considerations into all aspects of their operations and internal functioning'.[43] Prevention of human rights violations should be given high priority, and if violations occur nevertheless, 'measures for mitigating the impact thereof and mechanisms of accountability and redress should be put into place'.[44] In the clause proposed for inclusion in the policies of the IFIs, the negative nature of their obligation is reconfirmed: ie not to finance projects (in the case of the World Bank) or not to enter in financial agreements (in the case of the IMF) 'that contravene applicable international human rights law'.[45] In addition,

37 UN Norms, para 1. This seems to be an attempt to combine the tripartite typology now commonly used with regard to economic, social and cultural rights (respect, protect and fulfil) and the one found in Art 2 of the ICCPR (respect and ensure).

38 Kinley and Chambers have argued that that is the 'correct obligation', Kinley and Chambers (n 6), 29, fn 121.

39 UNGPs, para 11.

40 UNGPs, para 11.

41 UNGPs, para 13.

42 Compare N Jägers, 'UN Guiding Principles on Business and Human Rights: Making Headway towards Real Corporate Accountability?' (2011) 29 Netherlands Quarterly of Human Rights 159–163, at 162.

43 Tilburg Guiding Principles, paras 23–24.

44 Tilburg Guiding Principles, para 24.

45 Tilburg Guiding Principles, paras 30–31.

procedural obligations of transparent decision-making and active participation of those affected have been identified.[46] The IFIs should also ensure accessibility of accountability mechanisms and undertake human rights impact assessments *ex ante* and *ex post*.[47]

In sum, the scope of transnational obligations can be defined in the abstract to some extent. The standard-setting exercises under review, with the exception of the Maastricht Principles, tend to focus on negative obligations. However, the scope of the obligations is bound to be variable, not only for specific obligations (eg with regard to the obligation to fulfil, inter alia, commensurate with capacities, resources and influence; with regard to the obligation to protect commensurate with varying degrees of positions to regulate or influence), but arguably also more generally in light of the degree of control or influence exercised. This position is in line with that of the European Court of Human Rights,[48] the Maastricht Commentary[49] and some of the literature.[50] The variable scope of the obligations attributed to a duty-bearer cannot be insulated from the discussion on the attribution test for obligations, as discussed in the previous section. How broad or narrow the scope of transnational obligations is defined, is as much a matter of policy as of rigorous legal analysis.

Distributive allocation of obligations

As long as there is only one actor carrying obligations, the question of apportioning of obligations among duty-bearers is not an issue. However, in the context of transnational obligations, typically more than one actor comes into the picture as a (potential) duty-bearer: the domestic State, one or more foreign States, as well as companies, the international financial institutions and other NSAs. There are basically two options to address the distributive allocation of obligations in a plural and diverse duty-bearer setting. One is to define in the abstract the distributive allocation of obligations (also in a number of specific relations, like the home State – host State – company setting, or the member State – international organisation setting), the other is to examine

46 Tilburg Guiding Principles, paras 32–33.

47 Tilburg Guiding Principles, paras 35 and 38.

48 *Al-Skeini and others v United Kingdom*, App no 55721/07 (ECtHR, 7 July 2011), paras 137–138.

49 De Schutter et al (n 18), 1108.

50 See Ryngaert's notion of jurisdiction over violations of economic, social and cultural rights as a continuum, C Ryngaert, 'Jurisdiction. Towards a Reasonableness Test', in M Langford, W Vandenhole, M Scheinin and W van Genugten (eds), *Global Justice, State Duties. The Extraterritorial Scope of Economic, Social and Cultural Rights in International Law* (CUP 2013) 192–211, at 210–211. Compare Ratner, who has developed 'a theory in four parts' to define the scope of direct obligations for companies, 'based on an inductive approach that reflects the actual operations of business enterprises', Ratner (n 13), 496. That scope is defined by four clusters of issues: 'the corporation's relationship with the government, its nexus to affected populations, the particular human right at issue, and the place of individuals violating human rights within the corporate structure' (496–497).

in each specific context *in concreto* the distribution of obligations. The abstract approach has the advantage of legal certainty, but becomes increasingly difficult and artificial as more and different duty-bearers are involved. The *ad hoc*, contextualised distributive allocation of obligations offers less foreseeability, but may be more feasible in complex plural and diverse duty-bearer settings. In both approaches, at least some principles are needed.

The Maastricht Principles are not very explicit on the distribution of obligations between the domestic State and foreign States. It seems to go unquestioned that the domestic State bears the primary obligation for the realisation of ESC rights on its territory. Principle 4 proclaims that each State has 'the obligation to realize economic, social and cultural rights, for all persons *within its territory* …' (emphasis added), and that all States '*also* have extraterritorial obligations …' (emphasis added).[51] In particular with regard to the obligation to *fulfil* ESC rights, the primary obligation of the domestic State has been emphasised: 'A State has the obligation to fulfil economic, social and cultural rights in its territory to the maximum of its ability',[52] and it is under the obligation to seek international assistance and cooperation when it is unable to realise ESC rights within its territory.[53] Logically, if the primary obligation rests with the domestic State, other States can only have a complementary obligation. That complementary obligation applies simultaneously: 'All States have obligations to respect, protect and fulfil human rights, including civil, cultural, economic, political and social rights, both within their territories and extraterritorially.'[54] The extraterritorial obligation to fulfil is defined as an obligation to *contribute* to that fulfilment.[55] Such an understanding not only limits the scope of the extraterritorial obligation to fulfil (see the preceding section), but also suggests that the extraterritorial obligation to fulfil is subsidiary. The obligations to provide international assistance and to cooperate in order to contribute to the fulfilment of ESC rights extraterritorially also seem to depend on a legitimate request from a State that is unable to realise ESC rights within its territory, which illustrates once more the subsidiary or secondary nature of the extraterritorial obligation to fulfil.[56]

The Maastricht Principles do not elucidate the apportioning of obligations among foreign States. Whereas they state repeatedly that all States 'must take action, separately and jointly through international cooperation',[57] that all

51 Compare Principles 19, 23 and 28.

52 Principle 31.

53 Principle 34.

54 Principle 4, and echoed for the obligations to respect, protect and fulfil in Principles 19, 23 and 28.

55 Principle 31. This is reiterated in particular also for the obligation to provide international assistance in Principle 33.

56 On the terminology of complementary and subsidiary obligations, see Vandenhole and Benedek (n 36), 337–338.

57 Principles 19, 23 and 28–29.

States must cooperate to protect ESC rights extraterritorially,[58] and that they 'should coordinate with each other in order to cooperate effectively', little is said on what *particular* States are expected to do. Some guidance can nevertheless be found. With regard to the extraterritorial obligation to protect, reference is made to those States that are in a position to regulate or to influence.[59] With regard to the extraterritorial obligations to fulfil, and more in particular the obligation to coordinate, it is clarified that lack of coordination 'does not exonerate a State from giving effect to its separate extraterritorial obligations'. The obligation to provide international assistance is confined to States 'in a position to do so'.[60] Their contribution is commensurate with, inter alia, capacities, resources and influence in international decision-making processes.[61] The Commentary aptly clarifies the challenge: '[I]nternational human rights law, at present, does not determine with precision a system of international coordination and allocation that would facilitate the discharging of obligations of a global character ... among those States "in a position to assist".'[62] The way the Maastricht Principles seek to answer that challenge is by establishing a procedural obligation to devise a division of distribution of obligations to give effect to the collective (substantive) obligation to cooperate internationally.[63]

The Norms too take it that States have the primary responsibility for human rights, including the obligation to protect against business enterprises. Moreover, there is a savings clause that, inter alia, provides that nothing in the Norms should be construed as diminishing the human rights obligations of States.[64] This suggests that business enterprises themselves have a complementary obligation, albeit simultaneously with States.[65] The Guiding Principles, which build on the 'protect, respect and remedy framework', rest on 'differentiated but complementary responsibilities'.[66] They assign primary human rights obligations, also with regard to corporate conduct, to States: primarily and as a strong obligation to the host State, and much more weakly to the home State of the business enterprise. Foundational Principle 1 holds

58 Principle 27.

59 Principles 24 and 26.

60 Principles 33 and 35.

61 The Commentary points out that historical causation is not excluded, see De Schutter et al (n 18), 1153.

62 De Schutter et al (n 18), 1149.

63 Ibid, 1150.

64 UN Norms, para 19.

65 See our conceptualisation of distributing and apportioning of obligations in Vandenhole and Benedek (n 36), 334–346; compare Kinley and Chambers who argue that 'the Norms provide for the imposition of contemporaneous and complementary human rights responsibilities on corporations within their "spheres of activity and influence"' (Kinley and Chambers (n 6), 467).

66 Report of the Special Representative of the Secretary-General on the Issue of Human Rights and Transnational Corporations and Other Business Enterprises, John Ruggie, 'Protect, Respect and Remedy: A Framework for Business and Human Rights', UN Doc A/HRC/8/5 of 7 April 2008, para 9.

that the host States 'must protect against human rights abuse within their territory and/or jurisdiction by ... business enterprises'. This host State duty to protect is said to be a standard of conduct.[67] The responsibility of the home State to regulate the extraterritorial activities of businesses domiciled in their territory and/or jurisdiction is framed much more weakly as a soft obligation 'to set out clearly the expectation' that these business enterprises respect human rights throughout their operations.[68] In the case of involvement of transnational corporations in *gross* human rights violations *in conflict-affected areas*, a more detailed distributive allocation scheme has been devised between the host and home State. The scheme tilts towards the home State, albeit that the commentary vaguely frames the home State obligation as having 'roles to play in assisting both those corporations and host States'. Justification for that home State obligation is sought in the fact that 'the "host" State may be unable to protect human rights adequately due to a lack of effective control'.[69] As to the relationship of State obligations with corporate 'responsibility', no clarification can be found in the Guiding Principles.

The Tilburg Guiding Principles are quite silent on the question of apportioning responsibility between the IFIs themselves and their member States, let alone *among* their member States. They too recall the basic tenet of current international human rights law that the 'primary responsibilities and obligations in the field of domestic human rights enjoyment ... remain with the State'. This is (also) intended as a clause against State escapism from human rights obligations, as the next sentence stipulates that 'States cannot "delegate" human rights obligations to, for instance, international institutions and relieve themselves of these obligations'.[70]

In conclusion, in recent standard-setting exercises distributive allocation of human rights obligations among duty-bearers is the dimension that is least developed. All take the primary obligation of the domestic State as the natural point of departure. This stance is open to challenge in light of a global obligations paradigm. The 'primary-secondary obligations' terminology also seems to have at least two different meanings. For some, it denotes a differential *scope* of obligations,[71] for others it also includes a temporal *sequencing* or derivative obligation. In order to avoid this amalgamation of meanings, we have suggested the language of complementary rather than secondary obligations. When complementary obligations apply simultaneously (eg the

67 UNGPs, para 1, Commentary.

68 UNGPs, para 2.

69 UNGPs, para 7, Commentary.

70 Tilburg Guiding Principles, para 5.

71 See, eg, Ruggie: 'The corporate responsibility to respect exists independently of States' duties. Therefore, there is no need for the slippery distinction between "primary" State and "secondary" corporate obligations' (Ruggie (n 22). Compare LC Backer, 'Rights and Accountability in Development (Raid) v. Das Air and Global Witness v. Afrimex-Small Steps towards an Autonomous Transnational Legal System for the Regulation of Multinational Corporations' (2009) 10 Melbourne Journal of International Law 258–307, at 294.

obligation to respect), they are called parallel. When obligations are only triggered due to the inability or unwillingness of the primary duty-bearer, they have been coined secondary or subsidiary.[72] Whereas this typology has been developed in the context of extraterritorial obligations, it can be expanded to transnational human rights obligations.

As to the distributive allocation of obligations among foreign States, it has been suggested to have a varying scope of the obligation for the different foreign States concerned, depending on their varying levels of control or influence.[73] The most challenging part may be to define the distributive allocation of obligations among foreign States with regard to their (individual) obligations to *fulfil*. Elsewhere, we have looked into concepts that may help to articulate which States are in a position to assist, what the scope of their obligation is, and towards whom they hold the obligation.[74] In essence, we propose a *differentiated* human rights obligations regime, in which specific obligations to fulfil are assigned *in abstracto* to specific foreign States. Salomon has identified several bases for assigning obligations of international cooperation, such as causation, historical responsibility and capacity. All tend to be more context-specific,[75] although her contribution to the Maastricht Principles and the Commentary seems to suggest that she favours an abstract system of allocation. Further inspiration for a differentiated human rights obligations regime may be found in international environmental law and in legal public law regimes for common interests or concerns more generally (see De Feyter, chapter 8 in this volume). The concept of differentiated obligations creates space for investigating how obligations need to be apportioned among different actors. An example of the operationalisation of differentiated obligations can be found in the 1992 United Nations Convention on Climate Change (UNFCCC). Based on a differentiation between developing and developed country parties to the Convention, developed country parties undertake specific legal obligations in Art 4.[76]

In a plural and diverse duty-holder setting of States and NSAs, an abstract differentiation of obligations among the duty-bearers is only in its infancy. A key question is whether their obligations are separate or joint obligations. A rare attempt to answer this question can be found with Skogly. She has identified substantive and procedural *separate* direct human rights obligations for

72 Vandenhole and Benedek (n 36), 340–346.

73 M Langford, W Vandenhole, M Scheinin and W van Genugten, 'Introduction: An Emerging Field', in M Langford, W Vandenhole, M Scheinin and W van Genugten (eds), *Global Justice, State Duties. The Extraterritorial Scope of Economic, Social and Cultural Rights in International Law* (CUP 2013), 3–31, s 27.

74 Vandenhole and Benedek (n 36), 341–350.

75 ME Salomon, 'Deprivation, Causation and the Law of International Cooperation', in M Langford, W Vandenhole, M Scheinin and W van Genugten (eds), *Global Justice, State Duties. The Extraterritorial Scope of Economic, Social and Cultural Rights in International Law* (CUP 2013), 259–298, at 283–284.

76 Further examples can be found in K De Feyter (ed), *Globalization and Common Responsibilities of States* (Ashgate 2013).

the IFIs, in addition to obligations that these institutions share with creditor States.[77]

Conclusions on obligations

In this section, we have examined whether emerging principles can be found to ground a plural and diverse human rights duty-bearer regime. We have looked into three questions in particular: how to assign human rights obligations to an actor in a particular instance; whether and how to define the scope of obligations incumbent on each actor; and how to distributively allocate obligations to a multiplicity of different actors.

The Maastricht Principles contain the most elaborate and refined set of principles. However, these Principles only deal with States, not with NSAs. It is doubtful whether they can simply be applied by analogy to NSAs.

With regard to the test for assigning human rights obligations, the notion of jurisdiction was found to be too much associated with States, but other notions like sphere of influence seem equally contentious. It was suggested to prioritise the elaboration of criteria rather than the coining of a new concept. A combination of more abstract criteria like control and proximity with more context-specific ones (causation, impact) is most amenable to operationalisation.

As to the *abstract* delineation of the scope of human rights obligations incumbent on each duty-bearer, it is proposed to include as a matter of principle the full range of obligations. However, the scope of the obligations is bound to be variable, not only for specific obligations (eg with regard to the obligation to fulfil, inter alia, commensurate with capacities, resources and influence; with regard to the obligation to protect commensurate with varying degrees of positions to regulate or influence), but arguably also more generally in light of the degree of control or proximity. In other words, the determination of the scope of obligations of each duty-bearer *in concreto* is closely connected to the allocation of obligations to different duty-bearers.

An abstract system of distributive allocation of obligations among duty-bearers is favoured, but has not yet been elaborated. It should be premised on a differentiation of obligations and distinguish independent and joint obligations. Most likely, in addition to some general principles, specific rules will be needed for specific relationships between, for example, home State and company, or between member State and IFIs.

77 SI Skogly, 'The Human Rights Obligations of the World Bank and the IMF', in W van Genugten, P Hunt and S Mathews (eds), *World Bank, IMF and Human Rights* (Wolf Legal Publishers 2003), 45–78, 57–69.

Responsibility

Integrating transnational human rights obligations into human rights law as a *normative* framework, ie a framework that spells out the applicable rules, is a slow and uphill endeavour. To make them also part and parcel of human rights law as an *accountability and remedy framework* may be even more challenging, although both functions of human rights law cannot be fully separated. It is telling to note that the attribution of responsibility for human rights violations committed during military operations undertaken under the EU has been 'one of the most difficult issues in the negotiations on the agreement on EU accession to the ECHR'.[78]

This section deals with the question under which conditions failure to abide by transnational human rights obligations amounts to a violation or infringement, ie to an internationally wrongful act, and therefore triggers responsibility. The current public international law regime of responsibility has been codified by the ILC in the Articles on State Responsibility (ASR) and in the Draft Articles on Responsibility of International Organizations (DARIO). However, I have argued elsewhere that this regime does not sufficiently accommodate human rights law in general.[79] *A fortiori*, it is ill-equipped to address human rights violations in plural and diverse human rights duty-bearer regime.

In situations where a plurality and diversity of actors across the State-non-State divide is involved, which all have human rights obligations and are implicated in the same human rights violations, questions of shared responsibility and apportioning of responsibility among duty-bearers will inevitably arise. Several legal framings are imaginable. One is to approach these types of situations primarily through the prism of independent responsibility of each of the actors involved. It has been argued that even the recognition of truly joint obligations does not preclude 'an individualized regime of legal responsibility in the event of a breach of those obligations' (footnote omitted).[80] The opposite approach would be to take shared responsibility as the principled starting point. Legal rules on the apportioning of responsibility for human rights violations to and among a plurality of actors should be devised in such a way that they do not unduly impede the establishment of that responsibility. From a victim perspective, a principle of shared responsibility is

78 J Polakiewicz, 'EU Law and the ECHR: Will EU Accession to the European Convention on Human Rights Square the Circle?' September 2013, *http://ssrn.com/abstract=2331497* (accessed 12 December 2014).

79 Vandenhole (n 9). Compare Skogly's call to develop a theoretical framework regarding State responsibility for human rights violations, SI Skogly, 'Causality and Extraterritorial Human Rights Obligations', in M Langford, W Vandenhole, M Scheinin and W van Genugten (eds), *Global Justice, State Duties. The Extraterritorial Scope of Economic, Social and Cultural Rights in International Law* (CUP 2013), 233–258, at 244–249.

80 De Schutter et al (n 18), 1152.

therefore most attractive, for it does not lay the burden of finding out who is responsible, and to what extent, with the victim.

However, international responsibility law is premised on *independent* responsibility, not on shared responsibility. The latter can only occur in case of a single course of conduct, when the *same* internationally wrongful act is attributable to several States. Causation of damage plays no role in the determination of responsibility,[81] what matters is that an internationally wrongful (illegal) act has been committed. The irrelevance of the causal link between violation and damage has been blamed for the difficulties in identifying and addressing situations of shared responsibility *sensu stricto*, for they are believed to arise 'in the cumulative presence of the indivisibility of the wrong and the indivisibility of the damage'.[82] Notwithstanding some inroads into the principle of independent responsibility in DARIO, shared responsibility clearly remains the exception, and is only possible in a (very) circumscribed way.[83]

An incremental development of a legal regime of shared responsibility of NSAs, building on ASR and DARIO, is therefore unlikely to happen, let alone to succeed. First of all, ASR is premised on independent rather than shared responsibility, and circumscribes restrictively the exceptional circumstances in which concurrent responsibility can occur (ie aiding and abetting; direction and control; coercion). Whereas DARIO could not but grapple with additional circumstances of shared responsibility (ie of international organisations and their members), that came at the price of disrupting the homogeneity of international responsibility law. Whereas international responsibility law is mainly based on the illegality of the act, addressing shared responsibility forced it to allow fault, causation and injury back in.[84] Taking another, quantitative leap towards a regime of shared responsibility that also includes NSAs, drawing on the tenets of ASR, risks being at odds with the foundations of international responsibility law even further and resulting in a shattered and conceptually incoherent law of international responsibility. An overall fresh look at responsibility for human rights violations committed by a multiplicity and variety of actors is therefore needed.

Secondly, the exceptional circumstances in which shared responsibility has been accepted so far may fail to deal satisfactorily with the realities on the ground, due to an overtly narrow construction of shared responsibility in a limited number of instances and the virtual absence of acknowledgement

81 J d'Aspremont, 'The Articles on the Responsibility of International Organizations: Magnifying the Fissures in the Law of International Responsibility' (2012) 9 International Organizations Law Review 15–28, 21–22.

82 Ibid, 22.

83 Compare ND White and S Macleod, 'EU Operations and Private Military Contractors: Issues of Corporate and Institutional Responsibility' (2008) 19 European Journal of International Law 965–988, at 973.

84 C Ahlborn, 'The Use of Analogies in Drafting the Articles on the Responsibility of International Organizations. An Appraisal of the "Copy-Paste Approach"' (2012) 9 International Organizations Law Review 53–66, at 65.

of differentiated responsibility, amongst others. The concept of *differentiated* responsibility challenges the separation of primary and secondary rules, for it corresponds to a differentiation of substantive obligations in the first place. In my view, the concept of shared responsibility should be taken seriously, and developed further, in particular in human rights law.[85] Interestingly, the draft agreement on EU accession to the ECHR elevates joint responsibility to the principle, and considers independent responsibility of a member State and the EU to be the exception under the co-respondent mechanism (Art 3(7)).[86]

In sum, both ASR and DARIO have obvious limitations for apportioning responsibility to and among multiple and diverse human rights violators, so that extending these regimes by analogy to NSAs may raise more questions than answers. This conclusion does not mean that a new human rights responsibility regime needs to be invented from scratch. Useful inspiration for the elaboration in human rights law of a shared responsibility regime for a multiplicity of diverse actors can be found in the (international) law of civil liability regime, with its emphasis on injury and reparation.

Three building blocks of an alternative responsibility regime, that is more suitable to address instances of plural and diverse human rights violators, have been identified: shared responsibility; differentiation of responsibility along a continuum; and liability for monetary compensation commensurate with the degree of responsibility. The regime proposed here is premised on two starting points. The first one is that law needs to respond to (new) realities. Part of today's realities is that human rights violations are not always attributable to one single actor, or to one category of actors. A plurality (more than one actor) and diversity of actors (different types of actors ranging from States and international organisations to NSAs such as companies, armed groups,[87] and non-governmental organisations) tend to be involved in a number of alleged human rights violations. Moreover, power relations among these actors may be difficult to determine. The second starting point is that the adequacy of a human rights responsibility regime should be assessed from a victim perspective.[88] As the ECtHR explained in a recent inter-State complaint: '… it must be always kept in mind that, according the very nature of the [ECHR], it is the individual … who is directly or indirectly harmed and primarily "injured" by a violation of one or several Convention rights. Therefore, if just satisfaction is afforded in an inter-State case, it should always be done for the benefit of individual victims'.[89] The key question is whether a human rights

85 Skogly (n 79), 244–249. See also Salomon (n 75), 178–181 for the exploration of shared and independent responsibility in the context of the IFIs.

86 Polakiewicz (n 78).

87 See also J-M Henckaerts and C Wiesener, 'Human Rights Obligations of Non-State Armed Groups: A Possible Contribution from Customary International Law', in R Kolb and G Gaggioli (eds), *Research Handbook on Human Rights and Humanitarian Law* (Edward Elgar Publishing 2013), 146–169.

88 *Velásquez Rodríguez v Honduras*, App no 7920 (IACtHR, 29 July 1988), para 134.

89 *Cyprus v Turkey*, App no 25781/94 (ECtHR, 12 May 2014), para 46.

responsibility regime is able to adequately respond to situations in which plural and diverse human rights violators are involved.

A first building block of the proposed human rights responsibility regime is the principle of shared responsibility rather than independent responsibility. Given the frequent lack of clarity about the distribution of power and the diffuse exercise of power among different actors involved in human rights violations, shared responsibility is key from a victim's perspective. In order to be able to better respond to a *plurality* of violators, the basis of shared responsibility should be a contribution to the same human rights violation(s) rather than a single course of conduct. In order to be able to better respond to the *diversity* of violators, a comprehensive and coherent regime that accepts shared responsibility of diverse actors is needed. Hence, shared responsibility should be possible beyond existing categories of conduct responsibility and derived responsibility, and beyond categories of State and NSAs.

Shared responsibility means that each of the actors involved in a human rights violation can be held accountable by the victim of a human rights violation, ie that the finding of a violation can take place against each and any of them. The finding of a violation in itself often constitutes reparation (in the sense of public acknowledgement)[90] in human rights law. The finding should not only acknowledge that a violation has occurred, it should also establish to the extent possible whom is to be blamed and to what extent. Therefore, acknowledgement of differentiated responsibility and establishing the degree of responsibility of each of the actors involved may be needed.

The degree of responsibility held by a certain actor may be influenced by the scope of the human rights obligations incumbent on that actor.

Differentiated responsibility is better reflected in a continuum than in fixed and narrowly defined categories, that have meanwhile been imbued with a specific meaning. It may therefore be desirable to replace (or complement) existing categories of aid or assistance; direction and control; and coercion (and also circumvention) with other notions that reflect the degree of contribution (control,[91] influence) or omission with regard to the violation, or of benefit from the violation. Concepts that may propound to reflect a continuum in contribution (and benefit) are, for example, complicity and/or influence, although they may have their own drawbacks. Complicity, for example, has been used to conceptualise the relationship between human rights obligations of States and direct human rights obligations of non-States. It has been introduced, in particular, in the discussion of direct human rights obligations

90 H Rombouts, P Sardaro and S Vandeginste, 'The Right to Reparation for Victims of Gross and Systematic Violations of Human Rights', in K De Feyter et al (eds), *Outh of the Ashes. Reparation for Victims of Gross and Systematic Human Rights Violations* (Intersentia 2005), 345–503, at 465–466.

91 C Ryngaert, 'Apportioning Responsibility between the UN and Member States in UN Peace-Support Operations: An Inquiry into the Application of the "Effective Control" Standard after Behrami' (2012) 45 Israel Law Review 151–178.

of companies, through the notion of 'corporate complicity'.[92] Complicity can be understood as aiding and abetting, or knowingly assisting and benefiting from abuses by others.[93] Clapham and Jerbi distinguish direct, indirect and silent complicity. Direct complicity requires intentional participation (but not necessarily the intention to do harm; knowledge of foreseeable harmful effects is sufficient). Indirect corporate complicity happens where companies knowingly benefit from human rights abuses. Silent complicity follows from failure to exercise influence.[94] However, a downside is the potential confusion of the notion of complicity with aid and assistance in ASR and DARIO, and its association with criminal law (with requirement of intention, see Gibney's criticism in chapter 5 in this volume). Moreover, complicity seems to suggest a hierarchy of responsibility, with a main, primary culprit, and an accomplice.

Degrees of responsibility may have a bearing on the differentiation of obligations for offering reparation other than acknowledgement, though these two issues do not necessarily coincide nor fully correspond to each other.

Thirdly, with regard to (monetary) compensation, the civil liability regime can be adopted, ie in principle each actor is liable for compensation commensurate with the degree of responsibility. If the extent of responsibility cannot be established, the monetary compensation is apportioned equally between the violators involved. Nonetheless, in light of the victim perspective, the entire compensation can be sought by the victim from any of the violators involved, even if the degree of responsibility of each violator can be determined. The violator who pays the monetary compensation can afterwards claim from the others to pay for their share (this has been called a several obligation to make contribution).

Conclusion

This chapter has sought to articulate foundational principles for the attribution of human rights obligations and the apportioning of responsibility for violations in a plural and diverse duty-bearer setting. Assigning particular obligations to a duty-bearer logically precedes the question as to whether that actor can subsequently be held responsible for a violation or infringement of a human right (ie constituting an internationally wrongful act).

Assigning human rights *obligations* often happens in a more abstract way, prior to and outside the realm of alleged violations. In principle, an abstract touchstone (degree of control; influence) is therefore to be preferred. The scope of transnational obligations too can be defined in the abstract. That scope is bound to be variable, not only for specific obligations (eg with regard

92 A Clapham and S Jerbi, 'Categories of Corporate Complicity in Human Rights Abuses' (2001–02) 24 Hastings International and Comparative Law Review 339–349; Ruggie (n 22), 73–81.

93 Clapham and Jerbi (n 92), 340; A Clapham, *Human Rights Obligations of Non-State Actors* (OUP 2006), 563.

94 Clapham and Jerbi (n 92), 342–349.

to the obligation to fulfil, inter alia, commensurate with capacities, resources and influence; with regard to the obligation to protect commensurate with varying degrees of positions to regulate or influence), but arguably also more generally in light of the degree of control or influence exercised. The distributive allocation of human rights obligations among duty-bearers is least developed. Whereas it may be open to challenge, the primary obligation of the domestic State still seems to be the logical point of departure. Other States and non-State actors have complementary obligations. When complementary obligations apply simultaneously (eg the obligation to respect), they are called parallel. When obligations are only triggered due to the inability or unwillingness of the primary duty-bearer, they are secondary or subsidiary. As to the distributive allocation of obligations to fulfil among other actors than the domestic State, we propose a *differentiated* human rights obligations regime based on an abstract system of allocation.

The second question was how to assign *responsibility* for human rights violations in case of a *plurality* and a *diversity* of violators (State and non-State). We found the international law responsibility regime unsatisfactory, and have suggested three building blocks for a human rights responsibility regime that is more suitable and appropriate to address instances of plural and diverse human rights violators. Such a regime is based on the principle of shared responsibility; it allows for differentiation of responsibility along a continuum; and liability for monetary compensation is commensurate with the degree of responsibility (nonetheless, in light of the victim perspective, the entire compensation can be sought by the victim from any of the violators involved).

For sure, all of this needs much more detailed elaboration, inter alia also to flesh out the implications for actor-specific regimes of the adoption of these common principles governing human rights obligations and responsibility of a multiplicity and diversity of actors. Nonetheless, we believe that this attempt at identifying some common principles may advance the research agenda on transnational human rights obligations in the years to come.

7 Transnational legal responsibility: some preliminaries

George Pavlakos[1]

Outline

The question about transnational human rights obligations forms part of the wider problem of the transnational scope of legal obligations and the responsibility they ground.[2] Arguably, human rights obligations form the core of legal obligations; indeed for many they constitute a key task of law or even a key reason for its existence.[3] To that extent, in what follows, the question about the transnational scope of human rights obligations will be understood as one about the transnational scope of legal obligations.

1 For valuable comments on a penultimate draft, I thank Tamo Atabongawung, Emmanuel Melissaris, Wouter Vandenhole, Arne Vandenbogaerde and an anonymous reviewer. Their comments have led to considerable refinement of the argument. An earlier version of the paper was given at the GLOTHRO final conference at the Åbo Akademi in Turku in March 2014. I am indebted to my three commentators – Daniel Augenstein, Sten Schaumburg-Müller and Kirsteen Shields – as well as Martin Scheinin, who was chairing the session, for raising a number of insightful points. Triantafyllos Gkouvas has been a constant and invaluable interlocutor for many of the ideas discussed herein. Research for the paper was supported by the long-term strategic development financing of the Institute of State and Law of the Academy of Sciences of the Czech Republic (RVO: 68378122).

2 Following W Vandenhole, chapter 6 in this volume, I will assume that ascription of responsibility requires the prior existence of an obligation.

3 Tellingly, human rights enjoy the status of constitutional principles not only within domestic but also international and supra-national legal orders. Thus the European Court pronounces: 'respect for human rights is a condition of the lawfulness of Community acts' (Opinion 2/94, European Court Reports (ECR) 1996, I-1759, para 34). Further, Article 6 of the Treaty on European Union (EU) now explicitly states that the 'Union is founded on the principles of liberty, democracy, respect for human rights and fundamental freedoms, and the rule of law, principles which are common to the Member States'. Breaches of these principles can entail sanctions (Article 7) and prevent admission to the EU (Article 49 EU Treaty). These pronouncements run *in tandem* with the philosophical tradition of political liberalism, which takes human rights to delimit the normative space within which all other legal obligations, powers, privileges and permissions arise. For a recent re-statement of the constitutional rank of human rights in the domain of international law, see M Kumm, 'The Moral Point of Constitutional Pluralism', in J Dickson and P Eleftheriadis (eds), *Philosophical Foundations of European Union Law* (OUP 2012), 216–246.

In this chapter I shall try to establish some conceptual ground for expanding the scope of legal obligation beyond the limits of national sovereignty. While the discussion will remain mainly theoretical, ultimately it will aim to contribute to the practical aim of the volume to account for the possibility of transnational human rights obligations. In particular, I shall work with an eye to two specific background questions: first, how can we plausibly understand the subjects of legal responsibility as including not only States but also non-State actors? Importantly, this question will be treated as an extension of the wider question about actors in international law. Second, how to allocate and distribute responsibility among multiple and diverse actors in transnational contexts?

The chapter will be organised as follows: in the second section I shall point out that the standard understanding of legal obligation takes it to be confined to the boundaries of State sovereignty. As a consequence, legal responsibility is understood primarily as State-based responsibility. In reaction to that, several scholars have suggested an overhaul of the current system of legal responsibility with a view to dealing with cases that reach beyond the boundaries of sovereign legal orders.[4] In contrast to arguing for an *ad hoc* overhaul that meets the specific challenges of transnational phenomena, I shall propose a *reconstruction* of the standard perception of legal obligation, which will aim at a unified understanding across legal orders, be they domestic or supra-national.

The third section will undertake in detail a reconstruction of the grounds of legal obligation. Very roughly, I will question the received view that legal obligations are grounded in institutional facts, which involve States as their authors (call this the *legal relation*). Instead, I will suggest that the legal relation, conceptually speaking, does not form the ultimate ground of legal obligations: rather, I will suggest, legal obligations obtain in virtue of a more basic, so-called *proto-legal* relation,[5] which does not necessarily involve the State. Proto-legal relations involve interactions between individuals such that generate enforceable claims among the participants. I will spend some time clarifying the conditions under which a class of interactions between persons may produce the effect. Interestingly, it will turn out that while State-based norms are sufficient for enforceability, they are not necessary for it; many other instances of interaction between agents are capable of producing that effect.

Finally, in the last section, I will discuss in broad terms how the proposed reconstruction of legal obligation and the new demarcation of legal actors that that proposes can bear on the allocation and distribution of legal responsibility

4 For an overview, see Vandenhole (n 2). More generally, the view that we need new conceptual categories to deal with transnational law seems to be a widespread trend in the literature on law and globalisation. For a recent overview, see N Walker, *Intimations of Global Law* (CUP, 2014).

5 The proto-legal relation is ultimately a political relation, but the term 'proto-legal' is more illuminating in the present context. By adopting that terminology I also wish to suggest that the scope of legal relations is wider than the boundaries of state sovereignty.

between plural and diverse actors. To begin with, I shall adumbrate a key consequence of the account with regard to the subjects of legal responsibility: legal responsibility, in arising from interactions among individuals, primarily involves individuals. Any other type of actor (States or other corporate bodies) may become subject for responsibility only derivatively, that is considered as the sum of those individuals that fall under the same obligation. No doubt this is a striking claim in the current climate of international law (IL) and one that asks for a major shift of our understanding of its subjects. In particular, it asks us to think of States and other corporate actors as lying downstream of individuals, only as instantiations of plural individuals who are collected together because they share the same obligation in a given context. The great advantage of this picture is that it disengages the answer to the question 'who is obligated?' from a preconceived test that renders States the primary focus of legal obligation. In fact, it takes obligations to determine actors, not vice-versa: pertinent actors become those individuals, alone or in some formation, which fall under the obligation at hand. Finally, in the light of those findings, I will suggest ways in which the law of international responsibility can become more receptive to shared responsibility, with an eye to addressing cases in which States and corporate agents are jointly involved in wrongdoing, beyond the limits of a singly domestic legal order.

The standard picture

The standard theoretical picture takes legal obligations to be grounded on facts about the State (henceforth *facts of sovereignty*[6]). This picture of law has been mainly developed against the background of the domestic legal order and yields the conclusion that legal obligation requires sovereign State action to come to life.

A key contention of the standard picture is that for any legal obligation to obtain there must exist a norm which has been created by some State official or, more broadly, institutional agent. In effect, facts of sovereignty count as *existence conditions* for the norms that ground legal obligations. Those existence conditions are further grouped together to form a pedigree test which is used to assess the existence of legal obligations across an unlimited range of cases.[7]

6 Under the term I group together, somewhat simplistically, any social fact that originates in state institutions and/or officials.

7 Interestingly, such pedigree tests may support a monistic understanding of law, whereby all law flows out of features or facts of the same type, facts that count as the uniquely identified set of existence conditions for applying correctly the concept 'law'. Such *formal* monism remains silent on the question about the justification of legal obligation. In contrast the position adumbrated in this chapter is canvassed against an idea of *substantive* monism, for it takes legal obligations to be grounded on sound principles of justice (part of which are human rights). For a more detailed exposition of the idea of substantive monism, see G Pavlakos and J Pauwelyn, 'Principled Monism and the Normative Conception of Coercion under International Law', in M Evans and P Koutrakos (eds), *Beyond the Established Legal Orders: Policy Interconnections between the EU and the Rest of the World* (Hart Publishing 2011), 317–341; G Pavlakos, 'Legal Obligation in the Global

Thus if a social arrangement does not instantiate the conditions enumerated in the test, then it falls outwith the purview of legal obligation. Hence, to judge whether an agent has a standing in law, we must ascertain whether the existence conditions of legal obligation have been fulfilled in the particular situation, antecedently to what agents owe to each other. In other words, no one is rendered a subject of obligation unless a fact of sovereignty says so.

Positivist lawyers tend to abide by such pedigree tests when they wish to capture the scope of legal obligations. Famously, HLA Hart identified a social rule of recognition, which depicts a set of facts about the practice of legal officials that in turn function as existence conditions (or criteria) for the obtaining of obligation-imposing norms.[8] Such accounts can be called *site-oriented*. Site-oriented accounts conclude from the existence of certain non-normative facts the obtaining of normative relations (obligations, powers, privileges and perhaps permissions). A site-oriented account typically renders the question about the existence conditions of legal obligations antecedent to the question of their scope, that is, the question about the range of persons who fall under the claims and duties arising from those obligations.[9] Further, the standard picture, wedded to facts about State practice, deems domestic law the standard site of legal obligation with supra-national law remaining an odd exception in need of explanation.[10]

Let us now turn to the counterpart of this (site-oriented) construction in IL. Roughly put, this is the maxim that legal obligations, in order to arise, need to have been endorsed by State action – the theory that IL is grounded on the consent of States is just a further instantiation of that maxim: on the face of the lack of a super-State whose institutions can generate obligations, those can arise only if States commit or consent to them. The need for State action dictates that if no single State can generate obligation-imposing norms, then the consent of many States is required in order to generate obligations. That consent introduces a fiction that mitigates for the lack of a super-State, whose institutional actions would give rise to obligation-imposing norms.

The issue ramifies: the fiction produced through consent supports the further view that the primary addressees of supra-national legal obligations are States, to the extent that those have consented to the relevant obligation-imposing norms. Additional subjects cannot in principle be added lest those disrupt the principle that legal obligation requires a norm that has been generated within the confines of a sovereign State. Should such actors be admitted, a disruption of the above maxim would occur: it would threaten

Context. Some Remarks on the Boundaries and Allegiances among Persons Beyond the State', EUI Working Papers No 16 (Robert Schuman Centre for Advanced Studies 2012).

8 HLA Hart, *The Concept of Law*, with an introduction by Leslie Green (3rd edn, OUP 2012).

9 Compare the structurally very similar discussion on obligations of distributive justice in A Abizadeh, 'Co-operation, Pervasive Impact and Coercion: On the Scope (not Site) of Distributive Justice' (2007) 35 Philosophy and Public Affairs 318–358, at 323.

10 See also the discussion in R Collins, 'No Longer at the Vanishing Point? International Law and the Analytical Tradition in Jurisprudence' (2014) 5 Jurisprudence 265–298.

to give rise to legal relations that would not be based on State-generated norms and, as a consequence, would lie beyond the control of States. Imagine a corporate actor who is active across plural sovereign territories. Should such an actor directly incur legal obligations,[11] those would lay beyond the law-making powers of a single sovereign State. That would lead to a slippery slope which would undermine and potentially dismantle the maxim that legal obligation is grounded on facts of sovereignty. For no sooner has that maxim receded, than States will find themselves becoming subjects of obligations irrespective or independently of their own self-commitment.[12]

If the maxim is to survive, the State should remain the primary source and subject of legal obligation. Yet the maxim, as it stands, has a clearly detrimental effect: it prevents non-State actors from being subject to legal obligations outside the confines of a sovereign legal order. This might have been acceptable at a time when actors were *de facto* confined within domestic legal orders, but becomes increasingly unacceptable in a world in which non-State actors have the capacity to affect and be affected beyond the boundaries of the established legal orders.[13]

Site versus scope

Omitting a fair amount of detail, that is the picture we have to adhere to when we make considerations of site the point of departure for an account of legal obligation in the international context. What is more, when we do that, we cannot accommodate intuitions about non-State actors unless we are also willing to undertake an overhaul of the entire system of IL as we know it. Theoretical coherence and consistency aside, such an overhaul is likely to meet with resistance from the adherents to the standard picture of legal obligation. Why, they would object, invent an account which sets apart the workings of legal obligation at the transnational and domestic levels?

11 For a corporate actor to incur obligations in a direct manner, it is not sufficient that an obligation is imposed by one or several national legal orders, as is the case when a state exercises extraterritorial regulation (eg the US Alien Tort Act). Rather, an obligation arises directly when it is grounded on the relation between the corporate actor and other actors. In contrast, extraterritorial regulation remains indirect in my account, because it requires that facts of sovereignty feature amongst its existence conditions (cf also with the analysis of the *proto-legal* relation offered in this chapter). I thank an anonymous reviewer for helping me to drive home this point.

12 The same erosion of the maxim takes place when any other non-state actors is admitted into the picture – eg when individuals are rendered subjects of international law outwith the limits of a sovereign legal order.

13 Although my claims about the standard picture relate primarily to legal subjects in transnational contexts, the picture is not very different in the domestic realm, for even here non-state actors become subjects under the condition that there exists a state-generated rule which make them so. Ultimately my analysis reads the standard picture as capturing both domestic and transnational contexts: for any legal obligations to arise a pedigree test is required which consists in the obtaining of facts of sovereignty. As a result, the capacity to render actors subjects of obligations remains within the jurisdiction of the sovereign state (see the discussion in this chapter).

I wish to suggest a route that avoids this impasse. The starting point is to question the direction of fit between site and scope. The standard picture, in taking site to determine scope, subscribes to a strong claim which is not self-evident. For a start, should it be true that site determines scope something like the site/scope thesis would obtain, that is, the thesis that the scope of legal obligations coincides with their site. The site/scope thesis is treated by the standard picture as a conceptual truth, that is a proposition that is true in virtue of its meaning.[14] However, the site/scope thesis, far from constituting a conceptual truth, is a substantive claim that requires specific argument in order to ground its truth.[15]

Contrariwise, one may have good reasons to start the inquiry on the side of *scope*.[16] It is actually a substantive question whether two or more agents stand in a relation of obligation, which is not exhausted by the obtaining of any singular property/fact (or sets of properties/facts) about State practice as we encountered earlier. Re-conceiving the relation between site and scope suggests further that site does not list existence conditions but merely *enabling or instrumental conditions*: it points at those facts which in a particular context instantiate the salient normative bond between the agents.[17] As such, the site of an obligation would be pointing at all those (institutional) arrangements that ought to be undertaken when an obligation obtains, with a view to securing the fulfilment of the obligation, rather than laying down conditions for the existence of the obligation. Such a reversal of the priority relationship between site and scope reflects more accurately the fact that there is no royal route from site to scope, because the question about the contribution of a site to a particular obligation depends on an antecedent normative judgment about scope. Besides, this account tallies better with our intuition that questions of obligation are 'practical', hence must be determined not by some agent-independent properties, but by agent-relevant considerations about what is permissible to do with respect to the impact of our actions on others.

There is a further reason to question the primacy of site over scope: recent phenomena, which we categorise under the heading of globalisation, strengthen the intuition that it becomes increasingly difficult to formalise the grounds of legal obligation into sets of criteria, which can generate some

14 Much as the proposition: 'bachelor is an unmarried man'.

15 I owe the contrast between site and scope and the questioning of the primacy of the former entirely to A Abizadeh (n 9), 318. Abizadeh discusses site and scope with respect to obligations of distributive justice, but his remarks apply *mutatis mutandis* to any obligations of justice. In addition to the arguments offered by Abizadeh, it would seem that drawing inferences from the actual sites to the potential scope of obligations might open one to the charge of a naturalistic fallacy or the fallacy involved in concluding to a normative truth from a purely descriptive sentence (in case S1: conditions XYZ exist when obligation O obtains -> lack of XYZ in S2 -> no obligation O).

16 Scope here refers not to the question whether law involves just negative or, in addition, also positive obligations, but to the question about the range of actors who are obligated. The use of the term is familiar from political philosophy, cf with Abizadeh (n 9).

17 Ibid, 322–340.

invariable formula that determines what counts as the site of legal obligation. This shows quite well in respect of views that render the State the primary site of legal obligation. Such views, usually originating in the tradition of legal positivist, take facts about State practice (eg facts about consent) to belong to the set of the existence conditions that fix a pedigree test for legal obligation. Yet, as Mattias Risse submits when discussing obligations of justice,

> At a time when States share the world stage with a network of treaties and global institutions, philosophers have had to consider not only whether the State can be justified to those living under it but whether the whole global political and economic order consisting of multiple States and global institutions can be justified to those living under it. And in a world in which the most salient inequalities are not within States but among them, philosophers have had to broaden their focus for justice, too, asking not only what counts as a just distribution within the State but also what counts as a just distribution *globally*.[18]

Replace 'justice' with 'legal obligation' and the salient point turns out to be common for obligations of law and justice, namely that any focus on facts about sovereignty will not explain obligations at the international level.

A scope-oriented account is actor-insensitive and wrongdoing-sensitive. It is actor-insensitive in the sense that it does not take any actor as settled, but looks to determine actors in the light of the obligations obtaining. On the other hand, it is wrongdoing-sensitive because in identifying grounds for obligations it focuses on principles which aim to facilitate exchanges between agents which are free from wrongdoing. To that extent, the account considers legal obligations to be normative constraints that block instances of wrongdoing in the dealings between agents.

Reconstruction

The standard picture, I argued, takes the site of sovereignty to determine the content and scope of legal obligation. It is only on the basis of facts about the creation of rules through the State that legal obligations come into existence. Such an account is actor-sensitive in the sense of presupposing a particular actor (the State) as part of the grounding base of legal obligations.

Such a site-oriented and actor-sensitive account yields a particular understanding of the *legal relation* or, in other words, the kind of relation in which agents need to stand in order to incur legal obligations. To spell it out concretely, the standard picture submits that two or more agents may stand in

18 M Risse, 'Introducing Pluralist Internationalism – An Alternative Approach to Questions of Global Justice' (2013) (online paper available on the author's web-site: *http://www.hks.harvard.edu/fs/mrisse/Papers/Current%20Research/IntroducingPluralistInternationalismWZBJuly2013.pdf* (accessed 4 February 2015)), 3.

the legal relation only if there exists a norm whose origin can be traced back to some fact of sovereignty.[19] In other words the site of legal obligation (facts of sovereignty) ends up determining its scope (the set of agents that stand in the legal relation).

The upshot of the standard picture is that the State becomes constitutive of the legal relation and, what may sound more surprising, the main subject of it. In the domestic level there are of course plural non-State actors that are subjects of the law. Ultimately, however, the question 'who counts as a subject of the law?' receives the answer 'those who stand in the legal relation', where *that* latter relation is configured in terms of facts of sovereignty.[20] The counterpart of this picture in trans- and international contexts is the condition of consent.

I wish next to provide definite steps to disentangle the question of the *scope* of the *legal relation* from the *site* of *legal obligation*. I will argue that the kind of relation that gives rise to obligations of the type we usually regard as legal is a relation that can and must be captured independently of facts about the site of legal obligation, at least to the extent to which the latter is understood by the standard picture. To highlight the contrast with the standard account, I shall label the pertinent relation *proto-legal* and argue that, conceptually speaking, it is more basic than the *legal relation* in so far as the grounding of legal obligations is concerned.[21]

The proto-legal relation

I shall refer to a relation as *proto-legal* when it obtains between agents independently of facts of sovereignty.[22] Importantly, the proto-legal relation is capable of grounding obligations which share a core feature with legal obligations, that is the property of *enforceability*. I will first discuss what renders a relation proto-legal and subsequently propose a way for understanding the property of enforceability.

First, proto-legal relations obtain through patterns of action which engage two or more individuals (*joint patterns of action*). Such patterns are ubiquitous

19 Facts of sovereignty comprise facts about the expression of state will, as is the case in international contracts and, more generally, agreements. Many thanks to an anonymous reviewer for bringing this point to my attention.

20 Even though it would be inaccurate to say that the main subject of domestic legal relations is the state, a related idea might survive scrutiny: namely, that the duty to create normative relations between non-state actors cannot but be self-imposed by the state. To that extent, the primary subject of domestic law is the state: the state has a self-imposed duty to regulate the relations of all non-state actors within its territory by generating norms that create normative relations (aside of obligations I include here powers, privileges and perhaps permissions).

21 Because it generates the same kind of obligations that are attributed to the legal relation, but does so without requiring reference to institutional legal facts.

22 To put it more sharply: facts of sovereignty are not *necessary* for the proto-legal relation to obtain even though their obtaining can also ground the proto-legal relation (in other words they are *sufficient* for proto-legality).

in our lives: from cooking or moving a heavy table together to constructing a levee that contains the flood or planning the economy of our community, we all become subjects of such patterns. Significantly, the set of processes which are usefully captured under the label of globalisation have *created* many new instances of joint patterns of action while typically expanding the circle of actors involved in them: parent companies set up subsidiary companies in distant locations, which in turn engage with the local people through plural and complex patterns of action; immigration policies establish new patterns of action that direct the choices of foreign populations; and so on. Crucially, in compressing the space between agents, globalisation has significantly contributed to transforming many of otherwise 'unilateral' choices and actions to instances of joint patterns of action. That is to say, globalisation has intensified joint patterns of action: not just those that are grounded on some shared intention of the parties involved to participate in them (as in the cooking example), but in addition those that join together the actions of agents who do not partake in the same intention, in virtue of the impact their actions have on one another.[23]

What is the salient normative effect of those occurrences? Joint patterns of action impose normative constraints on the behaviour of the parties involved, constraints which are grounded on the permissibility of each party's actions within the joint pattern. This applies to both types of joint pattern of action – those covered by shared intention but also, and more interestingly so, those that join the action of different agents independently of their sharing a common intention. To that extent the constraint of permissibility becomes part of, or even constitutes, the *normative structure* of joint patterns of action.[24] Before I attempt a more detailed formulation of the constraint of permissibility let me first take a closer look at the success and pathology of joint patterns of action. [25]

23 For the standard account of joint action as based on shared intentions, see the work of Michael Bratman (M Bratman, *Intention, Plans, and Practical Reason* (Harvard University Press 1987); 'Intention, Practical Rationality, and Self-Governance' (2009) 119 Ethics 411–443). For a prominent re-statement of Bratman's theory in the realm of law, see S Shapiro, *Legality* (Harvard University Press 2011). The account of joint action that I adumbrate in this chapter deems the idea of shared intention insufficient for capturing joint action.

24 Although I cannot discuss this further, it should be noted in passing that the normative structure is itself grounded on the autonomy of the agents engaged in the joint pattern. The capacity of joint undertakings for mutual impact on the agency of the parties involved renders them answerable to reasons, thus subjecting them to justification. To that extent joint endeavors have a second-personal structure in the sense that the parties who engage in them should look to take on board, or respect, the reasons of one another, ultimately aiming to help one another to realise the reasons each independently has. In other words, exchange, not coercion, should be the outcome of the joint endeavour. For accounts that place autonomy at the basis of joint action in law and politics, see R Forst, 'The Justification of Human Rights and the Basic Right to Justification: A Reflexive Approach' (2010) 120 Ethics 711–740; K Möller, *The Global Model of Constitutional Rights* (OUP 2012).

25 I would not have arrived at this account had it not been for the seminal work of AJ Julius. See his 'The Possibility of Exchange' (2013) 12 Politics, Philosophy and Economics 361–374;

On a good day, joint patterns turn out as *exchanges* between the parties. This means roughly that each party engages in the pattern for reasons she has independently of the doings and sayings or the motives of the other parties.[26] During an exchange the parties, in engaging in the joint pattern, help realise the reasons each of them independently has. Take, for instance, the joint action [You drive me to the station, I pay the fare] in which we often engage when hiring a taxi. Here the passenger and the driver partake in the joint action [You drive ..., I pay the fare] for reasons each has independently of the sayings and doings of the other.[27] Alas, good days often come few and far between.

On a bad day, the joint pattern fails to amount to an exchange and deteriorates into some kind of *exploitative* or *coercive* scenario: a clear instance would be something like [You drive ..., I refrain from shooting you]. But other, subtler instances of deterioration come to mind, when for instance the driver is driving the taxi for an exploitative taxi owner; here the joint activity between taxi owner and taxi driver might take the form [you drive the taxi 15 hours a day and give the earnings to me, I let you drive it for three more hours in order to make a living]. What makes this activity exploitative is the fact that the driver does not have any independent reason to perform his part of the joint pattern (that is, to drive the taxi 15 hours for another person), other than the fact that the taxi owner has rendered that a condition for the driver to earn a living. A more blunt case of exploitation is blackmail: when the boss says to the employee [you sleep with me, I promote you] the pattern proposed thereby lacks independent justification *vis-à-vis* the employee who is *coerced* to perform his/her part as a result of the employer's making it a condition for performing his/her part.

Such instances of exploitative action abound in the practices of transnational corporations, which increasingly vary their standards of operation depending on the location of their operations. In particular, in the developing South corporations often coerce workers to work in deplorable human rights conditions, by taking advantage of the fact that their livelihood depends on those corporations. Consider a case where a transnational corporation, or its subsidiary, is the sole employer in a community. Most locals rely on that corporation for earning living wages. The corporation disposes waste upstream, the only source of drinkable water. At the same time, it makes clear that any complaint would lead to loss of employment for the complainant. Most employees remain silent of the abusive relationship for fear of losing their job.

Reconstruction (book manuscript presented at the third Jurisprudence Seminar @ The Center for Law and Cosmopolitan Values, Faculty of Law, University of Antwerp, with comments by David Estlund, Japa Pallikkathayil and Thomas Scanlon; version of 7 December 2013, available on the author's website: *http://www.ajjulius.net/reconstruction.pdf* (accessed 4 February 2015)).

26 Julius (n 25).

27 Such reasons may be explained either with reference to the reciprocal promises actors make (contract) or – on a deeper explanation – the reasons that predate the promissory act (my reason to go to place X; the driver's reason to make a good living and so on).

Extreme as it may appear, our imaginary example finds support in recent allegations of workers who have been coerced to work in deplorable conditions in the apparel industry of Bangladesh.[28]

The pathology of coercion/exploitation contributes to an understanding of the salience of the *constraint of permissibility* in the context of joint patterns of action. Let me explain how: joint patterns of action succeed (*qua* exchanges) if and only if they do not contribute to the exploitation/coercion of any of the parties involved.[29] Instead, cases of coercion/exploitation count as instances of wrongdoing.[30] For the purposes of the present discussion a plausible way to understand wrongdoing is through the idea of hindrance of freedom.[31] Under this explication exploitative or coercive patterns hinder the freedom of the coercee, in disregarding the coercee's independent reasons for participating in the pattern.

What may count as a hindrance of freedom, on this understanding, is determined by the impact it has on the capacity of the coercee to determine her participation in the joint pattern according to the reasons she has. Thus any manipulation of the environment by the coercer, or any other intervention that modifies the reasons of the coercee in a manner that prevents the latter from acting on the reasons she actually has, would count as hindrance of freedom.[32] If a corporation imposes exploitative terms on its employees or otherwise coerces those who live in the environment in which it is active, these actions would constitute hindrances of freedom, violating the constraint of permissibility of the relevant joint pattern of action.[33]

The idea of hindrance of freedom can be usefully contrasted with the condition of considerable and asymmetrical power which is often employed by

28 Following the collapse of the Rana Plaza (2013), killing over a thousand workers, the commission of inquiry concluded that workers are often intimidated not to expose their condition. I owe the construction of the example and further feedback on real-life cases to Tamo Atabongawung.

29 Julius requires further that these patterns help realise the reasons of those involved; see Julius (n 25). We may remain agnostic about this stronger condition for present purposes.

30 Recall that the account was deemed wrongdoing-sensitive precisely for that reason. See previous section.

31 Wrongdoing is often defined through harm (see, for instance, the so-called *Maastricht Principles on Extraterritorial Obligations of States in the area of Economic, Social and Cultural Rights*). To the extent that the definition relies on a standard understanding of harm as reduction of welfare, one should caution against it. Wrongdoing does not overlap with reduction of harm so conceived, for wrongdoing aims to cover instances of interference with freedom/autonomy which do not amount to any loss of welfare (so-called instances of harmless wrongdoing: say, if I avail myself of your car without your permission, damage it, and subsequently replace it with a better one, I will still count as having wronged you). See for an excellent discussion of the relevant conceptual distinction, A Ripstein, *Force and Freedom* (Harvard University Press 2009), ch 2 (42–50).

32 Julius (n 25).

33 A more specific aspect of wrongdoing relates to the various kinds of means we each use to achieve our ends. The use of any material resources must comply with such conditions that ensure that the use of, say, chattels and land does not hinder the freedom of others. Notably, Kant believes that any unilateral use of property that is not based on publicly promulgated rules would count as wrongful. See for extensive discussion, Ripstein (n 31).

international human rights lawyers in order to extend international human rights obligations to non-State actors.[34] The argument, very roughly put, is that non-State actors should also be admitted to the realm of human rights obligations precisely because in their dealings with individuals they possess considerable and asymmetrical power akin to that of States.[35] An explanation of 'considerable and asymmetric power' in terms of wrongdoing has a clear advantage: it captures the salient normative relation between actors without relying on specific characteristics of any one actor (ie the State). As such, the explanation can helpfully point to the obligations arising among a diversity of actors *in virtue of the normative significance of their interactions* as opposed to inferring those obligations from certain properties possessed by States. For no sooner one feels compelled to do the latter than one has already conceded that normative salience is a property of particular actors (State) and not of actions.

The most important normative consequence of the constraint of permissibility is that it requires joint patterns of action to contribute to each person's acting consistently with the actions of others.[36] Contribution of the required kind takes place when patterns of action facilitate exchange and, conversely, hinder coercion/exploitation. Patterns that facilitate exchange do so in virtue of certain features they possess (facilitating features), which are shared by each of them. These facilitating features can be formulated through general principles that generate obligations akin to those we encounter in human rights and other precepts of justice. Importantly, those obligations are jointly shared by everyone who partakes in the relevant patterns.

Let me take some stock and gesture at an interim conclusion: I argued that the proto-legal relation pertains to joint patterns of action such that trigger off a constraint of permissibility.[37] The normative environment of the proto-legal relation grounds general principles that impose obligations which are jointly shared by every actor that partakes of joint patterns of action of the kind described. If my account were sound, then it would seem that something like the proto-legal relation meets all the requirements of what I earlier labelled 'legal relation' without requiring any dedication to institutional facts of a certain kind. Focusing on the proto-legal relation would also take us beyond a site-oriented inquiry that is wedded to facts of sovereignty. What, instead, would become salient is the normative relation between agents in itself, not the social facts that determine one version of that relation (ie within the domestic State). Finally, the account would be able to draw the conclusion

34 See the chapters of Wouter Vandenhole (n 2) and Koen de Feyter, chapter 8 in this volume.

35 By possessing resources, influence and staff akin to those of states.

36 There exists of course a class of joint patterns of action in which permissibility does not feature prominently or at all. Such cases include *de minimis* infringements or special relations within which the hindrance of freedom is justified through some thick moral reasons (special relations such as family or club membership).

37 Such constraints of responsibility include human rights obligations and obligations from distributive justice alike. The formulation needs to remain general in order to capture any obligation-imposing principle which aims to enable exchange and/or disable exploitation.

that joint patterns of action *plus* the condition of permissibility (ie the two key ingredients of 'proto-legality') are capable of grounding obligations whose content and normative force is not dissimilar to the kind of obligation we usually call legal. Accordingly, it would open our eyes to all those other instances of interaction which can generate legal obligations, a fact that had been obfuscated by the dedication of the standard picture to one specific site for legal obligation. For, in disentangling the content of the salient normative relation from a preconceived test of site, proto-legality helps us recover the normative space, which is prominent in and largely constituted by transnational contexts.

Let me linger on the structural similarities between the proto-legal and legal relation, before I turn to the property of enforceability, which I believe is a core feature shared by the obligations that are grounded in the legal and proto-legal relation alike. Famously, Kant took instances of wrongdoing in the interaction between actors to constitute the opposite of the *rightful condition* as the condition that enables each actor to act consistently with the actions of everyone else.[38] Leaving out a lot of detail, Kant considered the rightful condition to be possible only within a system of publicly authorised norms which can exist only within the confines of a positive legal order. Legal norms, in being equipped with sanctions, have the capacity to 'hinder the hindrance of freedom' and thus restore instances of wrongdoing back to the rightful condition. The details of the Kantian account aside, it turns out that what I have called a proto-legal relation precisely aims at the whereabouts of the rightful condition, in Kant's terms. For the proto-legal relation displays a normative structure that is identical to that of the rightful condition, that of enabling each actor to act consistently with the actions of everyone else. Does this entail that the obligations grounded by the proto-legal relation are legal in the full sense, ie share the features of the obligations we have in the rightful condition?

A careful Kantian might caution against such an equation on two grounds: first, she would argue, obligations in the rightful condition take off the ground only as *publicly (omnilaterally) authorised* norms which are enshrined in positive rules of law.[39] If that objection were sound it would be damaging for the present account, as it would make anew State-related institutions part of the condition for the obtaining of the kind of obligations I am interested in. The second objection is somewhat different, albeit related: nothing can be called a legal obligation unless it is equipped with enforcement. Thus, even if one could conceive something like the proto-legal relation as a source of public or omnilateral obligations, those would not be the obligations of the

38 I Kant, 'The Doctrine of Right', Part I of the Metaphysics of Morals in *Practical Philosophy* (trans and ed Mary Gregor, CAP 1996); also the very instructive overview in the first chapter of Ripstein, *Force and Freedom* (n 31), 1–29.

39 For the idea of omnilateral authorisation, see Ripstein (n 31), 148–159.

rightful condition. Ultimately, a crude version of the objection would run, legal obligations require States and their institutions.

The objection from public authorisation is challenging. To begin with, Kant does not give to public or omnilateral authorisation any democratic gloss. Rather, his concern is that the norms introducing obligations should not originate unilaterally from any individual actor or else they would impose, in their unilateral character, an impermissible constraint on others. Whether the property of publicity requires a particular kind of institution (ie State) is a further issue that cannot be resolved solely by reference to publicity itself, not at least to the extent to which publicity does not require democratic authorisation. The structure of the proto-legal relation, as outlined earlier, can deal with the challenge of omnilateral authorisation without requiring reference to the State: we saw there that *that* relation grounds general principles which outline the general features of the joint patterns of action that facilitate mutual consistent action. Such principles make it the case that when acting within the joint pattern of action agents are acting out of reasons they themselves share, thereby rendering their joint endeavour an exchange rather than exploitation/coercion. To that extent, the obligations entailed by the principles that facilitate exchange purport to be omnilaterally authorised, for they purport to prevent wrongdoing. While the precise nature of omnilateral authorisation will need to be elaborated further, it suffices for now to point out that it does not stand in opposition to the normative structure of the proto-legal relation.

The second objection is stronger, but for that reason perhaps easier to rebut: it says, in a nutshell, that no obligation can be rendered legal unless it is coupled with enforcement. I believe that this view rests on a misunderstanding which I will look to dispel in the subsection that follows. Very briefly, the point will be that proto-legal obligations share with law a property with a much deeper significance than enforcement: that is, the property of enforceability. I will argue that enforceability is distinct from enforcement and at that a more fundamental feature of legal obligation than the latter. It is more fundamental to the extent to which it meets the conditions set by the rightful condition when it comes to the grounding of legal obligations. Conversely, enforcement plays no role in the grounding of legal obligations and only refers to the various factual possibilities for the realisation of enforceable obligations. That said, enforcement still retains a normative significance, however one that can be appreciated only in the light of the normative significance of enforceability.

Enforceability and enforcement

I shall now turn to argue that a key feature of the obligations grounded by proto-legal relations is enforceability. Earlier I argued that the proto-legal relation grounds principles that account for the general features of joint patterns of action which help persons to act consistently with the action of others. Further, I submitted that those principles entail obligations which are jointly shared by everyone within the overall scheme of joint patterns of action. I will now look to explain a further claim about such obligations, ie the claim that they are enforceable. Subsequently I shall suggest that the same property of enforceability is shared by the obligations of the rightful condition, which are the standard instances of legal obligation. This will help me to corroborate the conclusion that proto-legal obligations are much like the obligations of the rightful condition. I will conclude with some remarks on the significance of enforcement.

Proto-legal obligations are *enforceable* in the sense that the 'coercee' has a claim *vis-à-vis* the coercer that she abide by the relevant course of action or that she be made to perform some other action/omission for failing to do so. The claim/right of the coercee is part of the content/meaning of the obligation, which makes it the case that there arises an authorisation or 'standing' over the coercers' agency that she be made to do as the obligation says. That is to say, the precise content of any such obligation to F is 'you ought to F and *can be made* to F'. Suppose, for the sake of demonstration, that I pass on to someone false information in the context of a promise or, more broadly, some other assurance-evoking exchange: eg I indicate to Mary that she can have my car tomorrow in order to pick up her friend from the airport, but proceed to give my car to John instead. My obligation to Mary is enforceable, for part of its content is that I be made to comply with it, irrespective of whether I am motivated (intend, etc) to do so or not.[40] Similarly, acts of corporations can give rise to enforceable obligations irrespective of whether a mechanism of enforcement is in place. While the objection of the standard picture theorist is that lack of any mechanism of enforcement would deprive those obligations of enforceability, there is an emerging consensus amongst scholars that this is not so.[41]

Arguably, this is what obligations are like in the rightful condition. The rightful condition, much as the proto-legal relation, aims to facilitate persons'

40 This case can be helpfully contrasted with one of a purely moral, non-enforceable obligation: Take a general obligation not to lie: suppose I am boasting to someone about being very prominent in some way (say, in being on first name terms with President Obama). Should it turn out that I am lying, the other person may think ill of me or pass negative judgment about my character. However, there is no ground to suggest that they have a claim that I retract my lie or that I otherwise compensate them for having lied to them. As a result, enforceability sets apart the relevant joint obligations from other moral obligations which are owed in a first instance merely unilaterally.

41 The argument has been developed in regard of the binding force of *ius cogens* and its impact on determining the scope of obligations under international law. In summary, it is argued that *ius cogens* determines the content and scope of international law obligations irrespective of the consent of actors, or the undertaking of any institutional acts relating to its validation or enforcement. Cf with R Dworkin, 'A New Philosophy for International Law' (2013) 41 Philosophy and Public Affairs 2–30; and, placing the focus on questions of transnational corporate responsibility, T Atabongawung, *Diamonds, Corporate Responsibility and International Law. Case Study: Antwerp Diamond Sector* (PhD thesis University of Antwerp 2014).

acting in a way that is consistent with the actions of others. In it legal norms formulate patterns of action which regulate the action of everyone in a manner that is consistent with the action of every other person, much as the patterns established by the proto-legal relation do. Crucially, what generates enforceability in the strictly legal case (ie the rightful condition) is not the possibility of enforcement, which is attached to institutional norms, but the normative structure of the relation that pertains among agents: enforceability is part and parcel of any joint pattern that aims to help agents to engage in a consistent scheme of coinciding actions. For in any such scheme the reasons for acting are removed from the disposal of each agent individually and become subject to a normative constraint about what counts as action that is consistent with the action of every other.

Notice what may, at first glance, strike us as paradoxical: what would count, within a joint scheme/pattern, as acting for the reasons I have (and not as a 'reaction' to others' coercive moves) would after all be determined not by me but by the pattern in which I partake. There is no paradox here, however. Because acting (as part of a joint pattern) for the reasons 'I have' does not mean that the reasons I choose to act on are 'up to me'. The reasons I have are the reasons I *may* (as in: may permissibly) have; and I may have only those reasons that make my action compossible with the actions of others, or else permissible. Such reasons turn out to be determined by the principles that outline the general features of the joint scheme of compossible action.

Helpfully, this way of understanding enforceable obligations sheds a lot of light on a feature of law, which often is expressed by saying that the law aims to regulate *external conduct* leaving outwith its purview the internal conviction of agents. Now, if regulating 'external conduct' would just mean that the law imposes on people obligations irrespective of the reasons those people have, the law would be achieving consistency of action without aiming at exchange. Such an interpretation – consistent as it may be with the standard picture of legal obligation – falls massively short of the standard set by the *rightful condition*. Rather, to grasp the point about law's focus on 'external conduct', in a manner consistent with the rightful condition, we need to interpret legal obligations as proto-legal, that is enforceable obligations that aim to safeguard joint patterns of action through which consistency of action is achieved. Now at last the point about confining legal regulation to external conduct becomes clear: in the proto-legal relation the reasons of the agents and the obligations imposed by the joint pattern do not come apart. The agents are jointly obligated to act on patterns of external conduct which secure consistency of action. These are their reasons, and at that they are external reasons.[42]

42 See for an attempt to spell out this argument in the context of Kant's legal philosophy, G Pavlakos 'Coercion and the Grounds of Legal Obligation: Arthur Ripstein's *Force and Freedom*' (2010) 1 Jurisprudence 305–316; G Pavlakos, 'Why is Willing Irrelevant to the Grounding of (Any) Obligation? Remarks on Arthur Ripstein's Conception of Omni-lateral Willing', in S Kisilevsky and MJ Stone (eds), *Freedom and Force: Essays on Kant's Legal Philosophy* (Hart Publishing forthcoming 2015).

Accordingly, any obligations that arise from proto-legal relations have already 'one foot' in the legal realm because they also possess the same property of enforceability as legal obligations. A key feature of this property, you will recall, is that the content of the obligation contains an authorisation over the conduct of the agent who is subject to it. If the earlier analysis is correct then there is no independent account of the legal relation or 'legality' upon which a distinction between some special legal and other enforceable obligations can rest. Any account of the legality of an obligation will have to first demonstrate its enforceability, before it can lay claim to its legality. But if that is the right order of the explanation, then 'legality' is on course to a slippery slope which makes it very difficult to recover its autonomy through reference to more facts (including facts of enforcement) about the State and its institutions.

The role of enforcement

It turns out that the proto-legal relation can ground by itself the property of enforceability, which arguably counts as the key feature of legal obligations. I argued that in two steps: first by suggesting that the legal relation, *qua* relation that grounds legal obligations, aims to secure a rightful condition; in a further step I suggested that the rightful condition simply is a proto-legal relation. To the extent to which the conclusion stands, it supplies a strong argument against any views that wish to distinguish legal obligation as a special kind of enforceable obligation. Typically, such views focus on enforcement (or sanctions) in order to support that distinction.

For the moment I will rely on the strong indication that my account offers against such views and, instead of putting forward a more detailed argument, shall seek to explore the function and role of enforcement with respect to enforceable obligations. For even though my account suggests that enforcement does not play any special role in the grounding of (any) enforceable obligation, it still considers enforcement to have normative significance in respect of enforceable obligations, which otherwise are grounded independently of it. What is interesting is that the role of enforcement I am about to adumbrate is not confined to only some enforceable obligations. Having argued against any fundamental distinction between legal and any other enforceable obligation, I will suggest that the normative significance played by enforcement, whatever that turns out to be, will attach, in principle, to all enforceable obligations.[43]

The relation that accounts for the property of enforceability of obligations needs to be strictly divorced from enforcement (actual or possible,

43 I need to draw a caveat here: for some enforceable obligations, it might even be inappropriate to actually introduce enforcement. Take, for instance, a joint pattern of action aiming at moving a heavy object (eg a large table). In this case, and despite the fact that an enforceable obligation is in place, it would be otiose to argue that some enforcement mechanism ought to be in place – at least for as long as the stakes remain low.

within some available institutional context). Facts of enforcement are not constitutive to the proto-legal relation, hence, to the obligations pertaining to it. However, enforcement remains normatively relevant in the following sense: the proto-legal relation, in realising the rightful condition, cannot afford a unilateral imposition of enforceable obligations; in other words, it frowns upon any of the actors involved who take upon themselves the task of enforcing the obligation. For any such unilateral enforcement would disable the prospect of a scheme of acting consistently with the action of everyone else, which after all is part of what the rightful condition requires. Instead, enforcement should be entrusted to institutional arrangements which form a public or omnilateral scheme for realising the relevant enforceable obligations. Accordingly, the requirement for the publicity of enforcement in fact becomes part of the content of the principles that formulate the general features of the joint scheme that aims at consistency of action.

While the requirement of publicity confers a *prima facie* presumption in favour of State-based enforcement, nothing precludes other institutional arrangements to take up that role. To that extent a certain amount of *pluralism* is in order: it is conceivable that public/omnilateral institutions of a non-State (ie sub-State or supra-State) nature can meet the task of enforcement.[44] As a result, different parts of the existing international legal order can be combined with a view to addressing instances of wrongdoing which cut across the established domestic legal orders.[45]

Finally, one other aspect of the normative significance of enforcement comes in play: because public or omnilateral enforcement is an obligation grounded by the principles that determine the scheme for the consistency of action, it can be plausibly argued that the actors involved incur secondary obligations to set up institutions which can appropriately enforce the obligations that arise from those principles.[46] Notice, however, that here it is anew

44 For creative suggestions along the lines of a pluralist system of institutions of accountability, see Khalfan and Seiderman, chapter 2 in this volume.

45 A prominent example of combining the enforcement mechanisms of different institutional orders is displayed by the reasoning strategy of the European Court of Justice in Case T-315/01 *Kadi v Council and Commission* [2005] ECR II-3649. For additional examples and some useful comparisons, see the discussion in G Pavlakos and J Pauwelyn (n 7).

46 A comparison with Kant's obligation to enter the rightful condition might be instructive at this juncture: Kant famously argued that everyone in the state of nature has an obligation, and one that is enforceable, to enter the rightful condition. This formulation might give rise to a misunderstanding that Kant's obligation merely focuses on setting up institutional mechanisms of enforcement. The account of the chapter helpfully dispels the misunderstanding: Kant's obligation to enter the rightful condition is explained as the sum of all those obligations which are generated by the principles which formulate the general features of the rightful condition (ie a joint scheme of action that aims to generate consistency). For, on the present account, we become subject to those principles each time we engage in joint patterns of action in virtue of the constraint of permissibility that such patterns trigger off. Accordingly, enforcement makes no distinct contribution to the existence conditions of the rightful condition. The obligation to set up appropriate mechanisms of enforcement is just one amongst the obligations of the rightful condition, and at that one that serves an instrumental goal.

the force of the enforceable obligations of the proto-legal relation that explain the secondary obligation to set up institutions of enforcement rather than the other way around.

Towards shared responsibility in international responsibility law

Encouragingly, transnational human rights obligations have been increasingly recognised as part and parcel of international human rights law. Yet, this improvement is not reflected adequately in the current scheme of IL responsibility.[47] Setting aside various motivational failures that relate to the strategic considerations of the actors involved, a significant part of the failure can be attributed to the lack of conceptual clarity in respect of the grounds and scope of legal obligations in international law.[48] Tellingly, any progress that has been made in recognising the extraterritorial and transnational dimension of human rights obligations has been more the outcome of indignation and reaction towards a proliferation of instances of wrongdoing rather than any sustained reflection on the limitations of the standard statist understanding of international law. Lacking a deeper understanding of the problem, however, quickly reveals the limitations of such positive developments: no sooner the question of allocation of responsibility arises, than the statist foundations of the standard picture resurface to support the received regime of responsibility.

While a detailed reconstruction of the current regime of IL responsibility would fall outwith the limits of this chapter,[49] I shall focus on one of its central limitations and discuss it in the light of the conclusions drawn in the previous sections of the chapter. In this manner, I hope to showcase the advantages of the preceding analysis of legal obligation, while highlighting its contribution to developing a regime of responsibility that is more in line with the increasing recognition of transnational human rights obligations in international law. To the extent to which the overall aim of the volume is to push the current regime of responsibility in that direction, what follows can be understood as making a contribution to its theoretical underpinning.

The central feature of current international responsibility law is its reliance on independent (monadic[50]) not shared responsibility.[51] The result is a very coarse normative frame which fails to deal with a large number of instances of wrongdoing. The shortcomings of the regime can be ordered

47 See Vandenhole (n 2).

48 Ibid (n 2) for an attempt to survey the literature and identify shortcomings.

49 Instead, see Khalfan and Seiderman, chapter 2, van Genugten, chapter 3 and Letnar Černič, chapter 4 in this volume.

50 In conformity with standard usage in international law, I shall use 'independent' responsibility to denote the opposite of shared responsibility. I thank Wouter Vandenhole for pointing this out.

51 See Vandenhole, chapter 6 in this volume.

along two dimensions: the dimension of plural actors; and the dimension of diverse actors. Along the dimension of plural actors, monadic responsibility is weak in grouping together actors of the same kind (ie States, given that monadic responsibility usually rests on the statist picture) in order to render them accountable for committed wrongdoings. Along the dimension of diversity, the monadic model is weak in recognising other types of actors which alongside States contribute to wrongdoing.[52]

Frequently, the tendency has been to deal with those shortcomings by introducing ad hoc mechanisms, often through reference to other more well-established regimes of responsibility from the domestic legal order.[53] Those mechanisms are helpful and also lend more detail and sophistication to the field of international human rights responsibility, which is still a work in progress. That said, unless those mechanisms are integrated within a theoretically coherent and better-founded scheme of explanation, their ad-hocness will make them vulnerable to the standard objections stemming from the statist picture.

To begin with, the account adumbrated in the previous sections promotes a regime of *shared responsibility*: the analysis of the proto-legal relation has illustrated that the principles, which formulate the general features of a scheme of joint patterns of action, generate enforceable obligations that are jointly shared by all actors involved in the scheme, for example a scheme which involves international organisations, States, companies and individuals (in its most extensive form this could be the global trade regime; a more limited version would include some investment scheme whereby company C, based in State A, sets up a subsidiary S-C in State B, which engages members of the local population). All of the above actors,[54] on the account I presented, become joint subjects of the obligations enshrined in the principles that formulate the general features of the scheme (for simplicity you may take such principles to be human rights and/or principles of (distributive) justice). Now take a case in which S-C systematically exploits the local population with the help of local State B. Under the analysis offered earlier, despite the lack of a unique legal order, there exists a proto-legal relation which connects all actors by generating obligations that are shared jointly by them. Further, given the

52 See for more details Vandenhole, chapter 6 in this volume.

53 In particular, by bringing on board domestic tort and criminal law. For a recent comprehensive discussion, see instead of others, Atabongawung (n 41).

54 The joint subject of our example will include the state, the corporate actors and the individual members of the population. All of the above actors will be jointly subjected to the obligations enshrined in the principles that formulate the general features of the scheme. Failure to comply with any of the relevant obligations will make one or more of these actors responsible towards those actors to whom the obligation is owed. To that extent, individual persons can be understood as incurring human rights responsibility on a par with states and corporations. That is so even in cases in which individual responsibility is formulated in terms of criminal responsibility, for the grounds for imposing criminal responsibility attach to general human rights principles.

violations of their obligations to the local population all three (C, A and B) are jointly responsible.[55]

There is a deeper, structural reason why my account opens up the gate to a regime of shared responsibility, one that relates to the capacity of the account to deal with plural and diverse actors: the account, in making individual persons the building blocks of the proto-legal relation, resists any pre-conceived limitations to the understanding of actors. In contrast, notice how those accounts that limit the scope of obligations to composite actors (ie the State), end up 'freezing' the characteristics of those actors into necessary conditions for recognising any actor as a subject of obligations (and further responsibility) in international law. Thus, when an account (such as the standard picture) renders the State the primary/basic subject of international human rights obligations, it has a very hard time expanding its scope to include other corporate actors or even more simple ones, such as individuals.

Instead, by introducing individuals as the building block of obligations, the proposed account ultimately introduces a wide range of actors who can become subjects of the obligations that arise within what I called the proto-legal relation: for, recall, in that account what determines who is the pertinent actor is not a pedigree test but the question 'who shares the same obligation?'. The answer to that question sets out from persons as the elementary unit for attributing responsibility[56] and proceeds, by way of identifying instances of shared obligations, to group together individuals into composite agents. Thus, on this account, corporate actors and States are downstream of persons and what individuates them as agents is the fact that a set of individuals are grouped together in virtue of having become the joint subject of the same obligation. To avail myself of a simplified example, when we say that someone's (say Mary's) right is infringed by 'the State', my account calls for the following re-description: 'all of us/everyone in the community is wronging Mary'. The right of Mary here is the reason that groups together everyone else into a joint agent, which – by adding some additional detail[57] – coincides with the State. Or take again the earlier example about a company C from State A which sets up a subsidiary S-C in State B. The rights of those wronged by the exploitative activity of S-C collect together C, A, B and S-C into an extended joint actor who is responsible for the violation.

55 The question concerning the enforcement of the obligation needs to be dealt separately. However, as submitted in an earlier subsection (this chapter) it bears no relation to the grounding of the obligation.

56 Considering that attributing responsibility to sub-personal segments (say: half a person; or 'my right arm and left leg' and so on – absurd examples abound!) would prove rather hard.

57 These details refer to particular rules and practices of institutional organisation, which may have delegated the governance of the society to particular agents and offices. However, notice that even in the absence of such formalised institutional organisation, the joint agent would not change in its composition: it would include exactly the same individuals as it does in the case of a more formalised state.

In conclusion, the account presented herein is well-suited to deliver the conditions for shared responsibility: it shows how plural and diverse actors can be brought jointly under the same ground of responsibility. Notably, it does so by moving away from a preconceived notion of actors and demonstrating how individuals can be grouped together, under proto-legal relations, to form a wide array of joint actors that include States and non-State actors, such as corporations and individuals in their own right. As such the account presents an attractive alternative to the principle of monadic responsibility that seems to dominate the current picture of IL responsibility.

Crucially, such an alternative approach would need to spell out principles for apportioning responsibility between plural and diverse actors. While an exhaustive treatment of this aspect cannot be undertaken at present, some early hints might suffice at this juncture: the reconstruction of the *legal relation* in terms of a *proto-legal relation* has generated an understanding of joint subjects in IL which favours shared over monadic (independent) responsibility. This comprehensive understanding of joint subjects would further suggest principles of apportionment which – in line with the comprehensive understanding of subjects – would inflate responsibility along two dimensions: first, by distributing responsibility among everyone who is part of the joint subject, whatever that turned out to be; second, by allowing claim-holders to pursue a wide range of claims against all those involved in the joint subject of the breach. Two immediate consequences suggest themselves here: on the one hand, the *burden of proof* would rest in principle with the violator, not the victim; second, a scheme of *joint and several responsibility* would present itself as the appropriate candidate for apportioning responsibility. While a lot of detail needs to be filled in in order to work out such a comprehensive scheme of IL responsibility, this enterprise will not unfold at the level of principle but at the level of implementation. With that accomplished a lot of important ground has been gained.

8 The common interest in international law: implications for human rights

Koen De Feyter

Introduction

This chapter researches whether treaties aiming to protect global common interests may inspire the further development of human rights law.

An initial word of caution is in order. Public international law is only gradually moving towards the protection of global common interests. Historically, public international law is State-centric and consensual, while the protection of common interests ideally requires the cooperation of *all* States and other relevant actors. Current systems for the protection of global common interests are imperfect, and, when evaluated on their own merits, are only partially effective in achieving their objectives. Nevertheless, some aspects of these systems are of interest from a human rights perspective, particularly those dealing with the assignment, sharing and monitoring of responsibilities of various actors.

The concept of the global common interest is briefly discussed first. The use of the term in treaties and case-law is reviewed, and its implications are analysed. The term appears infrequently in international human rights law.

Most systems protecting global common interests take territorial sovereignty as their point of departure but require that sovereignty is exercised responsibly, ie that the exercise of sovereignty contributes to the protection of the global common interest. As capacities of States and conditions within States differ, States are granted a degree of policy space in the implementation of obligations. The international community has the dual role of providing implementation aid and of monitoring the responsible exercise of sovereignty.

Treaties protecting global common interests are based on a State duty to cooperate. They also require the cooperation of other actors, leading, for example, to the emergence of multi-stakeholder initiatives adopting hybrid instruments aiming at influencing the behaviour of a variety of actors.

Rule-making processes on global common interests, including multi-stakeholder initiatives, need to be scrutinised carefully, particularly in terms of the inclusiveness of the decision-making process. Each time, the possible implications of these various legal developments for the further elaboration of human rights law are discussed.

The global common interest in international law

International law offers no definition of the global common interest.[1] Common interest language is used in several treaties,[2] and in some international judgments, but no authoritative list of global common interests in international law exists. The terminology varies, but for the purposes of this research terms such as 'common concern',[3] 'common heritage of mankind',[4] 'crimes against humanity',[5] 'obligations of the international community',[6] '*erga omnes* obligations',[7] '*ius cogens* obligations'[8] have all been considered relevant.

1 This section of the paper makes use of W Benedek, K De Feyter, MC Kettemann, C Voigt (eds), *The Common Interest in International Law* (Intersentia 2014). The book was the outcome of a GLOTHRO-sponsored joint research project on the common interest in international law. For a collection of historical writings on the subject, see K De Feyter (ed), *Globalization and Common Responsibilities of States* (Ashgate 2013). I am indebted to Ashfaq Khalfan, Martin Scheinin and Kirsteen Shields for their criticism of an earlier version, which I may not have been able to refute completely in the final text.

2 Most notably in the second paragraph of the Preamble to the UN Charter (26 June 1945): '... that armed force shall not be used, save in the common interest'.

3 See Preamble UN Framework Convention on Climate Change: 'Acknowledging that change in the Earth's climate and its adverse effects are a common concern of humankind'; preamble UN Biodiversity Convention: 'Affirming that the conservation of biological diversity is a common concern of humankind.' Consider also ICJ, Case concerning the Gabcikovo-Nagymaros project (*Hungary v Slovakia*) ICJ Reports 1997, 7, para 140: 'Throughout the ages, mankind has, for economic and other reasons, constantly interfered with nature. In the past, this was often done without consideration of the effects upon the environment. Owing to new scientific insights and to a growing awareness of the risks for mankind – for present and future generations – of pursuit of such interventions at an unconsidered and unabated pace, new norms and standards have been developed, set forth in a great number of instruments during the last two decades. Such new norms have to be taken into consideration, and such new standards given proper weight, not only when States contemplate new activities but also when continuing with activities begun in the past. This need to reconcile economic development with protection of the environment is aptly expressed in the concept of sustainable development', and ICJ, Pulp Mills judgment, para 204.

4 See Article 136 of the UN Convention on the Law of the Sea: 'The Area and its resources are the common heritage of mankind' in Article 136 of the UN Convention on the Law of the Sea; Article 4(1) of the Moon Agreement: 'The exploration and use of the moon shall be the province of all mankind and shall be carried out for the benefit and in the interest of all countries, irrespective of their degree of economic or scientific development.'

5 See preamble to the ICC Statute: 'Determined to these ends and for the sake of present and future generations, to establish an independent permanent International Criminal Court ... with jurisdiction over the most serious crimes of concern to the international community as a whole.'

6 See Article 6(1) of the UNESCO Convention concerning the Protection of World Cultural and Natural Heritage: 'Such heritage constitutes a world heritage for whose protection it is the duty of the international community as a whole to cooperate'; Paragraph 2 of the UN Millennium Declaration: 'We recognize that, in addition to our separate responsibilities to our individual societies, we have a collective responsibility to uphold the principles of human dignity, equality and equity at the global level.'

7 See Article 48(1) of the Articles on State Responsibility: 'Any State other than the injured State is entitled to invoke the responsibility of another State if ... the obligation breached is owed to the international community as a whole.'

8 Article 53 of the Vienna Convention Law of Treaties: 'A peremptory norm of general international law is a norm accepted and recognised by the international community of States as a whole.'

Global common interests are recognised in the two main substantive fields of international law: the law of international peace and security (encompassing for our purposes international humanitarian law, international criminal law, and universal jurisdiction) and the law of sustainable development (with economic growth, environmental protection and social justice as its pillars).

When defining the common interest in abstract terms, a first option is to ground the common interest in common values.[9] In this approach, international law is perceived of as a legal system underpinned by strong moral values. Such common values are the basis for the identification of the common interest that is protected in international law through cooperation and collective commitment, and the frustration of which is considered to be an issue that affects the community as a whole. A second option is to take the measure of support that an interest enjoys within the international community as a criterion: common interests are those that are backed by a communal legal spirit – the *opinio juris communis.*[10] A third option is to designate interests as common when they can only be safeguarded through common action.[11]

In any case, interests are identified as global common interests on an ad hoc basis. So far, the terminology has not been used in order to deal with issues such as hunger or free migration – for reasons discussed in the final section of this chapter. The list of global common interests is thus in a (possibly perennial) state of fluctuation.

Treaties dealing with spatial areas beyond national jurisdiction disallow State appropriation and establish an international system of regulation – that may or may not include a global governance institution. Most international treaties aiming to protect a global common interest, however, take the territorial sovereignty of State parties as their point of departure. Human rights treaties are also anchored in State sovereignty, and therefore the latter 'type' of common interest treaty is of particular interest for our purposes.

Global common interest treaties based on territorial sovereignty require from the State in territorial control that it exercises sovereignty responsibly: the State needs to preserve the global common interest through the exercise of sovereignty. The territorially responsible State acts as the custodian of the global common interest. Hence, the territorially responsible State is under

9 For some, common values are the foundation of the recognition of common interests in international law. According to this view, international law is based on certain normative elements that are constitutive of the international community, and that find expression in the notion of communality of interests. Compare A Kulick, *Global Public Interest in International Investment Law* (CUP 2012), 85–91.

10 Compare C Voigt, *Sustainable Development as a Principle of International Law* (Martinus Nijhoff Publishers 2009).

11 A variation that resonates with economists is to link common interests to global public goods that can only be provided through cooperation, as discussed in I Kaul, P Conceição, K Le Goulven and RU Mendoza, *Providing Global Public Goods* (OUP 2003) and in N Krisch, 'The Decay of Consent: International Law in the Age of Public Goods' (2014) 108 American Journal of International Law 1–40.

an obligation to report on the responsible exercise of sovereignty to all other State parties to the treaty.

Other States have a legal interest in ensuring that the territorially responsible State exercises its sovereignty in the global common interest. Issues defined as of global common interest do not fall within exclusive domestic jurisdiction. The actions that other States are entitled/required to undertake broadly fall within two complementary categories: assistance and review. Other States have a duty to support the territorially responsible State in its custodial role through the provision of financial and technical assistance when necessary, and are expected not to take unilateral measures that hamper the territorially responsible State in protecting the common interest. A wide variety of interventions may fall under the review category, ranging from the right to criticise, the right to monitor implementation (eg through a global body) to the right to take enforcement measures (including, in the UN Charter, the use of force) against the State failing in the responsible exercise of sovereignty.

Several treaties use the language of 'common heritage of mankind' or of 'common concern of humanity'. The use of these words indicates that the drafters wished to go beyond the realm of inter-State relations: global common interests are of interest to the international community as a whole including other actors than States. Global common interest treaties thus invariably recognise that the cooperation of other actors than States is required to fully protect the global common interest. Various avenues for participation of other actors than States are opened, although the treaties may fall short of establishing clear obligations or enforcement mechanisms. As the treaty approach inevitably remains State centric, multi-stakeholder initiatives may provide an interesting supplement or alternative.

In human rights law, references to human rights as common interest are few and far apart. The Universal Declaration of Human Rights is 'a common standard of achievement for all peoples and all nations, to the end that every individual and every organ of society shall strive'.[12] The Vienna Declaration of the World Conference on Human Rights confirmed that the promotion and protection of human rights 'is a legitimate concern of the international community'.[13] Benvenisti points out that the Universal Declaration does not allocate responsibilities, and that the duty bearers therefore collectively share the duty to attain the common standard.[14] The human rights treaty regime that was built on the basis of the Universal Declaration, however, strongly emphasises individual State responsibility based on jurisdiction, and contains far less detail on collective State responsibilities or on duties of other actors

12 See final paragraph of the Preamble to the Universal Declaration of Human Rights (10 December 1948). In Article 56 of the UN Charter all Member States pledge to take joint and separate action for the achievement of the UN's purposes including human rights.

13 Vienna Declaration and Programme of Action (25 June 1993), para 4.

14 E Benvenisti, 'Sovereigns as Trustees of Humanity: On the Accountability of States to Foreign Stakeholders' (2013) 107 American Journal of International Law 295–303, 307.

than States. It could be argued that the universal periodic review procedure at the UN Human Rights Council reflects the legal conviction of States that human rights are of common concern to all States,[15] given the applicability of the procedure to all States.

The Genocide Convention declares that international cooperation is required to liberate mankind from the scourge of genocide.[16] The International Court of Justice has found that in the Genocide Convention States 'do not have any interests of their own; they merely have one and all, a common interest, namely the accomplishment of those high purposes which are the raison d'être of the convention'.[17] In *Belgium v Senegal*[18] the International Court of Justice held that all States parties to the UN Convention against Torture 'have a common interest to ensure, in view of their shared values, that acts of torture are prevented and that, if they occur, their authors do not enjoy impunity'. All the other States parties had a common interest in compliance with these obligations by the State in whose territory the alleged offender is present; the obligations of the territorially responsible State were held *erga omnes partes.* The common interest in compliance implied the entitlement of each State party to the Convention to make a claim concerning the cessation of an alleged breach by another State party. Clearly, the concept of obligations owed to all treaty parties is much more limited in scope than the concept of obligations owed to humanity or mankind – but it may still prove useful, particularly when the relevant treaty is widely ratified.

What reasons may explain the scarcity of references to human rights as a global common interest? First, human rights violations take place locally, and may not have any impact outside of the territory where they take place. In a purely domestic situation, the objectives of a human rights treaty can be achieved fully when the territorially responsible State properly complies with its treaty obligations. In contrast, the emission of greenhouse gasses affects the global climate, and can only be addressed by the cumulative effort of emitting States to halt dangerous anthropogenic interference in the climate system. Even a State fully complying with the Kyoto Protoco, remains dependent on other States' performance in order to protect its own population from harm. Climate change by its nature affects everyone, while human rights violations injure only the victims. Human rights may be perceived of as an instrument that first and foremost protects the interests of specific individuals or

15 See UN General Assembly resolution 60/251 (15 March 2006), para 5(e).

16 See third preambular paragraph of the Genocide Convention (9 December 1948).

17 ICJ, Reservations to the Convention on the Prevention and Punishment of the Crime of Genocide (Advisory Opinion), ICJ Reports 1951, 15. The African Charter on Human and Peoples' Rights (27 June 1981) provides that 'the rights and freedoms of each individual shall be exercised with due regard to the rights of others, collective security, morality and common interest' (Article 27(2) but the provision most probably refers to domestic rather than global common interest).

18 ICJ, Questions relating to the Obligation to Prosecute or Extradite (*Belgium v Senegal*), (Merits), ICJ Reports 2012, 422, paras 68–69.

communities, rather than a global common interest.[19] In order to characterise human rights as a global common concern, other arguments have to be relied on: the notion that human rights represent shared global values (raising difficult issues of evidence) or are backed by an *opinio juris communis*. In this context, gravity and scale of violations matter. The distinction goes back all the way to the immediate post-Second World War period, when a binding treaty was adopted on genocide on 9 December 1948, and a non-binding declaration one day later listing individual human rights. It would seem that the distinction lingers on today: grave and systematic violations of human rights are arguably of global common concern, eg triggering (at least in theory) a responsibility to protect on the part of the international community when the domestic State fails to protect its population against genocide, war crimes, ethnic cleansing and crimes against humanity[20] – while the human rights treaty system remains highly dependent on compliance by the individual territorially responsible State when violations are considered incidental or less grave.

The UNESCO Convention concerning the Protection of World Cultural Heritage demonstrates that it is possible to characterise an issue as of a global common concern even in circumstances when there is no extraterritorial impact, and the issue may be resolved by the effort of the individual State. The UNESCO Convention applies to cultural and natural heritage sites within the territory of the State parties. When damage occurs to these sites, there may be no impact outside of the source country. Nevertheless, the UNESCO Convention establishes a *duty of cooperation* for the international community, and does so in more certain terms than those used in human rights treaties:[21]

> Whilst fully respecting the sovereignty of the States on whose territory the cultural and natural heritage mentioned in Articles 1 and 2 is situated, and without prejudice to property right provided by national legislation, the States Parties to this Convention recognize that such heritage constitutes a world heritage for whose protection it is the duty of the international community as a whole to co-operate.[22]

19 Human rights law arguably recognises – through the inclusion of limitation clauses – that there may be a tension between individual rights and certain (domestic) public concerns.

20 See UN General Assembly resolution 60/1 (24 October 2005), paras 138–139.

21 Compare Article 28 of the Universal Declaration of Human Rights (10 December 1948), and Articles 2 and 23 of the International Covenant on Economic, Social and Cultural Rights (16 December 1966). In Article 23, the States Parties to the Covenant agree that international action for the achievement of the rights recognised in the Covenant 'includes such methods as the conclusion of conventions, the adoption of recommendations, the furnishing of technical assistance and the holding of regional meetings and technical meetings'.

22 Article 6(1) of the UNESCO Convention concerning the Protection of World Cultural and Natural Heritage (16 November 1972).

The preamble to the UNESCO Convention explains that the safeguarding of the sites and monuments is of importance to all peoples of the world, particularly, when they are of outstanding universal value from an historical, aesthetic, ethnological or anthropological point of view.

Responsible sovereignty and the incapacity/implementation aid nexus

When the protection of the global common interest is entrusted to the territorially responsible State, the capacity of that State to ensure protection becomes of global concern. The financial, technological and other capacities of States differ. A feature shared by most common interest regimes is that they include an element of differentiation among the States that are parties to the regime (as an exception to the traditional starting point in international law of sovereign equality). Lesser obligations for the State exercising territorial sovereignty are compensated by duties to provide assistance for States with stronger capacities. Common interest regimes thus imply an element of solidarity.

Differentiation requires an identification of both the States that are entitled to benefit from solidarity and of those expected to contribute to solidarity. This may be achieved through a categorisation of countries. In international treaties based on common but differentiated responsibility the main dichotomy is between developing and developed countries. Since there is no general definition of these two categories in international law, instruments and organisations define the terms in the light of their specific objectives on the basis of criteria laid down in the treaty or in the rules of the organisation. It may also be left to each State to self-identify as a member of a category. As an alternative to categorisation, ad hoc lists of States for the purposes of attribution of different obligations may be drawn up.

Apart from capacity, other factors play a role in justifying differentiation. These include: historical responsibility (past injury should be redressed through additional current effort); harm caused (countries currently contributing more to injury should contribute more to reparation); and sustainable development needs (efforts required under treaty commitments should not disable countries from satisfying the sustainable development needs of their population). By way of example, Article 3 of the UN Framework Convention on Climate Change (9 May 1992) listing the principles at the heart of the treaty, refers to a mix of factors to construe a heavier responsibility for developed States. According to the provision, developed States should take the lead in combating climate change, given: their differentiated responsibility and capacity (para 1); that full consideration is required of the special needs and special circumstances of developing country parties, and of those parties that would have to bear a disproportionate or abnormal burden under the Convention (para 2); and because change measures should be appropriate for the specific conditions of each party and should be integrated with national development programs, 'taking into account that economic development is essential for adopting measures to address climate change' (para 4).

For States with limited capacities, differentiation may be organised in various ways. Treaties may contain uniform obligations for all States, but:

- may allow States with limited capacities a grace period in the fulfilment of uniform obligations;[23]
- may make the fulfilment of obligations by these States conditional on the prior fulfilment of obligations of assistance by other States. Conditional obligations of developing countries exert pressure on developed States to honour their own commitment to provide implementation aid if they wish developing States to comply;[24]
- may allow for contextualisation of obligations.

The most 'radical' form of differentiation consists of the inclusion of non-uniform obligations within a single treaty regime. The inclusion of core substantive obligations that are binding for some State parties, but voluntary or non-existent for States with limited capacities, amounts to the establishment of sub-regimes within the same treaty.

While categorisation as a group may remain useful for some time to come for least developed countries, for other countries contextual obligations as

23 For example, Article 5(1) of the Montreal Protocol on Substances that deplete the Ozone Layer (16 September 1987, as amended).

24 For example, The Convention on Biological Diversity (5 June 1992) requires that developed States provide access both to (bio-)technology to developing countries under fair and most favourable terms, including on concessional and preferential terms (Article 16(2)), and obliges them to provide new and additional financial resources to enable developing country Parties to meet the agreed full incremental costs to them of implementing measures which fulfil the obligations of the Convention (Article 20(2)). A Financial Mechanism (Article 21) is set up that manages the flow of financial resources, on the basis of an agreed indicative list of the incremental costs and a burden-sharing agreement among the contributing parties. Pressure on developed States to honour their duties to provide assistance is exerted through the inclusion of Article 20(4):

> The extent to which developing country Parties will effectively implement their commitments under this Convention will depend on the effective implementation by developed country Parties of their commitments under this Convention related to financial resources and transfer of technology and will take fully into account the fact that economic and social development and eradication of poverty are the first and overriding priorities of the developing country Parties.

Conditional obligations raise intricate problems. It is not straightforward to determine when developed countries have satisfied their obligations of financial and technological assistance: the concept of 'full incremental costs' is open to debate, as is the assessment of the sufficiency of technology transfer. Given this difficulty, there is a risk that developing countries postpone fulfilment of their domestic obligations under the Convention indefinitely. The use by developing countries of the financial and technological transfers provided through the Convention mechanism may also be contested if domestic management of environmental protection shows no improvement.

part of a collective system for the protection of global common interests offer more promise. Given the diversity of countries across the world, systems aimed at protecting global common interests provide domestic policy space for countries when it comes to implementation. Contextual obligations are uniform obligations applying to all State parties, but they include a reference to certain characteristics that will (legitimately) affect domestic implementation. These varying characteristics – which may or may not be explicitly listed in the treaty[25] – lead to different expectations of implementation.

Grace periods, conditional obligations and non-uniform obligations are absent from current human rights law. Human rights treaties differ from treaties providing for common but differentiated responsibility in that they do not only provide for intra-State obligations, but also endow individuals and groups with rights.[26] These rights are deemed to reflect the dignity and worth of 'each member of the human family',[27] regardless of where the person is located. If everyone is inherently entitled to rights protection, it is difficult to see how postponement or non-existence of entitlement of rights holders can be justified.

Article 2(1) of the International Covenant on Economic, Social and Cultural Rights[28] provides a contextual obligation applicable to all State parties to progressively realise economic, social and cultural rights to the maximum of their available resources. The availability of resources (even when supplemented by international assistance and cooperation) differs from country to country, and therefore the expectation of the actual level of realisation of these rights at a given point in time also differs. According to the UN Committee on Economic, Social and Cultural Rights, the reference to progressive realisation is 'a necessary flexibility device, reflecting the realities of the real word and the difficulties involved for any country in ensuring full realization of economic, social and cultural rights'.[29] It is noteworthy that availability of resources is the only characteristic of context explicitly taken into account. The Vienna Declaration, while reaffirming uniform human rights obligations for all States, refers more broadly to the need to bear in

25 On contextual obligations, see DB Magraw, 'Legal Treatment of Developing Countries: Differential, Contextual and Absolute Norms' (1990) 1 Columbia Journal of International Environmental Law and Policy 69–99.

26 Compare Human Rights Committee, General Comment No 24: Reservations to the ICCPR, 2 November 1994, CCPR/C/21/Rev.1/Add.6 (1994), para 17.

27 Preamble to the Universal Declaration of Human Rights (10 December 1948).

28 Article 2(1) of the International Covenant on Economic, Social and Cultural Rights, 16 December 1966, reads: 'Each State Party to the present Covenant undertakes to take steps, individually and through international assistance and co-operation, especially economic and technical, to the maximum of its available resources, with a view to achieving progressively the full realization of the rights recognized in the present Covenant by all appropriate means, including particularly the adoption of legislative measures. The Covenant lacks a mechanism that ensures international assistance and co-operation for the realization of the treaty's objectives.'

29 UN Committee on Economic, Social and Cultural Rights, General Comment No 3: The Nature of States Parties Obligations, UN doc E/1991/23, para 9.

mind national and regional particularities and various historical, cultural and religious backgrounds.[30]

The UNESCO Convention concerning the Protection of the World Cultural and Natural Heritage provides another example of a regime based on contextual obligations[31] that allows broader flexibility than the Covenant, but also provides a solidarity mechanism (see below), which the Covenant does not. According to the Convention, each State party is required to invest the utmost of its resources in measures for the protection of cultural and natural heritage that are appropriate for the country. Again, all States are bound by this obligation, but a wide margin of discretion is left to each State as to the manner of implementation.

Importantly, contextual obligations allow navigating between the global and the local. They imply a joint commitment to the protection of a common interest, while at the same time providing appropriate policy space on how to take up responsibility at the domestic level. In the area of human rights, existing human rights treaties provide uniform norms, while what constitutes appropriate use of policy space can potentially be determined on the basis of how rights can be made practical and effective[32] in the circumstances prevailing in the relevant country (see below, in the final section).

International human rights monitoring bodies, however, tend to interpret contextual characteristics – in practice, primarily: availability of resources – restrictively, out of concern that giving weight to context will render the protection of rights illusory rather than effective. The view adopted by the UN Human Rights Committee in *Mukong v Cameroon* is exemplary. The case dealt *inter alia* with inhumane detention conditions. Clearly, providing proper detention conditions requires priority investment of resources by the State. According to the Human Rights Committee:

> As to the conditions of detention in general, the Committee observes that certain minimum standards regarding the conditions of detention must be observed regardless of a State party's level of development. These include ... minimum floor space and cubic content of air for each prisoner,

30 Vienna Declaration and Programme of Action (25 June 1993), para 1. Onuma argues that 'for human rights to be accepted by people all over the world and become truly universal, it must overcome its peculiarities stemming from its [Western] historicity'. See On Yasuaki, *A Transcivilizational Perspective on International Law* (Martinus Nijhoff 2010), 387.

31 UNESCO Convention concerning the Protection of the World Cultural and Natural Heritage (21 November 1972). Article 4 requires (in part) that each State Party 'will do all it can' to protect cultural and natural heritage, 'to the utmost of its own resources and, where appropriate, with any international assistance and co-operation, in particular, financial, artistic, scientific and technical, which it may be able to obtain'. Article 5 requires that each State party 'shall endeavour, in so far as possible, and as appropriate for each country' a range of measures.

32 Paraphrasing the European Court of Human Rights, see *Artico v Italy*, App no 6694/74 (ECtHR, 13 May 1980), para 33. See also K De Feyter, 'Sites of Rights Resistance', in K De Feyter, S Parmentier, C Timmerman and G Ulrich (eds), *The Local Relevance of Human Rights* (CUP 2011), 11–39.

> adequate sanitary facilities, clothing which shall be in no manner degrading or humiliating, provision of a separate bed and provision of food of nutritional value adequate for health and strength. It should be noted that these are minimum requirements which the Committee considers should always be observed, even if economic or budgetary considerations may make compliance with these obligations difficult.[33]

The UN Committee on Economic, Social and Cultural Rights has been reluctant to make broad use of the explicit reference in Article 2 of the Covenant to availability of resources. In its General Comment on Article 2, the Committee took the position that a minimum core obligation to ensure the satisfaction of, at the very least, minimum essential levels of each of the rights is incumbent upon every State party.[34] According to the Committee, a State party in which any significant number of individuals is deprived of essential foodstuffs, of essential primary health care, of basic shelter and housing, or of the most basic forms of education is *prima facie* failing to discharge its obligations under the Covenant. In order for a State party to be able to attribute its failure to meet at least its minimum core obligations to a lack of available resources, the Committee held, it must demonstrate that every effort has been made to use all resources that are at its disposition in an effort to satisfy, as a matter of priority, those minimum obligations. Even where the available resources are 'demonstrably inadequate', the obligation remains for a State party to strive to ensure the widest possible enjoyment of the relevant rights under the prevailing circumstances.[35] In a Statement adopted as a contribution to the drafting process of the Optional Protocol to the ICESCR, the Committee points out that availability of resources does not impact on the immediacy of the obligation, and that resource constraints alone cannot justify inaction.[36] As regards the core obligations under the Covenant, the Committee reaffirmed that 'in order for a State party to be able to attribute its failure to meet its core obligations to a lack of available resources, it must demonstrate that every effort has been made to use all resources that are at its disposal in an effort to satisfy, as a matter of priority, those core obligations'.[37]

In its General Comment on the Right to Health, the Committee goes further, in particular in the section dealing with 'Violations'. After once again stressing that in a situation where resource constraints render full compliance impossible, the burden of proof is on the State to justify that every effort has

33 UN Human Rights Committee, *Mukong v Cameroon*, CCPR/C/51/D/458/1991 (10 August 1994), para 9.3.

34 UN Committee on Economic, Social and Cultural Rights, General Comment No 3, E/1991/23, para 9.

35 Ibid, para 10.

36 UN Committee on Economic, Social and Cultural Rights, Statement on an Evaluation of the Obligation to take Steps to the 'Maximum of Available Resources' under an Optional Protocol to the Covenant, E/C.12/2007/1 (14 December 1990), para 4.

37 Ibid, para 6.

been made to use all available resources at its disposal as a matter of priority, the Committee adds:

> It should be stressed, however, that a State party cannot, under any circumstances whatsoever, justify its non-compliance with the core obligations set out in paragraph 43 above, which are non-derogable.[38]

In sum, the Committee interprets the *inadequate resources defence* under the Covenant stringently with a view to protecting particularly the rights of the most vulnerable.[39] The defence is rendered unavailable when the core content of the right to health is at stake. More than a decade ago Chapman and Russell commented that such an approach was 'somewhat abstract':

> States are assumed to have access to the resources needed to meet their minimum obligations, but in fact they may not; and wealthier States frequently disregard their international obligations.[40]

Since all individuals are equally entitled to rights, the territorially responsible State (even if it is least developed), rather than the complainant, is required to demonstrate that a violation of minimum core obligations is due to the unavailability of prioritised resources. No guidance is offered by the Committee on how a State should demonstrate such incapacity. No significant practice of exchanges between the monitoring body and resource scarce countries on whether the resource defence applies in a particular situation appears to have developed. No reality check is engaged in, and it is uncertain whether the Committee is equipped to engage in such an empirical enquiry. As a result, the presumption prevails that even the least developed countries have sufficient capacity to realise minimum essential levels of rights realisation.

As domestic capacity is presumed, the provision of implementation aid by other States becomes less urgent. In contrast to global common interest treaties based on common but differentiated responsibility, the Covenant does not include a *system* to enforce the provision of implementation aid. There

38 UN Committee on Economic, Social and Cultural Rights, General Comment No 14, E/C.12/2000/4, para 47. In the General Comment on the right to food, the Committee states that 'violations of the Covenant occur when a State fails to ensure the satisfaction of, at the very least, the minimum essential level required to be free from hunger; … A State claiming that it is unable to carry out its obligation for reasons beyond its control therefore has the burden of proving that this is the case and that it has unsuccessfully sought to obtain international support to ensure the availability and accessibility of the necessary food'. See UN Committee on Economic, Social and Cultural Rights, General Comment No 12, E/C.12/1995/5, para 17.

39 The Committee held that even in times of severe resources constraints whether caused by a process of adjustment, of economic recession, or by other factors the vulnerable members of society 'can and indeed must be protected by the adoption of relatively low-cost targeted programmes'.

40 A Chapman and S Russell, 'Introduction', in A Chapman and S Russell, *Core Obligations: Building a Framework for Economic, Social and Cultural Rights* (Intersentia 2002), 11.

is no doubt that the reference to 'maximum available resources' includes resources available from the international community through international cooperation and assistance.[41] International cooperation for the realisation of economic, social and cultural rights is an obligation of all States, and particularly of 'States which are in a position to assist others in this regard'.[42] It is recognised that in the absence of an active programme of international assistance and cooperation the full realisation of economic, social and cultural rights will remain an unfulfilled aspiration in many countries.[43] But, again, the approach is an abstract one: increasingly detailed international obligations and recommendations to Third States and other actors to contribute to the realisation of human rights are formulated,[44] but no obligations of financial assistance or of other transfers are established, nor is a system of enforcement provided for. States are entitled to receive resources offered by the international community,[45] but there is no mechanism that backs up the entitlement or that ensures that the offer is forthcoming.

There is increasing evidence that a number of countries do not have access to the available domestic and international resources to realise their core obligations. Most health practitioners with experience in developing countries agree that the attainment of the minimum essential level of the right to health is a distant dream, even if domestic levels of government expenditure would increase to the maximum of what can be reasonably be spent on health.[46] A similar finding founds the proposal for the establishment of a global fund for social protection by Olivier De Schutter and Magdalena Sepulveda. In a paper,[47] the two then Special Rapporteurs of the UN Human Rights Council recognise that '(a)lthough the costs of providing basic social protection may be affordable when estimated globally, *for many countries the domestic costs still may be beyond their capacity, even if they were to devote their maximum available resources to that objective*'[48] (emphasis added). What is needed, according to the authors, is 'a mechanism guaranteeing the support of the international community for

41 UN Committee on Economic, Social and Cultural Rights, General Comment No 3, E/1991/23, para 13.

42 Ibid, para 14. 'States in a position to assist' are not further defined.

43 Ibid, para 14.

44 Compare UN Committee on Economic, Social and Cultural Rights, General Comment No 14, E/C.12/2000/4, paras 38–42, 45.

45 UN Committee on Economic, Social and Cultural Rights, Statement on an Evaluation of the Obligation to take Steps to the 'Maximum of Available Resources' under an Optional Protocol to the Covenant, E/C.12/2007/1 (14 December 1990), para 5.

46 For an empirical study on the issue, see G Ooms and R Hammonds, 'Correcting Globalisation in Health: Transnational Entitlements versus the Ethical Imperative of Reducing Aid-Dependency' (2008) Public Health Ethics 154–170.

47 O De Schutter and M Sepúlveda, 'Underwriting the Poor. A Global Fund for Social Protection' (October 2012), available at *http://www.srfood.org/images/stories/pdf/otherdocuments/20121009_gfsp_en.pdf* (accessed 5 February 2015).

48 Ibid, 10.

commitments to provide basic social safety nets if the costs exceed the capacities of individual States' budgets both today and tomorrow'.[49]

So the question is whether it is wise and legally sound[50] to find a violation by a resource scarce country while domestic resources are demonstrably inadequate to realise core obligations, and the entitlement to international assistance is not enforceable? Does such an approach not contribute to the reduction of human rights to 'unfulfilled aspirations'? Should human rights law require the impossible in order to drive policies gradually in the right direction?

Global common interest treaties may provide some inspiration. In such treaties, differentiated responsibility *for the least developed countries* is not controversial. While there is no general definition of 'developing country' in international law, there is a clear definition of 'least developed country' that is widely used.[51] The uniform obligation to devote the maximum of available

49 Ibid, 11.

50 In honor of the old maxim *Ad impossibile nemo tenetur*. Impossibility of performance is discussed in Article 61 of the Vienna Convention on the Law of Treaties (23 May 1969), that envisages suspension of a treaty in case of temporary impossibility of performance. Suspension would not be an appropriate response to inadequacy of resources, as even in those circumstances the obligation remains for a State party to strive to ensure the widest possible enjoyment of the relevant rights. But clearly the impossibility of performance doctrine is well established in contractual law, and may, given certain conditions, lead to a finding that an obligation should not be performed.

51 Within the United Nations, the Committee for Development Policy (CDP), an ECOSOC subsidiary body, is responsible for reviewing the status of least developed countries. The CDP defines least developed countries (LDCs) as low-income countries suffering from the most severe structural impediments to sustainable development. Three criteria are currently taken into account: per capita gross national income (GNI), human assets and economic vulnerability to external shocks; the latter two criteria are measured through indices. To be added to the category, a country must score below a given threshold level for all three selected criteria and have a population no larger than 75 million inhabitants. CDP undertakes a review of the list (currently consisting of 49 countries – South Sudan is the most recent addition) every three years, on the basis of which it advises the ECOSOC regarding countries which should be added to or graduated from the list.

The UN definition of least developed countries is used within the entire UN system [including by UNCTAD – which produces an annual Least Developed Countries Report – and by the UN High Representative for the Least Developed Countries, Landlocked Developing Countries and the Small Island Developing States (UN-OHRLLS)], and equally by other international organisations, such as the World Trade Organization, the OECD or the EU, and in numerous international treaties.

Least developed countries are typically accorded more generous differential treatment, including preferences and exemptions from treaty obligations not granted to other developing countries. Examples include: Article 66 of the WTO TRIPS (Agreement on Trade-Related Aspects of Intellectual Property Rights) (15 April 1994) provides a grace period for implementation of numerous TRIPS provisions to least developing countries; Article 32(1) of the International Tropical Timber Agreement (27 January 2006) that enables least developed countries to apply for special measures to the convention's governing body; the EU's 'Everything But Arms' (EBA) arrangement gives all LDCs full duty-free and quota-free access to the EU for all their exports with the exception of arms and armaments. The arrangement was created in 2001, see Council Regulation (EC) No 416/2001 (28 February 2001).

resources to the realisation of human rights should remain also for the least developed countries, but the presumption that the commitment of the maximum available resources will suffice to realise core obligations should be abandoned. Rather than focusing on the establishment of a violation in cases where resources are demonstrably inadequate, a finding of non-compliance with core obligations would be more appropriate. Least developed countries could also volunteer that they are unable to comply due to inadequacy of resources. A finding of non-compliance by the monitoring body would be non-confrontational and trigger the duty of cooperation of all other treaty parties to jointly agree the technical and financial assistance that is required to redress the situation. If human rights were truly to be considered as a global common interest, situations of non-compliance due to demonstrable inadequacy of resources in the relevant least developed country should be systematically addressed through the provision of implementation aid.[52]

Third States: assistance and review

In global common interest regimes, Third States have the duty to provide implementation aid to States that lack the capacity to sufficiently safeguard the global common interest on their territory. Third States also have a right of review over how the territorially responsible State exercises sovereignty for the protection of the global common interest. Implementation aid may be financial in nature, or consist of transfer of technology or knowledge, or aim at capacity-building.

As a minimum, Third States are required to take into account the interests of States with lesser capacities when they take unilateral measures that have an impact on those States. In the United States – Import Prohibition of Certain Shrimp and Shrimp Products (*US Shrimp-Turtle* case)[53] the WTO Appellate Body held that a US import prohibition of shrimp and shrimp products from non-certified countries constituted unjustified discrimination, because it did not take 'into consideration different conditions which may occur in the territories of those other Members'.[54]

Article XXXVII:3 of GATT 1947 requires developed countries to 'have special regard to the trade interests of developing contracting parties when considering the application of other measures permitted under this Agreement to meet particular problems …'. Article 15 of the WTO Anti-Dumping Agreement provides that developed countries give consideration to

52 See the following section for examples of such an approach in global common interest treaties.

53 Appellate Body Report, United States – Import Prohibition of Certain Shrimp and Shrimp Products, WT/DS58/AB/R (6 November 1998), DSR 1998:VII, 2755.

54 Ibid, para 164. See also Panel Report, United States – Import Prohibition of Certain Shrimp and Shrimp Products. Recourse to article 21.5 by Malaysia, WT/DS58/RW (15 June 2001), para 5.46: 'We believe that another reason for the Appellate Body finding is that the United States, by unilaterally defining and implementing criteria for applying Section 609, failed to take into account the different situations which may exist in the exporting countries'.

the special situation of developing countries before applying anti-dumping measures. Constructive remedies should be explored first when the essential interests of developing countries are at stake.[55] In WTO dispute settlement, such rules have been interpreted as not requiring that developed countries undertake a specific action or ensure a given outcome. What needs to be shown is only that other remedies than anti-dumping measures were explored.[56] It has been suggested that WTO requirements on developed members to take into consideration the needs of developing members should be construed as obligations of due diligence on their part.[57]

In the *Bosnia Genocide* case, the International Court of Justice held – all be it in a very different area of international law – that what is required under a 'due diligence' standard depends on an assessment *in concreto*.[58] According to the Court, various parameters operate when assessing whether a State has duly discharged its due diligence obligation. This includes the capacity to influence the actions of others, which 'varies greatly from one State to another', and depends on geographical proximity and the strength of political and other links between the authorities of the relevant States. The capacity to influence may be affected by the limits permitted by international law.[59]

Building on these examples, the due diligence required from Third States when they take unilateral measures impacting on global common interests could be construed as including:

- a duty to avoid measures that adversely affect the capacity of the territorially responsible State to protect the common interest;
- and a duty to influence (within the limits permitted by international law) the State exercising jurisdiction, so that it uses its sovereignty responsibly, ie for the protection of the global common interest.

55 Article 15 of the Agreement on Implementation of Article VI GATT (15 March 1994), reads: 'It is recognized that special regard must be given by developed country Members to the special situation of developing country Members when considering the application of anti-dumping measures under this Agreement. Possibilities of constructive remedies provided for by this Agreement shall be explored before applying anti-dumping duties where they would affect the essential interests of developing country Members.'

56 For a review, see A Alavi, *Legalization of Development in the WTO* (Kluwer Law International 2009), 163–166. Muchlinski notes that in the area of protection of foreign investment, arbitral tribunals rarely take into account the level of development of the host country in determining the investor's legitimate expectations as to treatment. See P Muchlinski, 'Holistic Approaches to Development and International Investment Law: The Role of International Investment Agreements', in J Faundez and C Tan (eds), *International Economic Law, Globalization and Developing Countries* (Edward Elgar 2010), 185. For a plea in favour of the inclusion of contextualised obligations in international investment law, see E Alexander, 'Taking Account of Reality: Adopting Contextual Standards for Developing Countries in International Investment Law' (2008) 48 Virginia Journal of International Law 815-839.

57 SE Rolland, *Development at the WTO* (OUP 2012), 122; note also 166–169.

58 ICJ, *Application of the Convention on the Prevention and Punishment of the Crime of Genocide* (*Bosnia-Herzegovina v Serbia and Montenegro*), Judgment (26 February 2007), para 430.

59 Article 1 of the Genocide Convention (9 December 1948) explicitly provides a duty for all States to prevent genocide – hence the due diligence obligation to use influence.

On the other hand, within global common interest regimes there is a bias against unilateralism, and in favour of cooperation. These regimes offer little on extraterritorial State obligations beyond what was mentioned immediately above. The preferred option is that measures are agreed between relevant States, and that such measures reflect the varying capacities of States. The UN Convention on the Law of the Sea thus encourages cooperation between States with regard to the conservation and management of living resources on the high seas: in *jointly determining* the allowable catch and other conservation measures, measures should be agreed to produce a sustainable yield, while taking into account *inter alia* 'the special requirements of developing States'.[60] In United States – Import Prohibition of Certain Shrimp and Shrimp Products (*US Shrimp-Turtle* case) the WTO Appellate Body held that the United States should have engaged in 'serious, across-the-board negotiations with the objective of concluding bilateral or multilateral agreements for the protection and conservation of sea turtles', before enforcing the import prohibition against the shrimp exports of those other Members.[61] Principle 12 of the Rio Declaration on Environment and Development (14 June 1992) states (in part):

> ... Unilateral actions to deal with environmental challenges outside the jurisdiction of the importing country should be avoided. Environmental measures addressing transboundary or global environmental problems should, as far as possible, be based on an international consensus.

The emphasis on cooperation in global common interest treaties results in the inclusion of systems that organise implementation aid to States in need of assistance. Such systems may consist of the establishment of a collective mechanism such as a Fund (to which all or some States are obliged to contribute), or of obligations to bilaterally support capacity-building in countries in need of assistance.

The UNESCO World Heritage Convention sets up a collective body, the World Heritage Committee, to which requests for assistance can be addressed, particularly by States that lack the resources to safeguard threatened property by their own means.[62] The Convention creates a Fund to support the Committee's activities, to which all State parties are required to contribute – although a reservation to the relevant provision is permissible. Article 10 of the Montreal Protocol on Substances that Deplete the Ozone Layer (16 September 1987; Article 10 was included in the 1990 Amendments) creates a Financial Mechanism that provides financial and technical coopera-

60 UN Convention on the Law of the Sea (10 December 1982), Article 119(1a). See also for a similar approach: Articles 61–62 of the Convention.

61 Appellate Body Report, United States – Import Prohibition of Certain Shrimp and Shrimp Products, WT/DS58/AB/R (6 November 1998), DSR 1998:VII, 2755, para 166.

62 Article 13(4) of the UNESCO Convention concerning the Protection of World Cultural and Natural Heritage (16 November 1972).

tion including the transfer of technologies to developing countries [63] with a low level of consumption of the substances controlled by the Protocol. The Financial Mechanism strives to meet all agreed incremental costs developing countries face in order to comply with the control measures of the Protocol. A multilateral fund supports the mechanism. The fund is financed by contributions from developed countries.[64] The level of contribution required is calculated on the basis of the United Nations scale of assessments. The creation of the Financial Mechanism was crucial to attracting the participation of developing countries in the Protocol.[65] In 2009, the Montreal Protocol achieved universal ratification.

The UN Convention to Combat Desertification (17 June 1994) provides obligations of developed countries to directly assist country parties affected by desertification.[66] Developed country parties undertake to provide assistance to affected countries in order to enable these countries to develop and implement their own long-term plans and strategies to combat desertification and mitigate the effects of drought. The Convention also includes a section (Article 5) obliging affected countries to allocate adequate resources to combat desertification in accordance with their circumstances and capabilities.[67] Assistance to build domestic capacity to design and engage in action for the protection of global common interests makes eminent sense in the context of an approach based on contextual obligations.

A global common interest approach to human rights would not replace, but complement, existing human rights treaties that focus on unilateral obligations of States *vis-à-vis* individuals and groups with inter-State obligations to cooperate for the realisation of human rights. Inter-State obligations belong to the realm of classic public international law, and also reflect the principle of mutuality that grounds international cooperation for development. The principle of mutuality suggests that development objectives – in this instance, human rights – need to be realised through agreements between partner countries based on mutual commitments. Parties make such commitments voluntarily to each other, but once they are undertaken, they become binding. Mutual accountability is one of the five core pillars in the OECD Paris Declaration on Aid Effectiveness.[68] The concept was included in the Paris Declaration in order to signal a move away from the traditional one-way

63 Article 5 of the Montreal Protocol on Substances that Deplete the Ozone Layer (16 September 1987, as amended), entitled 'Special Situation of Developing Countries'.

64 That is, non-Article 5 parties.

65 P Sands and J Peel, *Principles of International Environmental Law* (CUP 2012), 272.

66 UN Convention to Combat Desertification (17 June 1994), Article 6. See also Article 20 on financial resources.

67 In addition, the Conference of the Parties in 1988 established a Global Mechanism as a body of the UN Convention to Combat Desertification specifically mandated to support developing countries to increase investments into sustainable land management to help reverse, control and prevent land degradation and desertification.

68 OECD Paris Declaration on Aid Effectiveness (2 March 2005), available at *http://www.oecd.org/development/effectiveness/34428351.pdf* (accessed 6 February 2015).

donor to recipient accountability towards a contractual approach, where each party is understood to have obligations, and where mutual progress is jointly assessed. This joint assessment needs to take place within an institutional set-up, such as a compliance committee (see below).

Mutual accountability also has a broader significance, as:

> a process through which commitment to, and ownership of, shared agendas is created and reinforced by: building trust and understanding; shifting incentives towards results in achievement of shared objectives; embedding common values; deepening responsibilities and strengthening partnership; and openness to external scrutiny for assessing results in relation to goals.[69]

When applied to human rights, the principle suggests that bi- or multilateral solutions based on international cooperation and consensus are the most effective way to tackle a problem of a global nature. As Rumu Sarkar puts it: '… both developed and developing nations should bargain with each other in good faith, and facilitate, where practicable, the development of other nations. More importantly, the act of cooperating with each other is more than joint or simultaneous action; it is the unity of action to a common end or a common result.'[70]

In international environmental law, the monitoring of inter-State obligations is entrusted to compliance committees. Compliance committees are cooperative rather than adversarial in nature. They have been characterised[71] as institutions which:

- aim to avoid complexity;
- are non-confrontational;
- are transparent;
- leave the competence for the taking of decisions to be determined by the contracting parties;
- leave the contracting parties to each convention to consider what technical and financial assistance may be required, within the context of the specific agreement;
- include a transparent and revealing reporting system and procedures, as agreed to by the parties.

69 J Droop, P Isenman and B Mlalazi, *OECD Paris Declaration on Aid Effectiveness: Study of Existing Mechanisms to Promote Mutual Accountability between Donors and Partner Countries at the International Level. Final Report* (Oxford Policy Management 2008), 10, available at *http://www.oecd.org/dac/effectiveness/43163465.pdf* (accessed 6 February 2015).

70 R Sarkar, *International Development Law* (OUP 2009), 100.

71 See the UN/ECE Luzern Declaration (30 April 1993), para 23(1), available at *http://www.unece.org/fileadmin/DAM/env/efe/history%20of%20EfE/Luzern.E.pdf* (accessed 6 February 2015).

The Compliance Committee attached to the Kyoto Protocol to the UN Framework Convention on Climate Change consists of members serving in their individual capacity, and includes both a facilitative and an enforcement branch.[72]

From a human rights perspective, membership of individual experts would certainly be a requirement. Some form of accountability by the partnership (as constituted by their mutual obligations) to rights holders would need to be included, as this is an essential feature of human rights law. Rights holders should be able to request that the Compliance Committee reviews conduct against human rights law; and when conduct cannot be justified, some form of remedial action would need to be ensured.

Multiple actors

The use in global common interest treaties of terms such as 'mankind', 'humanity' or 'humankind' makes it clear that the protection of the common interest is not of concern to States only, but to the international community as a whole.

The International Court of Justice famously held that only the State possesses the totality of international rights and duties recognised by international law. The rights and duties of intergovernmental organisations depend on their purposes and functions as specified or implied in their constituent documents and developed in practice.[73] The international personality of private actors – individuals, groups, companies, NGOs – is limited, and 'determined by political exigencies'.[74] Private actors become international persons to the extent that international law recognises their rights and duties, enables them to bring a claim and holds them accountable for wrongful acts. The attainment of international legal personality is a gradual process that depends on the willingness of the entities and of established international legal persons (States) to make international law applicable to their relationships with IGOs and private actors.[75]

Lack of international legal personality acts as an obstacle, because it may prevent these entities from acting at the international level for the protection

72 See, in detail, Rules of Procedure of the Compliance Committee of the Kyoto Protocol (consolidated version of 3 February 2014), available at *http://unfccc.int/files/kyoto_protocol/compliance/application/pdf/consolidated_rop_with_cmp_4&cmp9_amend_2014feb03.pdf* (accessed 6 February 2015).

73 International Court of Justice, Advisory Opinion on Reparation for Injuries Suffered in the Service of the United Nations, 11 April 1949, ICJ Reports 1949, 180.

74 J Klabbers, *International Law* (CUP 2013), 88.

75 There is thus a circular dimension to Article 3 of the Vienna Convention on the Law of Treaties, 23 May 1969 that provides that international agreements concluded between States and other subjects of international law can have legal force. Entities become 'other subjects of international law' to the extent that they conclude agreements to which international law applies. Nevertheless, Article 3 of the VCLT is an important provision in that it clarifies that there is no obstacle to making international law applicable to a variety of transboundary relationships, as long as the parties consent. For an interesting analysis of international agreements and non-State actors, see A-K Lindblom, *Non-governmental Organizations in International Law* (CUP 2005), 487–509.

of the common interest, and may obstruct the establishment of responsibility when actions of these entities run counter to the common interest.[76]

Nevertheless, the concept of global common interest acts as a catalyst for further legal development in this area. The concept implies that full protection of global common interests is dependent on compliance by these actors with a duty to cooperate for the protection of the global common interest even if institutions of enforcement do not yet exist.

The inclusion of other actors than States in global common interest regimes can be achieved in two ways. The first option is to provide participation within treaties that are open for ratification only to States, and thus remain situated firmly within the Article 38 ICJ Statute framework. Even within such a State-centric approach, cooperation with other actors than States at both the drafting and implementation stages can be developed to a certain extent. The second option is to design multi-stakeholder instruments that are most often of a recommendatory nature, but may nevertheless exert significant influence on the behaviour of the participants.

Treaties using the global common interest terminology invariably provide for a degree of involvement of non-State actors.

Intergovernmental organisations have played a significant role in the normative process leading up to various global common interest treaties by providing the institutional framework where negotiations took place.[77] The World Health Organization made use for the first time of its legislative powers[78] when it set in motion[79] negotiations on the Tobacco Control Convention.[80] The drafting process[81] was initiated with a report by the WHO

76 For example, the polluter-pays principle in international environmental law often operates as a principle for the establishment of State responsibility, even if pollution is caused by industry. Nevertheless, some international civil liability regimes for high-risk activities which are likely to create environmental damage seek to hold private operators (such as ship owners and carriers) directly liable. See P Schwartz, 'The Polluter-Pays Principle', in M Fitzmaurice, DM Ong and P Merkouris (eds), *Research Handbook on International Environmental Law* (Edward Elgar 2010), 252. Article 6 of Annex VI to the Protocol on Environmental Protection to the Antarctic Treaty: Liability Arising From Environmental Emergencies (17 June 2005, not yet entered into force) thus provides that a private operator that fails to take prompt and effective response action with respect to environmental emergencies arising from its activities shall be liable to pay the costs of response action taken by the Parties to the treaty.

77 For example, on the negotiations processes leading up to the Framework Convention on Climate Change and the Convention on Biological Diversity, see P Sands, *Principles of International Environmental Law* (CUP 2003), respectively 357–361 and 515–516.

78 Constitution of the World Health Organization (22 July 1946), Article 2(k).

79 WHA Resolution 48.11 (12 May 1995).

80 The preamble to the Tobacco Control Convention states that 'the spread of the tobacco epidemic is a global problem with serious consequences for public health that calls for the widest possible international cooperation and the participation of all countries in an effective, appropriate and comprehensive international Response'. See WHO Framework Convention on Tobacco Control (21 May 2003).

81 The drafting process is described in Annex 2 to WHO Framework Convention on Tobacco Control (21 May 2003).

Director-General on the feasibility of developing an international instrument. At the end of the eight-year long process, the Convention was adopted by consensus by the World Health Assembly.[82] In commenting on the negotiation process, Boyle and Chinkin point out that the WHO did not draft the Convention – drafting remained the prerogative of States – but that the organisation provided the leadership and the necessary technical expertise that were essential to the success of the law-making exercise.[83]

Susskind and Ozawa have advocated an expanded role for NGOs in negotiation processes, because international agreements, and arguably common interest agreements in particular, depend for implementation on domestic measures. This requires a domestic constituency willing to push for implementation. Involvement of NGOs in the negotiation process increases the chances that such a constituency will emerge.[84] The Tobacco Control Convention echoes the authors' concerns by recognising that 'the participation of civil society is essential in achieving the objectives of the Convention and its protocols'.[85] In the course of the negotiation process leading up to the Convention, two NGOs were invited to send representatives to participate in the sessions of the intergovernmental negotiating body.[86] Currently, 22 NGOs have been accredited as observers to the Conference of the Parties.[87] The Tobacco Control Convention also provides a role for NGOs in the activities in the context of the Convention, most notably on awareness raising.[88] Other global common interest conventions provide observer status for NGOs usually under the condition that no one-third of the Parties to the Convention objects to admission.[89]

The Convention on Biological Diversity includes a specific regime on the participation of indigenous and local communities. The Conference of the Parties set up an open-ended Working group on Article 8(j)[90] and related

82 WHA Resolution 56.1 (21 May 2003).

83 A Boyle and C Chinkin, *The Making of International Law* (OUP 2007), 131.

84 L Susskind and C Ozawa, 'Negotiating International Agreements', in A Hurrell and B Kingsbury (eds), *The International Politics of the Environment* (Clarendon Press 1992), 158.

85 WHO Framework Convention on Tobacco Control (21 May 2003), Article 4(7).

86 See A/FCTC/INB2/6, Add.1, 26 April 2001.

87 For the list, see *http://www.who.int/fctc/cop/observers_ngo/en/index.html* (accessed 6 February 2015). Accreditation procedures for NGOs are regulated in Rule 31 of the COP Rules of Procedures (adopted in February 2006).

88 WHO Framework Convention on Tobacco Control (21 May 2003), Article 12(e). See also Article 23(5g).

89 Vienna Convention for the Protection of the Ozone Layer (22 March 1985), Article 6(5); Convention on Biological Diversity (5 June 1992), Article 23(5); UN Framework Convention on Climate Change (9 May 1992), Article 7(2l).

90 Article 8(j) of the Convention provides that State parties shall, subject to national legislation, respect the knowledge of indigenous and local communities embodying traditional lifestyles relevant for biodiversity, and shall promote their wider application with the approval and involvement of the holders of such knowledge, and shall encourage equitable sharing of benefits. The terms 'indigenous and local communities' are not defined in the Convention; the term 'indigenous peoples' is not used in the Convention. For a commentary on the provision as a whole, see E Desmet, *Indigenous Rights Entwined with Nature Conservation* (Intersentia 2011), 131–132.

provisions in 1998. Efforts have been made to ensure the participation of indigenous and local communities in the meetings. The mechanisms that have been developed within the Convention include financial and logistical support to facilitate attendance. In 2005, the Secretariat established an Advisory Group/Steering Committee[91] in which indigenous and local communities are represented, in order to ensure their participation in work programmes. In 2004, the parties adopted the Akwé: Kon Voluntary Guidelines for the conduct of cultural, environmental and social impact assessments regarding developments proposed to take place or which are likely to impact on sacred sites and on lands and waters traditionally occupied or used by indigenous and local communities.[92] The guidelines are intended to provide a collaborative framework ensuring the full involvement of indigenous and local communities in the assessment of cultural, environmental and social concerns and interests of indigenous and local communities of proposed developments.

The provision in the Nagoya Protocol[93] on cooperation on capacity-building for the implementation of the Protocol, particularly in developing countries, also refers to the need to involve private actors, including NGOs and the private sector.[94] Parties should also encourage the use of voluntary codes of conduct, guidelines and best practices in relation to access and benefit-sharing.[95] The provision is a partial response to the challenge of using an inter-State treaty for the purpose of regulating transactions that in practice occur mainly between private actors.[96]

The WHO Framework Convention on Tobacco Control takes a critical view of the influence of business: the Convention provides that in setting and implementing tobacco control policies, States 'shall act to protect these policies from commercial and other vested interests of the tobacco industry in accordance with national law'.[97] The Convention on Biological Diversity, on

91 See *http://www.cbd.int/traditional/list-ac.shtml* (accessed 6 February 2015).

92 Available at *http://www.cbd.int/doc/publications/akwe-brochure-en.pdf* (accessed 6 February 2015).

93 See Article 6 of the Nagoya Protocol on Access to Genetic Resources and the Fair and Equitable Sharing of Benefits arising from their Utilization to the Convention on Biological Diversity (29 October 2010).

94 Ibid, Article 22(1).

95 Ibid, Article 20(1).

96 M Buc and C Hamilton, 'The Nagoya Protocol on Access to Genetic Resources and the Fair and Equitable Sharing of Benefits arising from their Utilization to the Convention on Biological Diversity' (2011) 20 Review of European Community and International Environmental Law 47–61, at 48. Compare the Nagoya Protocol on Access to Genetic Resources and the Fair and Equitable Sharing of Benefits arising from their Utilization to the Convention on Biological Diversity (29 October 2010), Article 4(1).

97 WHO Framework Convention on Tobacco Control (21 May 2003), Article 5(3). The preamble recognised 'the need to be alert to any efforts by the tobacco industry to undermine or subvert tobacco control efforts'. On WHO efforts to 'ensure that tobacco industry lobbying could not undermine the negotiations' leading up to the Convention, see Boyle and Chinkin (n 83), 129–130. Article 19 of the Convention encourages States to consider taking legislative action or promoting their existing laws, where necessary, to deal with criminal and civil liability, including compensation where appropriate. The Protocol to Eliminate Illicit Trade in Tobacco

the other hand, encourages cooperation between government and the private sector in developing methods for sustainable use of biological resources.[98]

A final category of non-State actors involved in the preparation and implementation of global common interest conventions is the relevant scientific community. Peter Haas has written extensively about the role of 'epistemic communities' in international policy-making, which he defines as 'a network of professionals with recognised expertise and competence in a particular domain and an authoritative claim to policy-relevant knowledge within that domain or issue-area'.[99] These professionals may be employed in intergovernmental organisations, work-in-state administrations or at research institutes: as a community of knowledge they provide information that influences decision-makers.

The Vienna Convention for the Protection of the Ozone Layer states that the application of the general obligations provisions 'shall be based on relevant scientific and technical considerations',[100] and the Conference of the Parties keeps scientific information on the ozone layer under continuous review.[101] The Executive Body of the Convention on Long-range Transboundary Air Pollution relies on the Steering Body of EMEP, the European Monitoring and Evaluation Programme, for data collection and scientific cooperation.[102] EMEP regularly provides governments and subsidiary bodies under the LRTAP Convention with qualified scientific information to support the development and further evaluation of the international protocols on emission reductions negotiated within the Convention. The Steering Body consists of government representatives, as do the subsidiary bodies for scientific and technological advice[103] set up under the biodiversity and climate change conventions. In both bodies all State parties participate through representatives 'competent in the relevant field of expertise'.[104] In the context of the Convention of Biological Diversity, an additional instrument providing scientific expertise

Products prohibits State parties from delegating their obligations under the Protocol to the tobacco industry, while at the same time permitting them to require that the tobacco industry bears the costs associated with their obligations. See Protocol to Eliminate Illicit Trade in Tobacco Products (12 November 2012), Article 8 (12 and 14). For an example of a State obligation to regulate the behaviour of private actors through domestic law, see the State duty to ensure that masters of a ship flying their flag abide by the duty to provide assistance to persons in distress at sea. See Chapter V, Regulation 33(1) of the International Convention for the Safety of Life at Sea (1 November 1974) and Article 98(1) of the UN Convention on the Law of the Sea (10 December 1982).

98 Convention on Biological Diversity (5 June 1992), Article 10(e).

99 PM Haas, 'Epistemic Communities and International Policy Coordination' (1992) 46 International Organization 3.

100 Vienna Convention for the Protection of the Ozone Layer, 22 March 1985, Article 2(4).

101 Ibid, Article 6(4b).

102 Convention on Long-range Transboundary Air Pollution (13 November 1979), Article 10(3).

103 Convention on Biological Diversity (5 June 1992), Article 25; UN Framework Convention on Climate Change (9 May 1992), Article 9.

104 Convention on Biological Diversity (5 June 1992), Article 25(1); UN Framework Convention on Climate Change (9 May 1992), Article 9(1).

was created in 2006 when a memorandum of understanding was signed with six scientific institutions. Today, 22 institutions act as a scientific consortium 'in order to implement education and training activities to support developing countries that are building scientific, technical and policy skills in the area of biodiversity'.[105]

In human rights law, the Human Rights Council Advisory Committee currently functions as the Human Rights Council's expert body.[106] The Advisory Committee prepares studies and research-based advice. Members are appointed in their individual capacity. The Advisory Committee has proposed or acted on new standard-setting initiatives to the HR Council, including on the right to peace, the right to international solidarity, the rights of peasants and the possible establishment of a world court of human rights. NGOs in consultative status with ECOSOC can participate in the meetings, and have influenced standard-setting initiatives. Experts may also contribute to standard-setting as members of treaty bodies (in particular through the adoption of general comments) or as mandate holders (detecting gaps in the law through their practice-oriented work). Private initiatives include the mixed expert group that drafted the Maastricht Principles on Extraterritorial Obligations in the Area of Economic, Social and Cultural Rights.[107] The Scientific Consortium idea developed in the context of the Biodiversity Convention would be a welcome addition to current instruments providing for expert input in the area of human rights.

In multi-stakeholder approaches the State centrism of public international law is largely abandoned in favour of a fully inclusive approach. It has been argued that the development of multi-stakeholder partnerships is a sign of a crisis of purely intergovernmental diplomacy.[108] Multi-stakeholderism mimics the consensual nature of traditional public international law: international obligations come into existence when parties consent, and therefore the consent of non-State actors needs to be sought in order to establish direct obligations for them in international law. The consent is expressed through joining a multi-stakeholder partnership.

105 For more information, see *https://www.cbd.int/cooperation/csp* (accessed 6 February 2015).

106 The Advisory Committee replaced the Sub-Commission on the Promotion and Protection of Human Rights and was established through Human Rights Council resolution 5/1 (18 June 2007).

107 The experts 'came from universities and organizations located in all regions of the world and included current and former members of international human rights treaty bodies, regional human rights bodies, and former and current Special Rapporteurs of the United Nations Human Rights Council'. See O De Schutter, A Eide, A Khalfan, M Orrelana, M Salomon and I Seiderman, 'Commentary on the Maastricht Principles on Extraterritorial Obligations in the Area of Economic, Social and Cultural Rights' (2012) Human Rights Quarterly 1084–1169. This was a private initiative aiming to influence the direction of legislative efforts. As such private initiatives to propose new human rights standards come in all shapes and sizes, colours and scents, further research on criteria to assess their legitimacy would be useful.

108 J Martens, *Multistakeholder Partnerships – Future Models of Multilateralism?* (Friedrich Ebert Stiftung 2007), 62.

Article 3 of the VCLT (23 May 1969) does not preclude the conclusion of binding multi-stakeholder agreements under international law, but so far instruments that have been adopted are mostly of a soft-law or hybrid (regulatory/self-regulatory) nature.[109] Arguably, the soft law nature of the documents contributes to the formation of a joint understanding between stakeholders that may have conflicting initial positions. Ideally, the joint understanding is transformed at a later stage into either international or domestic regulation or self-regulation that may target each stakeholder separately.

Multi-stakeholder initiatives (MSIs) tend to have highly formalised governance structures offering detail on the stakeholder types that are included, and the roles they are expected to fulfil. Rights holders (ie individuals and communities) affected by the MSI are usually not directly involved. Multi-stakeholder initiatives focus on standard-setting, and provide reporting obligations for members in order to encourage implementation. In the regulation of the internet, it is argued that multi-stakeholderism provides for a strong legitimation base because it includes the three relevant key stakeholder groups (States, the private sector and civil society).[110]

Wolfgang Benedek perceives of multi-stakeholderism as a potentially more inclusive form of governance but only if certain principles are respected[111]: if all relevant stakeholders are represented and their interests properly taken into account; inclusiveness, if the process is transparent to ensure that all stakeholders are informed about the structure and the dynamics of the multi-stakeholder partnership and can participate in decision-making; if internal and external accountability both to the members and the public at large who might be affected by the partnership are provided for. The author recognises that in practice such principles are often not followed; particular concerns have been expressed about the risk that the interests of powerful business lobbies might prevail.[112]

Inclusive decision-making may imply that progress in the effective protection of global common interests is slow. There is thus a need to create mechanisms providing incentives to encourage all countries to strengthen their commitments to reaching global goals. As a minimum, the cumulative effect of efforts made towards achievement of global goals as originally agreed

109 An interesting hybrid is the Global Fund to Fight Aids, Tuberculosis and Malaria. According to Article 1 of its By-Laws (as amended 21 November 2014) the Fund is 'a multi-stakeholder international financing institution duly formed as a non-profit foundation under the laws of Switzerland and recognized as an international organization by various national governments'. Voting members include both developing and developed States, actors from civil society, and actors from the private sector.

110 See the contribution by MC Kettemann, 'The Common Interest in the Protection of the Internet: An International Legal Perspective', in W Benedek, K De Feyter, MC Kettemann and C Voigt (eds), *The Common Interest in International Law* (Intersentia 2014), 167–184.

111 W Benedek, 'Multi-Stakeholderism in the Development of International Law', in U Fastenrath, R Geiger, D-E Khan, A Paulus, S von Schorlemer and C Vedder, *From Bilateralism to Community Interest. Essays in Honour of Judge Bruno Simma* (OUP 2011), 209–210.

112 Martens (n 108), 62.

should be systemically measured, so that the gap between aspiration and success can, when necessary, be closed through additional agreements.

In any case, a global common interest approach to human rights would suggest that a legitimation base that includes all relevant stakeholders is important. It would perceive a departure from an overly State-centred international human rights law to a structure that accommodates the proliferation of other participants as progress. As has been pointed out, this may be particularly important when the nexus between perpetrators of human rights violations and victims is weak.[113] Multi-stakeholder initiatives providing for cooperation by the international community for the realisation of human rights could be of a soft law nature, and would need to include an accountability mechanism to rights holders.

Legitimate law-making

In legal writing on public international law, concerns have been raised with regard to the legitimacy of law-making, particularly by authors from 'the rest of the World', ie not from the West. These concerns certainly apply to the identification of global common interests. Why do some interests make it to the public international law catalogue? Clearly, the process of identifying what counts as a global common interest is actor (or institution)-driven. Hence, it is crucial to carefully analyse the legitimacy of the actor or the institution defining the global common interest.

Arguably, international law tends to reflect the interests of dominant actors. There is thus a risk that only interests that coincide with the self-interest of dominant actors are recognised as global common interests.

There is a growing trend in writings on international law and development to read the history of international law as continuously disempowering the non-European world[114] through the maintenance of 'juridical mechanisms in the form, for example, of sources doctrine, personality doctrine, consent doctrine and so forth, which resist any challenge being made to the colonial past and sovereignty's role within it'.[115] The common history of subjugation through international law, first to colonialism, and later to economic policies by hegemonic powers, is constitutive of the identity of the Third World[116]

113 See the contribution by W Scholtz, 'Human Rights and Climate Change: Extending the Extraterritorial Dimension via the Common Concern', in W Benedek, K De Feyter, MC Kettemann and C Voigt (eds), *The Common Interest in International Law* (Intersentia 2014), 127–142.

114 A Anghie, *Imperialism, Sovereignty and the Making of International Law* (CUP 2004) 312. For an analysis arguing that international law through its exclusive focus on statehood has contributed to global inequality, see K Shields, 'Rewriting the Centricity of the State in Pursuit of Global Justice', in A Perry-Kessaris (ed), *Socio-legal Approaches to International Economic Law: Text, Context, Subtext* (Routledge 2012), 235–249.

115 Ibid, 313.

116 As reflected in dependency theories that explain disparities in development as ensuing from a conscious effort by the West to create wealth by keeping the Third Wealth in a state of dependency, see Q Qerimi, *Development in International Law* (Brill 2012), 33.

that remains a political grouping because of this history and regardless of its growing economic heterogeneity.[117] Celine Tan thus argues that the concept of the 'Third World' should be retained as 'a continuing form of resistance to hegemonic attempts to disperse the collective voice and organizing unity of third world states and third world peoples'.[118]

Given this perception of the history of international law, it does not come as a surprise that the process of identification of global common interests in international law is viewed with suspicion. Reality may be far removed from the Rio+20 Summit Outcome Document's recognition that people should be able to influence their lives and thus participate in decision-making and voice their concerns, and that action for sustainable development requires a broad alliance of people, governments, civil society and the private sector, all working together to secure the future for present and future generations.[119]

A similar criticism can be levelled at the history and practice of human rights international law-making. As codification progressed from the Universal Declaration onwards, the earlier norms set the direction. Proposals on new (aspects of) human rights had to fit within the confines of existing legal norms, and within the confines of existing legal techniques. For Upendra Baxi, the adoption of the Universal Declaration was of great importance, because it meant recognition by the international community of those whose suffered abuse, regardless of where they were. Peoples and communities, he argues, are the primary authors of human rights. Their resistance to (abusive) power:

> ... at a second order level [is] translated into standards and norms adopted by a community of states. In the making of human rights it is the local that translates into global languages the reality of their aspiration for a just world.[120]

The codification process following the Universal Declaration was, however, based on negotiations among governments, who are entrusted with law-making powers in international law. The adoption of international human rights law created a distance between those experiencing abuse, and those deciding what abuse qualified as a human rights violation:

> ... when read sociologically, the coverage, content, inclusions and exclusions of rights texts tell us not only who is protected against what, but also the sort of people and the aspects of social relations that are especially

117 Compare S Pahuja, *Decolonising International Law* (CUP 2011), 261.
118 C Tan, *Governance through Development* (Routledge 2011), xv.
119 UN doc A/RES/66/288 (22 June 2012), para 13.
120 U Baxi, *The Future of Human Rights* (OUP 2002), 101.

> valued (or not) by the governmental body responsible for constructing, approving and enforcing the regime.[121]

Governmental negotiations on human rights reflect the same power relations that determine the whole of international relations, and so outcomes will reflect the interest of hegemonic States. In the increasingly complex UN human rights architecture, little remains of the bottom-up process of rights discovery that Baxi celebrates, so much so that rediscovering peoples and communities as primary authors – a process I have described elsewhere as *localising* human rights[122] – is now a major challenge for the global human rights system, at least if the local relevance of human rights to Everyman is to improve. As Rajagopol argues:

> the mainstream human-rights discourse ... does not have the cognitive ability to 'see' much of the resistance of social movements. Engaging with the theory and practice of social movements is necessary to convert human-rights discourse from its narrow, state-centred, elitist basis to a grassroots-oriented practice of the subalterns.[123]

Engagement with the practice of social movements also supports the extension of human rights duties beyond the State – regardless of the current state of international human rights law. Social movements tend to perceive of any actor having an adverse impact on effective protection of human rights as a duty holder. In local social settings, effective human rights protection often does not depend on the law, but on the willingness of actors to engage in human rights conduct – hence the insistence by social movements that all actors adversely affecting human dignity are bound by human rights.

Conclusion

The global human rights regime aims to offer effective protection to individuals and groups whose human dignity is under threat. Threats to human dignity emerge in a local context and vary across the globe. The use of the global language of human rights permits lifting a local problem to the global level through the discovery of similarities in human rights problems (eg as a consequence of economic globalisation) and the building of human rights solidarity across borders. Taking this starting point into account, what can be learned from efforts to deal with global common interests in international law?

121 A Woodiwiss, 'The Law Cannot be Enough', in S Meckled-Garcia and B Cali (eds), *The Legalization of Human Rights* (Routledge 2006), 30–44, at 33.

122 K De Feyter, 'Localizing Human Rights', in W Benedek, K De Feyter and F Marrella (eds), *Economic Globalisation and Human Rights* (CUP 2007), 67–92.

123 B Rajagopol, *International Law from Below* (CUP 2003), 271.

The exercise of responsible sovereignty is key to the protection of global common interests. This also remains valid for human rights. The international human rights regime is a decentralised regime that places the heaviest responsibility on the jurisdictionally responsible State. Responsible sovereignty requires that global human rights are implemented domestically in such a way as to result in effective and practical protection of rights holders.

The emphasis on responsible sovereignty also implies that the capacity of States to provide effective human rights protection is tested empirically. The assessment of such capacity should be evidence-based rather than dogmatic. Fictitiously assuming capacity in law while there is insufficient capacity in reality amounts to an abandonment of rights holders.

It should not be presumed that sufficient resources are available to realise the core content of human rights in least-developed countries. This does not affect their obligation to strive to ensure the widest possible enjoyment of the relevant rights in the prevailing circumstances, nor does it affect the entitlement of rights holders to protection. A finding of non-compliance with core content obligations due to inadequacy of resources should therefore trigger a system of implementation aid for which State parties take responsibility, with a view to creating a domestic enabling environment to ensure effective human rights protection.

The inclusion of mutually agreed inter-State obligations would reinforce the international solidarity dimension of human rights as a global common interest. In a global common interest approach, joint State efforts need to be complemented by responsible action by multiple other actors. A global common interest approach acts as a catalyst for the further development of the international legal personality of these actors. The full protection of human rights as global common interest is dependent on compliance by other actors than States with a duty to cooperate for the protection of human rights even if institutions of enforcement do not yet exist.

9 You say you want a revolution: challenges of market primacy for the human rights project*

Margot E Salomon

Introduction: the primacy of the market

Like everything else, human rights have entered an era of hypercapitalism – of a global commitment to what I will call 'market primacy'. This chapter serves as a warning against the risk of human rights being subsumed into the ruinous mainstream, whatever revolutionary ambition they might once have promised. The concern is that now we fight to soften the worst tendencies of economic globalisation but do not try, or worse no longer notice, that the human rights project has in fact internalised the status quo of market primacy. The primacy of the market is so pervasive as a doctrine that the reasons why we adhere to its supremacy as a global community no longer even require justification; in important ways they are no longer even questioned. Are human rights then sufficiently cognizant of where they are positioned in what is now the mainstream, of what role they play in supporting the primacy of markets, and at what costs to their noble ambitions?

This chapter might begin with a word on terminology: my observation is that there is today little difference in speaking of 'neoliberalism' or the 'free market' understood as either the 'free play of market forces'[1] or liberalised markets, or 'market capitalism' or just 'the markets' not to mention 'market fundamentalism' or indeed 'global capitalism'. Central premises shared by them all are that human well-being is best satisfied by the market and the role of the state is to guarantee the conditions that best allow markets to function; that the public good is served by shaping policy to reflect what the owners

* The ideas for this chapter were presented at the Globalization and Transnational Human Rights Obligations (GLOTHRO) workshop held at the University of Antwerp in February 2014 and delivered in a keynote address at the GLOTHRO Final Conference, Åbo Akademi Institute for Human Rights, March 2014, and in September 2014 at the Centre for International Governance and Justice and the Centre for Moral, Social and Political Theory, Australian National University. My thanks to participants for the thoughtful comments received at all events and to Ali Kadri for his valuable insights on a draft of this chapter. The views herein are those of the author alone.

1 W Streeck, 'The Crisis of Democratic Capitalism' (2011) 71 New Left Review 5–29, at 7.

and managers of capital want;[2] and that the turn to new markets in finance as the most recent change in capitalism is a natural and welcome addition to the current system. Dedication to 'private accumulation',[3] to privatisation and to the development of the private sector are key characteristics of market primacy, along with the creation of new areas for commodification, for example land, water, seeds, seed reproduction and much else. Today, market primacy requires that capital can roam the globe in search of profit maximisation, as such far-reaching cross-border trade and investment are also defining features. Finally, there are at least two other unifying features: devotion to economic growth and reliance on debt to expand financialisation, that is, credit afforded to the financial and private sector.[4]

In addition to the utilitarian selling point on the market meeting human needs best and moreover that the 'social good will be maximised by maximising the reach and frequency of market transactions',[5] it is often argued that the primacy of markets not only offers an instrumental good but that it is an inherent good fulfilling our real potential as self-interested individuals. But in so far as one can recognise both the individual and common merits of a system that allows for free markets, free enterprise and private ownership, the market primacy we know today, as pointed out by the Governor of the Bank of England, supports the pre-eminence of the individual at the expense of the system on which it relies.[6] Put in the starker terms of Araghi, it would seem

2 This definition is derived from Wade's description of neoliberalism in RH Wade, 'Capitalism and Democracy at Cross-Purposes' (2013) 28 New Zealand Sociology 208–236, at 209.

3 D Harvey, 'Ponzi Scheme Capitalism: An interview with David Harvey, Review 31', available at *review31.co.uk/interview/view/16/ponzi-scheme-capitalism-an-interview-with-david-harvey*.

4 'The deregulation in the financial markets and the consequent innovations in mortgage backed securities, collateralised debt obligations and credit default swaps facilitated the debt-led growth model. These innovations and the "originate and distribute" model of banking have multiplied the amount of credit that the banks could extend given the limits of their capital. The premiums earned by the bankers, the commissions of the banks, the high CEO incomes thanks to high bank profits, the commissions of the rating agencies all created a perverse mechanism of investments that led to short-termism and ignorance about the risks of this banking model. In the short-run in the sub-prime credit segment, even if the risk of default was known, this was not perceived as a major issue: first, parts of these credits were anyway sold further to other investors, thanks to the generous ratings assigned by the rating agencies. Second, when there is a credit default, the houses, which serve as collateral, could be taken over and as long as house prices kept increasing, this was a profitable business for the creditor. However, this banking model led to a very risky economic model and a time bomb, which was destined to explode eventually. The bad news from the sub-prime markets triggered the explosion eventually, and first the market for collateralised debt obligations (CDOs) and then the interbank market, and finally the whole credit market collapsed at a global scale' (Ö Onaran, 'A Crisis of Distribution' (2009) XLIV Economic and Political Weekly 171–178, at 173).

5 D Harvey, *A Brief History of Neoliberalism* (OUP 2007), 3.

6 M Carney, *Inclusive Capitalism: Creating a sense of the systemic*, Governor of the Bank of England (2014), 5, available at *http://www.inclusivecapitalism.org/*.

we have nurtured a 'social system that is parasitically consuming life, labour, and nature as it is dying'.[7]

In exposing dangers that market primacy has for the human rights project, this chapter will proceed as follows: drawing on a range of examples, the second section will explore the ubiquity of markets, where market primacy has had influence and how, and the implications for human well-being. To these ends, this section will also interrogate the new development policy of the UK's Department for International Development (DfID) recently launched at the London Stock Exchange at which DfID's 'strategic partnership' with UK business and its 'new, ambitious approach to economic development' in developing countries was unveiled.[8] The third section will highlight the role of law in sustaining the primacy of markets and in underpinning the deceptive ideas that law is somehow not central to the creation of the permissive environment so conducive to market primacy. The fourth section will unpack the UK's National Action Plan to implement the UN Guiding Principles on Business and Human Rights for how it seeks to advance the cause of business and harnesses human rights in that effort. In conclusion, the final section will present some alternatives to the ethic of market primacy and motions to the human rights project to be wary of inadvertently ceding its revolutionary capacity.

Market ubiquity and why we should care

The commitment to market primacy is reflected in the entrenched adherence to economic growth in policy-making. Growth is the trophy, growth is indicative of there being no more financial crisis and of development; growth is indicative of a 'strong economy' and a strong economy is an unequivocal good, so we are told.

In the case of Britain we were expected to celebrate the end of the Great Recession when growth was predicted to go from 1.8 to 2.4 per cent between 2013 and 2014.[9] This would require ignoring figures that show, as Skidelsky calculates, that the lost output from the financial crisis is £210 billion with the 'government's revenue 70 billion less – that is say, 70 hospitals, 1000 schools and 250,000 housing units not built', just as 650,000 people that would have been employed are now unemployed.[10] Growth, of course, tells us little about its distribution and about the relative share of the poorest;[11]

7 F Araghi, 'The End of "Cheap Ecology" and the Crisis of "Long Keynesianism"' (2010) XLV Economic and Political Weekly 39–41, at 41.

8 The Right Honourable Justine Greening, MP, *Smart Aid: Why It's All About Jobs*, 27 January 2014, available at *https://www.gov.uk/government/speeches/smart-aid-why-its-all-about-jobs*.

9 R Skidelsky, 'The Economic Consequences of Mr Osborne: What We have Learned From Four Years of Austerity' *New Statesman* (14–20 March 2014), 23.

10 Ibid.

11 See, for example, T Pogge, 'Growth and Inequality: Understanding Recent Trends and Political Choices' (2008) 55 Dissent 66–75, at 70: '*All* countries should conceive growth much more from

it is silent on means – the forms of callous dispossession – that capital accumulation invites.[12] In non-industrialised countries it forecloses routes that support other meanings of development, for example strategies that directly target improving the living conditions of the people[13] and development understood as distinct from industrialisation and as a process directed at fostering traditional ways of life. Trickle down has been replaced by the idea that growth and a larger GDP bring in resources through taxation that the state can redistribute to the poor, but whether this gets realised is highly questionable since the condition for this growth is the offer of corporate enticements and investment 'incentives' in terms of disciplining workers and limiting their rights.[14] People and their well-being are not factored in as fundamental to economic management but instead are by-products of the benefits growth is alleged to bring. Processes and outcomes are dominated by the value judgments of hypercapitalism and not by norms that best equate with justice, which find expression today through the range of human rights standards and principles, including those that recognise individual rights as issued from collective social rights.

Meaningful efforts to revisit the growth model have quietly disappeared with the significant work of a 2008 UK Commission on 'Prosperity without

the standpoint of their poorer population segments. Doing so, they would do much better in terms of avoiding *both* poverty and environmental degradation.'

12 For example: 'The acceleration of growth [in India] is typically accompanied by a process of primitive accumulation of capital, entailing an expropriation of petty producers from their meagre means of production; but it does not create an adequate number of jobs where the expropriated could be absorbed as proletarians' (P Patnaik, 'A Left Approach to Development' (2010) XLV Economic and Political Weekly 33–37, at 33). 'Land grabs – the illegal expropriation of land by military and government officials – remain a major problem [in Myanmar since the shift to a nominally civilian regime in 2011]. The risk is that foreign investment could exacerbate the problem by encouraging officials to seize land, which can then be offered to investors' (Investment Policy Reform and Human Rights in Myanmar, interview with Dr Jonathan Bonnitcha, Investment and Human Rights Project, the Laboratory for Advanced Research on the Global Economy, LSE (2014), available at *http://blogs.lse.ac.uk/investment-and-human-rights/portfolio-items/myanmar/?portfolioID=5250*.

13 See Patnaik (n 12), 35.

14 Ibid, 34. Speaking of India but with application generally, Patnaik remarks: 'The hope that a part of this surplus value can be taxed away by the government to be spent upon the welfare of the poor, never gets realised. Since a condition for this high growth rate is the offer of enticements to capitalists to undertake investment, for which the state governments are made to vie with one and other ... ', ibid. See also an overview of Mynamar's new Foreign Investment Law of November 2012: 'The most eye-catching incentive is the increase from a three-year to a five-year tax holiday that begins when the enterprise starts production or services activities. Another interesting improvement is the granting of customs duty and internal tax exemption for the expansion of an existing investment, which was painfully absent from the 1988 law' (VDQ/Loi, Myanmar Legal Wire), available at *http://www.vdb-loi.com/mlw/new-foreign-investment-law-with-extensive-tax-incentives-enters-into-force/*. '[Pro-poor growth and growth-with-equity] ... is crucial to [those economists who support it] their theological role of appeasing the conscience of their wealthy constituents and of reconciling rich and poor alike to the great globalization push of the last twenty-five years' (Pogge (n 11), 66).

Growth' aimed at living within the 'ecological limits of a finite planet' offering a prime example.[15] If 'sustainable development' represents the international consensus, it is not obvious quite what it has done to challenge dominant thinking[16] or how it has provided clarity and direction on the role of growth *vis-à-vis* poverty, human-centred development, and protection of the environment. What is increasingly clear is the way in which business has been situated as the lynchpin between sustainability and growth, not least with solutions to be found in new technologies to be provided by the private sector.

The costs of awarding primacy to the market include the rapacious appropriation of natural resources and land globally, and the violent displacement of peasants (including what Nixon refers to as 'displacement without moving'[17]) from their lands, livelihoods and ways of life. Workers are divorced from the basis upon which their organisational power base might be built and quashed is 'anything that looks like communal control of the means of subsistence …'.[18] As growth is revered and market primacy embraced as its engine, the attendant costs include also grotesque inequality and widespread alienation, both acknowledged and sustained.[19] Governance colludes in sustaining this model including through the ability of the wealthy to have their preferences and interests translated into government policy,[20] while corporations use

15 'If we were true economists we would stop growth before the extra environmental and social costs that it causes exceed the extra production benefits it produces. GDP does not help us to discover this point since it is based on conflating costs and benefits into "economic activity" rather than comparing them at the margin … Once growth becomes uneconomic at the margin it begins to makes us poorer not richer … It makes it harder to fight poverty' (HE Daly, 'Foreword', in T Jackson, *Prosperity Without Growth: Economics for a Finite Planet* (Earthscan 2009), xii).

16 The Proposal to the General Assembly of the Open Working Group for Sustainable Development Goals (19 July 2014): 'Goal 8. Promote sustained, inclusive and sustainable economic growth, full and productive employment and decent work for all. 8.1 Sustain per capita economic growth in accordance with national circumstances, and in particular at least 7% per annum GDP growth in the least-developed countries', available at *https://sustainabledevelopment.un.org/content/documents/1579SDGs%20Proposal.pdf*.

17 '… I want to propose a more radical notion of displacement, one that, instead of referring solely to the movement of people from their place of belonging, refers rather to the loss of the land and resources beneath them, a loss that leaves communities stranded in a place stripped of the very characteristics that made it inhabitable' (R Nixon, *Slow Violence and the Environmentalism of the Poor* (Harvard University Press 2011), 19).

18 On the latter points and generally, see M Neocleous, 'International Law as Primitive Accumulation; Or, the Secret of Systematic Accumulation' (2012) 23 EJIL 941–962, at 960.

19 'Inequality remains high, with the top 10% of the world population owning 86% of global wealth, compared to barely 1% for the bottom half of all adults' (Credit Suisse, *Global Wealth Report 2013*, *https://publications.credit-suisse.com/tasks/render/file/?fileID=BCDB1364-A105-0560-1332EC9100FF5C83*.

20 Wade (n 2), 225. The incommensurability of democracy and wealth concentration is a danger long-recognised and captured in the famous remark by US Supreme Court Justice Louis Brandeis, 'We must make our choice. We may have democracy, or we may have wealth concentrated in the hands of a few, but we can't have both.'

their massive influence to shape democratic and intergovernmental processes in order to secure agendas conducive to the expansion of global capital.[21]

It is also market primacy that best captures the reasons for the 2008 global financial and economic crisis that rolled out across the world exemplified by the systemic flaws in national and international monetary and financial architecture brought about by regulatory failures including the over-reliance on market self-regulation. And it is market primacy that reflects the prevailing responses to the crises in Europe and elsewhere. The aims of austerity measures can be summed up in an IMF Memorandum of Understanding with Greece underlining the terms of its bailout package: 'To restore competitiveness and growth, we will accelerate implementation of far reaching structural reforms in the labor, product, and service markets ... To bring the fiscal deficit to a sustainable position, we will implement bold structural spending and revenue reforms. The adjustment will be achieved through permanent expenditure reductions ... We remain committed to our ambitious privatization plans.'[22] Many commentators have questioned the economic soundness of austerity as a response to recession with the severe social implications of this policy choice have been clear for all to see. Figures are emerging that show, for example, a 200 per cent rise in the incidence of HIV/AIDS in Greece during the period of cuts to health spending[23] with the austerity measures since 2010 having led to an increase in poverty within the EU of 24 per cent.[24] While stimulus spending on specific public health programmes has been shown in comprehensive studies to save lives and reduce debt by sparking new economic growth,[25] and with attempts to halt austerity coming from hundreds of economists who sought to highlight that 'inflicting austerity on a weak economy leads to deeper recession, rising unemployment and increasing misery',[26] austerity as the preferred policy response forged ahead with its key aim of inspiring the confidence of business.[27]

Another recent example comes by way of the UK government's shift in its development policy from aid to investment that boosts growth as announced by DfID in January 2014. The speech was given at the London Stock Exchange

21 See further the thoughtful work of U Baxi, *The Future of Human Rights* (OUP 2002), 150–151 and L Pingeot, *Corporate Influence in the Post-2015 Process*, Brot für die Welt, Global Policy and MISEREOR (January 2014), available at *https://www.globalpolicy.org/images/pdfs/GPFEurope/Corporate_influence_in_the_Post-2015_process_web.pdf*.

22 IMF, Greece: Letter of Intent, Memorandum of Economic and Financial Policies (15 March 2012).

23 D Stuckler and S Basu, *The Body Economic: Eight Experiments in Economic Recovery from Iceland to Greece* (Penguin Books 2013), xiv.

24 ILO, *World Social Protection Report 2014/15 Executive Summary: Building Economic Recovery, Inclusive Development and Social Justice* (2014), 7. Many of those affected are children, women, older persons and persons with disabilities, ibid.

25 Stuckler and Basu (n 23).

26 'Jobs and Growth, Not Austerity', Open letter signed by US economists, Institute for America's Future (December 2012), available at *http://jobsnotausterity.org/*.

27 M Blyth, *Austerity: The History of a Dangerous Idea* (OUP 2013), 2.

highlighting 'that DfID's economic development role will be focused on making it easier to do business in developing countries'. The International Development Secretary announced that 'I went to Tanzania with senior representatives from 18 British and international companies including Unilever, Diageo and the London Stock Exchange Group, and others, either already investing or keen to explore investing in Tanzania for the very first time ... expect more DfID trade delegations, in more DfID countries'.[28]

In our study of market primacy the concerns of this policy shift by DfID are numerous: the focus on economic development seems to sideline over a decade of effort on human-centred development and the lessons learned; DfID's policy ignores findings that economic growth in Africa is failing to translate into job creation and the broad-based development needed to reduce high poverty and rising inequality rates in many countries;[29] the international development objectives overtly and unapologetically shift to securing Britain's economic gains through growth in exports;[30] and DfID's new policy links liberalised trade, investment and finance with the dubious (Post-Washington Consensus) idea of 'pro-poor' policies.[31] The conclusions we can draw align with those of a study by Ruckert in 2006 in which we see perpetuated and supported 'market colonisation of all aspects of social life' under the idea of an 'inclusive-neoliberal development model'[32] and the sustained deployment of Western interests framed and sold as universal interests.[33] The embrace of market primacy in political-economic thinking and practice – 'that the market logic solves nearly all social, economic and political problems'[34] – is ubiquitous and has come to act as a proxy for all that humankind values.[35]

28 The Right Honourable Justine Greening (n 8).

29 M Tran, 'UK to boost aid for business in poor countries to £1.8bn', *The Guardian*, 27 January 2014.

30 'As a former Treasury Minister, I'm acutely aware that Britain's future economic strength depends on us increasing our global exports. As part of its long-term economic plan for building a stronger and more competitive economy, this government aims to double UK exports to £1 trillion by 2020. Success hinges on our goods and services being taken to new markets around the world' (The Right Honourable Justine Greening (n 8).

31 'In the *Sourcebook* [World Bank's *Sourcebook for Poverty Reduction Strategies*], financial and trade liberalization, policies that have been at the heart of the Washington Consensus, are considered pro-poor policies' (A Ruckert, 'Towards and Inclusive-Neoliberal Regime of Development: From the Washington to the Post-Washington Consensus' (2006) 39 Labour, Capital and Society 36–67, at 54).

32 Ibid, 59.

33 There is a rich and insightful literature from among critical international legal scholars on the danger of claims to universality. See, for example, Chimni (drawing on Pollin), 'The real problem is that cooperation from developed countries is presently forthcoming only when the economics of neo-liberalism informs the policies and programs of institutions' (BS Chimni, 'ECOSOC and International Economic Institutions' *United Nations Reform Through Practice*, Report of the International Law Association Study Group on Reform (December 2011), 48 at 52; and of course, A Anghie, *Imperialism, Sovereignty and the Making of International Law* (CUP 2007)).

34 *Report of the Commission of Experts of the President of the General Assembly on Reforms of the International Monetary and Financial System* (21 September 2009), 8 (Report by Stiglitz et al), available at *http://www.un.org/ga/president/63/commission/financial_commission.shtml*.

35 'An imperious economic perspective that has been implemented, often under duress, across the

The past decades have seen the tireless critique of structural adjustment policies of the international financial institutions for their failure to deliver robust growth, their failure to contribute to poverty reduction in the developing world, their over-zealous commitment to privatisation, and to trade liberalisation and export-led growth despite the negative impact on the exercise of basic socio-economic rights such as healthcare, education and the right to an adequate standard of living.[36] Nonetheless, comparable policies were recently imposed on the debtor countries of Europe ('the South within the North'[37]) in the form of austerity following the global financial crisis[38] while international development, as we have seen, shifts to focusing on the wholesale support of foreign investors thus reconstituting our understanding of the very beneficiaries of development assistance. Favoured is the violence and disenfranchisement of accumulation with the 'private appropriation'[39] and 'privatised solutions'[40] branded as the only viable way to address current challenges of food security, climate change and all else too.[41] Dissenting voices are many and at the same time alienated in assorted ways as the protests against the prescriptions of the market logic by the Uruguayan President attest[42] as does the chastisement of India and allies by the US, Europe and the mainstream press for withholding their support for an agreement (purportedly) to facilitate world trade in order

globe during the last 35 years take the perspective that the market logic solves nearly all social, economic and political problems. The well-known staples of economic policy complexity such as the need to address economic and non-economic sources of economic instability ("market failure"), the need to account for costs imposed on others and to redress the unfair appropriation of social benefits ("externalities"), the need for public intervention to provide for the conditions and values of sustainable life ("public goods" and "social equity") are all regarded as incidental rather than fundamental issues of economic management', ibid.

36 International Covenant on Economic, Social and Cultural Rights (1966), entered into force 3 January 1976, GA Res A/RES/2200A (XXI), 993 UNTS 3.

37 Araghi (n 7), 39.

38 ME Salomon, 'Of Austerity, Human Rights and International Institutions' (2015) 5 European Law Journal (forthcoming).

39 Harvey (n 3).

40 Araghi (n 7), 39: 'In the true spirit of neoliberalism, the [Copenhagen] climate summit turned into a convention for shifting costs to the weaker competitors and privatising solutions to the climate crisis such as the global commodification of pollution rights through carbon trading', ibid.

41 See, for example, the fascinating article, L Lohmann, 'Marketing and Making Carbon Dumps: Commodification, Calculation and Counterfactuals in Climate Change Mitigation' (2005) 14 Science as Culture 203–235. See further, Pingeot (n 21).

42 'I am just sick of the way things are. We're in an age in which we can't live without accepting the logic of the market [remarks of Uruguay's president José Mujica]. Contemporary politics are all about short-term pragmatism. We have abandoned religion and philosophy … What we have left is the automatisation of doing what the market tells us' (J Watts, 'No palace, no motorcade, no frills: meet Uruquay's unique president', *The Guardian*, 14 December 2013); On 'the tendency of Kyoto-style carbon accounting systems to marginalise non-corporate, non-state and non-expert contributions toward climatic stability', see Lohmann (n 41), 204.

to ensure proper consideration of their food security concerns.[43] These are all the markers of market primacy.

Market primacy and law

Market primacy and its allied philosophy of *laissez-faire* are not – as the latter term would suggest – based on non-intervention in a so-called free market economy. Instead, it requires legal intervention in favour of certain interests over others. As the US legal realists of the early 20th century reasoned, 'government and law are omnipresent – that if some people have a lot and others a little, law and legal coercion are a large part of the reason'.[44] As one of legal realisms most articulate proponents, Robert Hale, cogently argued: 'laissez-faire [is] in reality permeated with coercive restrictions of individual freedom, and with restrictions, moreover, out of conformity with any formula of "equal opportunity" or of "preserving the equal rights of others"'.[45] The central point, as Sunstein would express it, is that 'Economic value does not *predate* law; it is *created* by law'.[46]

Legal rules underpin today's 'predistribution' – the less scrutinised phenomenon described by Wade whereby laws allow for 'sluicing market incomes upwards'[47] and it is the law that determines redistribution, ie tax and public spending, all so central to the exercise of socio-economic rights. As highlighted above, market forces are a product of the choice of law (property, contract, etc); there is no *laissez-faire* really, it 'requires statecraft and repression to impose the logic of the market and its attendant risks on ordinary people'.[48] Poverty, inequality, hunger, and the array of widespread deprivations nationally and globally are quite simply borne of law and the policy choices thereof.

43 'India has threatened to withhold its support for trade facilitation, which would effectively scuttle the deal in the WTO's consensus-based process. The Indian government charges that there has been no serious movement on a re-tabled proposal from the so-called G-33 group of developing countries (which now includes 46 nations) to renegotiate parts of the WTO's agreement on agriculture so that government efforts to buy and distribute food to the poor are not treated as illegal agricultural subsidies' (TA Wise and J Capaldo, 'Will the WTO Fast-track Trade at the Expense of Food Security?' *Al Jazeera*, Opinion, 24 July 2014, available at *http://www.aljazeera.com/indepth/opinion/2014/07/wto-negotiations-food-security-20147237431402983.html*.

44 C Sunstein, *The Second Bill of Rights* (Basic Books 2004), 20–21.

45 R Hale, 'Coercion and Distribution in a Supposedly Non-Coercive State' (1923) 38 Political Science Quarterly 470–494, at 470.

46 Sunstein (n 44), 20, paraphrasing US Supreme Court Justice Oliver Wendell Holmes Jr.

47 'One has to examine the whole array of state laws, regulations and policies for their effects on the distribution of market income, before taxes, particularly to show how, in high-inequality developed countries, many parts of the array (including corporate governance law, trade union law, patent law, monetary policy, exchange rate policy, and more) have the effect of sluicing market incomes upwards' (Wade (n 2), 229).

48 F Block, 'Introduction' to Polanyi, *The Great Transformation: The Political and Economic Origins of Our Time* (1944), (Beacon Press 2001), xxvii; see also, L Wacquant, 'The Punitive Regulation of Poverty in the Neoliberal Age' *OpenDemocracy* (1 August 2011).

It is also law that allows for the transnational connivance of militarisation and marketisation; of the lucrative appropriations part and parcel of the 'peace and security' agenda.[49]

Market primacy is facilitated through regulation that favours capitalist accumulation – on a generous read it might be called 'light touch regulation',[50] commentators inclined to highlight its motives prefer the term 'profit-lead regulation',[51] with others rejecting the language of deregulation altogether and pointing instead to a regulatory shift in society towards benefiting the ruling class.[52] A system that invites speculative gains, for example, despite its rights-destabilising tendencies, is a product of regulatory choices[53] as is the international legal regime constructed to regulate foreign investment which, put otherwise, was set up to facilitate the untrammelled flow of funds of multinational corporations and the creation of wealth for rich shareholders largely in developed states.[54] 'The protection of the increasingly diminishing numbers of the rich and the consequent exploitation of the vast and growing numbers of the destitute' is a product of law[55] and the international judicial mechanisms that provide rigorous safeguards for threats to the maximisation of wealth (largely by the wealthy) but relatively feeble systems when it comes

49 Situating the 'war on terror' 'within the wider frame of neoliberalization', Neocleous concludes: 'The only term which properly describes this complex re-articulation of imperial war and international law in the global security project is "primitive accumulation"' (Neocleous (n 18) 960); see also, N Klein, *Shock Doctrine: The Rise of Disaster Capitalism* (Penguin Books 2007).

50 Carney (n 6), 3.

51 'Neo-liberal economists tend to argue that markets and property should be regulated in ways that promote flexibility and make it easier for businesses to invest and make profits (this is often called "deregulation", but might more appropriately be called "profit-lead regulation"' (R Balakrishnan, D Elson and R Patel, 'Rethinking Macreconomic Strategies from A Human Rights Perspective' (2010) 53 Development 27–36, at 35).

52 A Kadri, 'LAB "views"', *Laboratory for Advanced Research on the Global Economy,* Interview 3, Centre for the Study of Human Rights, LSE (July 2014), 1–10, at 3; 'What these supposed de-regulatory measures do is not to de-regulate, but to shift the power to regulate the flow of resources in society from the working class to the ruling class. As such, these are re-calibrations of the accounting parameters that allow value, signified in the money form, to wash back and forth within certain degrees between labour and capital; in the neoliberal case, it is capital that makes the bigger share', ibid. Available at *http://www.lse.ac.uk/humanRights/documents/projects/LABViewsKadri.pdf.*

53 P Patnaik, 'The Accumulation Process in the Period of Globalisation' (28 June 2008) Economic and Political Weekly 108–113, at 109. For a brief overview of speculation on physical and financial markets and its implications for access to food, see O De Schutter, 'Cracking Down On Speculation – A Safe Bet for Tackling Hunger, Hunger for … Justice', *Digital Development Debates*, Issue 10 (28 February 2013), available at *http://www.srfood.org/images/stories/pdf/press_cuts/20130102_giz_speculation.pdf.*

54 M Sornarajah, 'A Justice-based Regime for Foreign Investment Protection and the Counsel of the Osgoode Hall Statement', Special Section on International Law, Human Rights and the Global Economy: Innovations and Expectations for the 21st Century, Guest Editor ME Salomon (2012) 4(3) Global Policy 463–466, at 463.

55 Ibid.

to ensuring minimum essential levels of well-being for those in need are also a question of policy choice in the area of legal enforcement.[56]

It is also legal rules that insulate international organisations – such as the World Bank and International Monetary Fund – from having human rights obligations despite being deeply implicated in the ability of people to exercise their rights, just as it is those international financial institutions that continue to date to be protected from judicial challenge for the socio-economic harms committed via anachronistic immunity laws that essentially trump the human right to a remedy.[57] It is also our laws that continue to rely almost solely on a rights-holder's own state as the bearer of duties in the area of socio-economic rights despite extensive extraterritorial harms committed by states other than the rights-holder's own and despite the atrophying power of states in our globalised world generally.[58]

In a recent set of decisions against Greece under the 1961 European Social Charter,[59] Greece was found to have violated the right to social security due to its austerity measures. In its defence, Greece argued, *inter alia*, that, 'the modifications of the pensioners social protection … result from the Government's *other international obligations*, namely those deriving from a financial support mechanism agreed upon by the Government together with the European Commission, the European Central Bank and the International Monetary Fund ("the Troika") in 2010'.[60] The European Committee of Social Rights properly rejects this argument, and on the facts found Greece in violation of its obligations under the Charter. Various international organisations were and remain directly involved in the austerity measures undertaken by Greece and the resultant misery that descended on the people of Greece, but no responsibility has been forthcoming. It seems the law does not provide for it.[61] The shift from the national to the global arena – to transnational actors

56 ME Salomon, 'The Future of Human Rights', Special Section on International Law, Human Rights and the Global Economy: Innovations and Expectations for the 21st Century (2012) 4(3) Global Policy 455–457, at 455–456.

57 A Reinisch and J Wurm, 'International Financial Institutions before National Courts', in DD Bradlow and D Hunter (eds), *International Financial Institutions and International Law* (Kluwer 2010), 103–136 and S Herz, 'Rethinking International Financial Institution Immunity', ibid, 137–166.

58 For efforts to highlight the potential of international law in this area, see *Maastricht Principles on Extraterritorial Obligations of States in the area of Economic, Social and Cultural Rights* (2011), available at *http://www.maastrichtuniversity.nl/web/Institutes/MaastrichtCentreForHumanRights/MaastrichtETOPrinciples.htm*; F Coomans and R Künneman (eds), *Cases and Concepts on Extraterritorial Obligations in the Area of Economic, Social and Cultural Rights* (Intersentia 2012); M Gibney and W Vandenhole (eds), *Litigating Transnational Human Rights Obligations: Alternative Judgments* (Routledge 2014).

59 The complaint is part of a series of collective complaints concerning the same facts, registered as Nos 76/2012 to 80/2012 and on which the European Social Rights Committee provided the same assessment and rendered the same decision.

60 *Federation of Employed Pensioners of Greece (IKA-ETAM) v Greece*, European Committee of Social Rights, Decision on the Merits, Complaint No 76/2012, para 10.

61 Salomon (n 38).

and their influence and to international organisations and their power – is of paramount significance, but the law is suspiciously selective in its application and reach.

One can imagine that law is situated somewhere between its capacity to provide for the elite as well as the disenfranchised, as Pirie elegantly suggests: 'Law might serve the interests of domination … but as the Greeks realised, it offers justice for rich and poor alike.'[62] True, the law also offers guarantees when it comes to standards of living, food, healthcare, at least at the level of principle, and provides the difference between – as Sen and then the 'rights-based' thesis argues – 'food availability and food entitlement'.[63] Let us, then, consider its tempering effects.

Market primacy and the UK National Action Plan to implement the UN Guiding Principles on Business and Human Rights: a case study

The UK's National Action Plan to implement the UN Guiding Principles on Business and Human Rights was released in September 2013 and was perhaps the first such national action plan. The National Action Plan reflects the government's approach to implementing the UN Guiding Principles on Business and Human Rights which were endorsed in a consensus resolution by the UN Human Rights Council in 2011. The Guiding Principles indicate what states need to do to protect people from corporate human rights abuses and the actions that businesses should take to respect human rights. While the UN Guiding Principles have been the subject of some criticism, for example their weak legal basis when it comes to the corporate duty to respect human rights;[64] their disregard for positive corporate duties;[65] and as regards the treatment of extraterritorial obligations[66] (all examples that point to market primacy), they represent the current global benchmark and provide the basis upon which sector-specific standards are to be developed. The Guiding Principles have been significant in bringing together human rights – traditionally the purview of the public remit – and the private realm of commercial endeavour. The UK's National Action Plan has been endorsed by many prominent civil society groups, albeit anxious for proof that the action plan will actually prevent abuses of human rights by companies, that it will strengthen the means for vulnerable communities to seek redress

62 F Pirie, *The Anthropology of Law* (OUP 2013), 205.

63 A Sen, *Poverty and Famines: An Essay on Entitlements and Deprivation* (Clarendon Press 1981), 166.

64 A Khalfan and I Seiderman, chapter 2 in this volume.

65 D Bilchitz, 'Do Corporations Have Positive Fundamental Rights Obligations?' (2010) 57/125 Theoria 1–35.

66 D Augenstein and D Kinley, 'When Human Rights "Responsibilities" become "Duties": The Extraterritorial Obligations of States that Bind Corporations', in S Deva and D Bilchitz (eds), *Human Rights Obligations of Business: Beyond the Corporate Responsibility to Respect?* (CUP 2013), 271–294.

including access to justice for victims of corporate human rights abuse overseas, and that there will be a comprehensive set of actions following on from the references in the National Action Plan to protect human rights defenders and as regards investment agreements.[67]

The National Action Plan is entitled *Good Business: Implementing the UN Guiding Principles on Business and Human Rights* and begins with a joint Ministerial Foreword by the Minister for Foreign Affairs and the Minister for Business and Trade. They write that the National Action Plan 'embodies our commitment to protect human rights by helping UK companies to understand and manage (sic) human rights' and that the National Action Plan recognises the importance of 'securing a level playing field' so that no business is rendered less competitive by respecting human rights. So far so good. In the National Action Plan itself, the UK outlines what it is doing to bring human rights to bear on business, for example the UK explains how it secured G8 support for advancing responsible investment in Burma and funded the creation of a resource centre in Rangoon to sensitise incoming investors to the importance of human rights compliant business in Burma. It highlights that UK Export Finance will take account of any negative final Organization for Economic Cooperation and Development National Contact Point statements that a company has received in respect of its human rights record when considering a project for export credit. The National Action Plan explains that the UK will continue to work collaboratively to establish an international mechanism to monitor compliance with the International Code of Conduct for Private Security Service Providers. It also explains 'the Government expectation of business' indicating that business should seek to comply with human rights principles, adopt due diligence policies, consult with communities potentially affected by private sector projects, and, further, establish or participate in grievance mechanisms. For present purposes we will not venture to critique the National Action Plan on the basis of its weak language when it comes to the expectations of business that in many cases fall below international human rights requirements, its underambitious approach to extraterritorial obligations in this area,[68] or its lack of consideration as regards international investment and the myriad ways that legal

67 Press Release, *Action plan on human rights must go beyond business as usual.* The Corporate Responsibility Coalition (CORE Coalition) whose members include Amnesty International, Oxfam, CAFOD and War on Want, supported by the Trades Union Congress (4 September 2013), available at *http://corporate-responsibility.org/wp-content/uploads/2013/11/bhr-action-plan-PR_final.pdf.*

68 'The UK is subject to international human rights obligations under customary international law and as a result of the international legal instruments we have signed and ratified. Human rights obligations generally apply only within a State's territory and/or jurisdiction. Accordingly, there is no general requirement for States to regulate the extraterritorial activities of business enterprises domiciled in their jurisdiction, although there are limited exceptions to this, for instance under treaty regimes. The UK may also choose as a matter of policy in certain instances to regulate the overseas conduct of British businesses.'

regime impacts on human rights and democratic governance.[69] For current purposes the consideration is on what *assumptions* underpin the UK National Action Plan on business and human rights and with what implications for the human rights project.

First, the Ministerial Foreword, in providing the context for the purpose of interpreting the National Action Plan, axiomatically endorses liberal market values. In introducing the UK's commitment to human rights when it comes to business, it begins by privileging the role of the private sector and the commitment to having *commerce* flourish, the foreword states: 'Private sector entrepreneurship, industry and trade are key to Britain's economic success …', and Britain is 'working towards more liberal market environments internationally in which commerce can flourish …'. From this fertile environment 'consumers emerge'. It states that 'Personal freedoms contribute to economic development. The safeguards that are good for human rights – democratic freedoms, good governance, the rule of law, property rights, civil society – also create conditions for private sector led growth'. Further, the Ministers note: 'Responsible action by the private sector on human rights is good for business and communities; it helps create jobs, customers and a sense of fairness; it contributes to market's sustainability and therefore its potential to generate long-term growth.'

It is perhaps no accident that the title of the National Action Plan is 'Good Business'. Yes, business should *be* good and at a minimum respect human rights if not actively contribute to their realisation, but the bigger message is that business *is* good. The celebrated focus on business and human rights by the UK offers no challenge to basic assumptions of market primacy. It never entertains an alternative to advancing liberal market values and an environment wholly conducive to business. To these ends, as we have seen, it explicitly supports a discrete selection of human rights, ie 'personal freedoms' that contribute first and foremost to a good business environment. Reducing (or indeed misappropriating) human rights to those that act as instrumental tools of growth or as trade facilitators aim to empower individuals but as *economic* agents at the service of a particular economic strategy, not as political actors in the fuller sense or as rights-holders.[70] It is difficult to ignore the view that what is being advanced is the idea that healthy, able people are of

69 The National Action Plan contains only one paragraph and no elaboration on investment agreements, but the UK commits to: 'Ensuring that agreements facilitating investment overseas by UK or EU companies incorporate the responsibility of business to respect human rights, and do not undermine the host country's ability to meet its international human rights obligations nor to impose the same environmental and social regulation on foreign investors as it does on domestic firms.'

70 P Alston, 'Resisting the Merger and Acquisition of Human Rights by Trade Law: A Reply to Petersmann' (2002) 13 EJIL 815-844, at 826. For a libertarian argument as to why 'economic freedoms' are the 'human rights' necessary for development and poverty-reduction, see JP Chauffeur, *The Power of Freedom: Uniting Human Rights and Development* (Cato Institute 2009).

value in so far as they can participate as consumers and contribute to private sector led growth;[71] people are instrumentalised and reduced to consumers, the assumption being that they will be the ultimate beneficiaries of this thriving economy driven by corporate interests. We see in this brief Ministerial framing a privileged role for the private sector in driving change; development as co-terminus with the creation of customers; the assiduous 'fetishization of growth';[72] and foreshadowing DfID's new policy that was launched just three months after the National Action Plan, the peddling of the largely disingenuous proclamation as to the universal benefit of 'global growth and prosperity'.[73]

The Ministerial Foreword exposes the UK's business and human rights agenda as one that seeks to ensure human rights in so far as they are good for business, and as one that presupposes the primacy of markets and the protection of their interests. The risk to the human rights project is that by taking the gains that come from the explicit mapping of human rights onto the corporate agenda we accept what Wade refers to in his critique of the post-2008 centre-left agenda as 'diluted neoliberalism'.[74] In this way, the UK's National Action Plan on business and human rights carries the same message as DfID's new approach to business and international development which speaks of 'aligning interests'. The broader danger comes from the formidable alliance between corporation and state that underpin these developments, but the state is meant to function also as the bearer of human rights obligations raising the question as to whether it can reasonably serve two masters. The ominous answer is found in the speech unveiling DfID's new international development policy whereby Greening announces the establishment of corporate contact points within her Ministry, stating that: ' … DfID is open for business. We are partnering up with key industries and professions, as well as setting up new dedicated contact points in the department for our major partner companies.'

71 See, for example, Greening justifying DfID's 'Greater engagement with businesses': 'In 10 years, the number of middle-class African consumers has increased by 60% to 313 million. African consumer spending could reach $1.4 trillion by 2020' (The Right Honourable Justine Greening (n 8)).

72 Stuckler and Basu referring to the March 1968 speech by Senator Robert Kennedy where he eloquently rejects the idea that growth is capable of capturing the values of society ('… The gross national product counts air pollution and cigarette advertising … It counts special locks for our doors and jails for the people who break them … It counts the destruction of our redwoods … and it counts nuclear warheads … It does not include the beauty of our poetry or the strength of our marriages, the intelligence of our public debate or the integrity of our officials. It measures neither our wit or our courage; neither our wisdom or our learning … [I]t measures everything, in short, except that which makes life worthwhile …' (Stuckler and Basu (n 23), xv).

73 The Right Honourable Justine Greening (n 8).

74 Wade (n 2), 227.

Conclusion: of alternatives and warnings

We might be forgiven for assuming there is no 'alternative mode of being beyond capital',[75] but alternatives abound, alien as they may now sound to our ears trained by market reification. Onaran, for example, wants a determination as to which sectors are critical for society in order to ensure that ownership rights are not left to the private sector and to the private profit motive.[76] Patnaik outlines an alternative development strategy for India – but one that is surely relevant elsewhere – rooted in among other methods: land reforms, the protection and promotion of peasant agriculture and cooperatives, industrialisation based primarily on home markets, a spate of welfare measures to improve the quality of life of the working people, and where private capitalists are invited to set up projects governments 'must have a "reservation price", a level of concessions which they will not exceed in entertaining private project proposals. Such a threshold will have meaning insofar as alternatives such as public and cooperative sectors are available for taking up projects'.[77] Araghi calls for a 'global eco-socialism' to confront the 'cancerous growth and parasitic consumption' that define capitalism as we know it.[78] Elsewhere there are clear ideas presented for a 'solidarity-oriented global economy'.[79]

Anghie is right to point out that governance is designed in a way so as to further economic globalisation;[80] thus what we see increasingly are socio-economic rights understood as flowing from rather than directing governance. This is not only to reduce human rights to a fortuitous outgrowth of the capitalist agenda but to attribute to them worth in so far as their realisation reinforces global capitalism today. That would seem to be the message that DfID's new policy conveys and in significant ways the UK's National Action Plan too.

The effectiveness of the current human rights framework will have to contend with the pervasive values of economic globalisation; any attempt at advancing general principles that might drive a human rights-based agenda will have to be alive to the principles and objectives that form the meta-narrative of market primacy. Streeck is correct to suggest that 'People stubbornly refuse to give up on the idea of a "moral economy" under which they have rights that take precedence over the outcomes of market exchanges' that is, 'non-market notions of social justice'[81] but increasingly the sanctity of human rights are tied so tightly to the role of the market – economic rationalisation and the outcomes of (transnational) market exchanges – that we could be forgiven for internalising the dubious counsel that there can be

75 Neocleous (n 18), 960.
76 Onaran (n 4), 177.
77 Patnaik (n 12), 34–35.
78 Araghi (n 7), 41.
79 Onaran (n 4), 178.
80 Anghie (n 33), 253.
81 Streeck (n 1), 8.

no socio-economic rights without the maximal market. When human rights get into bed with business there is a risk, as we have seen above, that rights are resituated so as to be understood as dependent upon the capacity of the capitalist order thus inverting the logic that underpins human rights as first order principles the realisation of which should shape our economic arrangements. Any attempts to impose direct human rights obligations on non-state actors such as business – aspirations that so animate this edited volume – will be challenged on a range of grounds, not least that those constraints will serve to limit the contribution of the market to the so sought-after human rights.

The aim of this inquiry is to highlight the possibility that the role of human rights is increasingly to humanise the worst tendencies of market primacy but not to place our economic order at the service of human well-being and respect for the environment, much less offer an alternative vision. Perhaps in this era of entrenched market primacy we should be content with the gains that human rights carve out of the dominant market ethic. Perhaps we have silently reconciled ourselves to a world of greed and so struggle at least to cloak greed with a human face; perhaps the best we have, and the most we can hope for, is not a revolution at all but merely some form of justice for capitalist societies.[82]

82 I borrow the term 'justice for capitalist societies' from Nancy Fraser (N Fraser, *Fortunes of Feminism: From State-Managed Capitalism to Neoliberal Crisis* (Verso 2013), 194).

Index

For Product Safety Concerns and Information please contact our EU representative GPSR@taylorandfrancis.com Taylor & Francis Verlag GmbH, Kaufingerstraße 24, 80331 München, Germany